The Cambridge Companion to Shakespearean Comedy

This is an accessible, wide-ranging and informed introduction to Shakespeare's comedies and romances. Rather than taking each play in isolation, the chapters trace recurring issues, suggesting both the continuity and the variety of Shakespeare's practice and the creative use he made of the conventions he inherited. The first section puts Shakespeare in the context of classical and Renaissance comedy and comic theory, the work of his Elizabethan predecessors, and the traditions of popular festivity. The second section traces a number of themes through Shakespeare's early and middle comedies, dark comedies and late romances, establishing the key features of his comedy as a whole and illuminating particular plays by close analysis. Individual chapters draw on contemporary politics, rhetoric, and the history of Shakespeare production. Written by experts in the relevant fields, the chapters bring the reader up to date on current thinking and frequently challenge long-standing critical assumptions.

ALEXANDER LEGGATT is Professor of English at University College, University of Toronto. Among his books are *Citizen Comedy in the Age of Shakespeare* (1973), *Shakespeare's Comedy of Love* (1974), *Ben Jonson: his Vision and his Art* (1981), *English Drama: Shakespeare to the Restoration, 1590–1660* (1988), *Shakespeare's Political Drama* (1988), *Jacobean Public Theatre* (1992), *English Stage Comedy 1490–1990: Five Centuries of a Genre* (1998) and *Introduction to English Renaissance Comedy* (1999).

CAMBRIDGE COMPANIONS TO LITERATURE

CAMBRIDGE COMPANIONS TO CULTURE

THE CAMBRIDGE
COMPANION TO
SHAKESPEAREAN
COMEDY

EDITED BY
ALEXANDER LEGGATT

CAMBRIDGE
UNIVERSITY PRESS

CAMBRIDGE UNIVERSITY PRESS
Cambridge, New York, Melbourne, Madrid, Cape Town,
Singapore, São Paulo, Delhi, Tokyo, Mexico City

Cambridge University Press
The Edinburgh Building, Cambridge CB2 8RU, UK

Published in the United States of America by Cambridge University Press, New York

www.cambridge.org
Information on this title: www.cambridge.org/9780521779425

© Cambridge University Press 2002

First published 2002
Fifth printing 2010

A catalogue record for this publication is available from the British Library

Library of Congress Cataloguing in Publication data
The Cambridge companion to Shakespearean comedy / edited by Alexander Leggatt.
p.   cm. – (Cambridge companions to literature)
Includes bibliographical references and index.
ISBN 0 521 77044 0 (hardback) – ISBN 0 521 77942 1 (paperback)
1. Shakespeare, William, 1564–1616 – Comedies – Handbooks, manuals, etc.
2. Comedy – Handbooks, manuals, etc.   1. Title: Companion to Shakespearean comedy.
II. Leggatt, Alexander.   III. Series.
PR2981.C36   2001
822.3´3 – dc21   2001025933

ISBN 978-0-521-77044-6 Hardback
ISBN 978-0-521-77942-5 Paperback

CONTENTS

CONTENTS

NOTES ON CONTRIBUTORS

CATHERINE BATES is Senior Lecturer in the Department of English and Comparative Literary Studies at the University of Warwick. She is the author of *The Rhetoric of Courtship in Elizabethan Language and Literature* (1992) and *Play in a Godless World: the Theory and Practice of Play in Shakespeare, Nietzsche and Freud* (1999). She has edited the poems of Sir Philip Sidney and written numerous articles on Renaissance literature, psychoanalysis, and other topics.

EDWARD BERRY is Professor of English at the University of Victoria. He is the author of numerous articles on Shakespeare and early modern English literature, and of four books: *Patterns of Decay: Shakespeare's Early Histories* (1975), *Shakespeare's Comic Rites* (1984), *The Making of Sir Philip Sidney* (1998) and *Shakespeare and the Hunt* (2001).

LOUISE GEORGE CLUBB is Professor Emerita at the University of California, Berkeley, where she is a member of the Department of Comparative Literature and the Department of Italian Studies. She is General Editor of Biblioteca Italiana, the bilingual series published by the University of California Press and launched by her edition and translation of Della Porta's *Gli duoi fratelli rivali* (1980). A former President of the Renaissance Society of America, she has been Director of the University of California's Centro Studi at Padua and the Harvard Renaissance Center at Villa I Tatti, Florence, and is a member of the Accademia Galileiana di Scienze, Lettere ed Arti in Padua and the Comitato dei Garanti at the University of Siena. Her books include *Giambattista Della Porta, Dramatist* (1965), *Italian Plays (1500–1700) in the Folger Library* (1968), *Italian Drama in Shakespeare's Time* (1989) and (with Robert Black) *Romance and Aretine Humanism in Sienese Comedy* (Florence, 1993). She is the author of the chapter "Italian Renaissance Drama" in *The Oxford Illustrated History of Theatre* (reprinted 1997) and numerous studies of Renaissance comparative literature.

JOHN CREASER is Hildred Carlile Professor of English Literature at Royal Holloway, University of London, and Executive Secretary of the Malone Society. He has published extensively on Renaissance literature, especially on the work of John Milton, Ben Jonson and Andrew Marvell. He has edited Jonson's *Volpone* and collaborated on Malone Society editions of works by Middleton and "Anon." He is a contributing editor to the forthcoming Cambridge edition of the works of Ben Jonson, for which he is editing *Bartholomew Fair*.

JANETTE DILLON is Reader in Drama at the University of Nottingham. She works mainly on medieval and early modern drama, and her most recent books are *Language and Stage in Medieval and Renaissance England* (1998) and *Theatre, Court and City, 1595–1610* (2000). She is currently working on an edition of spectacles in the reign of Henry VIII in Hall's Chronicle.

DAVID GALBRAITH is Associate Professor of English at Victoria College, University of Toronto. He is the author of *Architectonics of Imitation in Spenser, Daniel and Drayton* (2000) and of essays on Petrarch, Erasmus, and Marlowe.

BARBARA HODGDON is Ellis and Nelle Levitt Distinguished Professor Emeritus of English at Drake University. She is the author of *The End Crowns All: Closure and Contradiction in Shakespeare's History* (1991), *Henry IV Part 2* in the Manchester University Press Shakespeare in Performance series (1996), *The First Part of Henry the Fourth: Texts and Contexts* (1997) and *The Shakespeare Trade: Performances and Appropriations* (1998). An associate editor of *ArdenOnline*, she is presently editing the Arden 3 *Taming of the Shrew* and, with Carol Rutter, working on a book about performers and performances.

FRANÇOIS LAROQUE is Professor of English at Sorbonne Nouvelle-Paris III. He is the author of *Shakespeare's Festive World* (1991; reprinted paperback 1993) and of *Shakespeare: Court, Crowd and Playhouse* (1993). He is currently working on a new book, *Shakespearean Re-creations*, and coediting thirty-five non-Shakespearean plays (from *Everyman* to *The Antipodes*), all in new translations into French, for éditions Gallimard, collection La Pléade (two volumes to appear in 2002 and 2004).

ALEXANDER LEGGATT is Professor of English at University College, University of Toronto. He has published extensively on drama, mostly on the work of Shakespeare and his contemporaries. His books include *Shakespeare's Comedy of Love* (1974), *Shakespeare's Political Drama*

(1988), *Jacobean Public Theatre* (1992), *English Stage Comedy 1490–1990* (1998), and *Introduction to English Renaissance Comedy* (1999).

LYNNE MAGNUSSON is Professor of English Language and Literature at Queen's University, Canada, and has published on Shakespeare's language, early modern women's writing, the genre of the letter, and discourse analysis. She is the author of *Shakespeare and Social Dialogue: Dramatic Language and Elizabethan Letters* (1999) and a coeditor of *Reading Shakespeare's Dramatic Language: a Guide* (Arden Shakespeare, 2000) and of *The Elizabethan Theatre*, volumes XI to XV. Currently she is working on a book on early modern women's letters and an edition of *Love's Labour's Lost*.

ANTHONY MILLER is Senior Lecturer in English at the University of Sydney. His research centers on the relations between early modern and classical literatures and between early modern literature and history. He has published a monograph on *Antony and Cleopatra* (1989), and editions of *Richard III* (1992) and *Julius Caesar* (1996). His book *Roman Triumphs and Early Modern English Culture* is forthcoming in the Palgrave series Early Modern Literature in History.

ROBERT S. MIOLA is the Gerard Manley Hopkins Professor of English and Lecturer in Classics at Loyola College of Maryland. He has written several books on Shakespeare's classical backgrounds and recently published the Revels edition of Ben Jonson's *Every Man in his Humour* (2000), as well as a volume for the Oxford Shakespeare Topics series, *Shakespeare's Reading* (2000). He is currently editing an anthology called *The Catholic Renaissance*.

MICHAEL O'CONNELL is Professor of English at the University of California, Santa Barbara. He has written on Catullus, Petrarch, Spenser, Shakespeare, Milton, and medieval and early modern theatre. He is the author of *Mirror and Veil: the Historical Dimension of Spenser's Faerie Queene* (1977), *Robert Burton* (1986), and *The Idolatrous Eye: Iconoclasm and Theater in Early Modern England* (2000). He is currently working on the relation between the mystery cycles and Shakespeare's theatre.

In our world comedy is available on a daily basis, packaged and processed like bread and milk: the comic strip in the newspaper, the situation comedy on television. As with bread and milk, predictability is the principle, and surprises are undesirable. The familiar characters, embodied on television by familiar actors, the familiar situations and the running gags, suggest a need to play for safety. Sometimes a strip is worth clipping out, a program (or a whole series) is worth taping and saving. But in general the product, taking few risks and making fewer demands, is disposable, and is meant to be disposable. Stand-up comedy, live or on television, deals, like the other forms, in quick and instantly recognizable effects. Some comedians will refuse to play it safe, evidently aiming to shock and offend: but there is such a thing as acceptable shock, and as a comic pushes the limits the limits simply get wider. Even the comedy of sheer craziness quickly develops its own conventions: for viewers of this editor's generation, the lunatic fantasies of *Monty Python*, the dead parrot and the Ministry of Silly Walks, getting into their thirties now, have become familiar old friends, as comfortable as a worn pair of slippers.

Home-delivery comedy of this sort operates in small units, dealing in quickly established situations rather than full stories. Comedy in the movies shares the qualities I have been describing: recurring conventions, familiar actors, the offensiveness that in crossing the line simply changes the line's position. But it can also develop stories, taking its characters through a period of confusion and misunderstanding towards a final resolution in a way that in broad terms would seem like business as usual not just to Shakespeare but to his predecessors as far back as classical Greece and Rome. Just before I wrote this preface I watched a movie that may be forgotten by the time you read it: the romantic comedy *Notting Hill* (1999, directed by Roger Michell) in which two lovers, played by Hugh Grant and Julia Roberts, overcome the obstacles presented by their social situation (he runs a small, struggling bookshop, she is an internationally famous movie star) on their way to that most traditional of comic endings, marriage. As the story develops, the comedy draws laughs from familiar human psychology (the difficulties of conversation between shy people), from the larger idiocies of society (the cult of celebrity in which the victim is raised to divinity, then killed and eaten) and familiar character types (the impossible flatmate, the gormless shop assistant, the pompous hotel desk clerk). If we could dig Shakespeare up and show him this or any one of a number of similar movies, he would need to have most of the jokes and nearly all of the technology explained to him, but he would recognize the basic conventions.

Moving into Shakespearean comedy means moving into a lost world, in which men wore swords, a gentleman's name would be entered on the burial register in larger letters than that of a social inferior, and children would be expected to kneel before their fathers every morning and ask their blessing. The unfamiliarity is cultural as well as social: his comedy throws off mythological references as our comedy throws off movie references; his requires footnotes, as ours will before long. Yet the purpose behind such references is fundamentally similar: to draw on a common pool of knowledge that not only highlights the meaning of a particular moment, but creates a sense of community between the story and its audience. We can see an equivalent play of similarity and difference if we look at the movie *10 Things I Hate About You* (1999, directed by Gil Junger), which transfers plot material from *The Taming of the Shrew* into the world of modern American teenagers. While the play deals with marriage and its expectation of a lasting relationship, the movie deals with dating, the only expectation being that one date may lead to another. This gives the story a different rhythm, a different structure. But when the Petruchio character is paid to date the Katherina character an issue arises that we recognize in Shakespeare, the interplay of personal relations and money.

Comedy is at once a traditional form in which conventions like mistaken identity, rival wooers, and parents who oppose love-matches are handed down through the centuries; and a form attuned to the changing society around it, commenting on manners, dress, and language in a way that as the years go by fixes a comedy in its period. It is formulaic, dealing in the familiar: yet its greatest artists can give new twists to a formula, and make us see the familiar with fresh eyes. This means that the play of similarity and difference we have noted between historical periods can also be seen within a period when a writer, drawing on stock material, deepens the experience it offers.

This collection is concerned first with the traditions Shakespeare inherited and second with the distinctive achievement of his own art. Part 1 begins with the theory of comedy available in his time and goes on to his dramatic sources in Rome, Italy, and Elizabethan England. It will be clear that "sources" does not just mean the stories he borrowed, and that the work in question commands attention in its own right, not just as background to Shakespeare. The section concludes with his nonliterary source in popular festivity, traditional in its own way. Part 2 examines his comedies, not taking each play in isolation but setting groups of plays together around recurring themes, structural principles, and comic techniques. As within the larger comic tradition, so within Shakespearean comedy itself there are conventions and preoccupations that appear in play after play but never look the same from one play to another. Shakespeare's comedies seem at times to speak to each other in a world of their own making, and some of the chapters trace their themes through a large number of plays, seeing each play in a context created by the others. Yet these comedies are also tuned to the world outside, a world in which they themselves can be transformed; other chapters accordingly relate the plays to contemporary politics and contemporary writing on rhetoric, and to theatrical practice through the centuries down to our own time.

The play of similarity and difference can be seen in the decision to include Shakespeare's final romances in this volume. While in some chapters they appear as part of a continuum that includes the earliest comedies, in the final chapter they appear as a distinctive form with their own tradition. Each approach has its value, and if this is inconsistency, it can be said that Shakespeare criticism has always thrived on inconsistency. Each chapter in the volume is free-standing and can be read on its own; but anyone who reads through the book as a whole will find some problems and questions recurring, as each contributor, from the angle of approach of that chapter, considers what to make of (for example) the taming of Katherina or the treatment of Shylock.

The results differ, as they are bound to do. On a technical level, there has been no attempt to make each contributor conform to a single standard text of Shakespeare for references, and this means that readers will find, just as in the Shakespeare section of a bookstore or library, a variety of texts. The exception, to ensure that we are inconstant about our inconsistency, is that the spelling of characters' names conforms to the Riverside edition, the one most commonly used by contributors. There is in the Shakespeare text itself, as in the history of its interpretation, a play of stability and shiftiness, which is reflected here.

Much of the comedy of Shakespeare's time, as of ours, was disposable, and through the centuries his own comedies have shifted in and out of favor, and have appeared in strange mutations. But they have never been off the boards for long, and there are very few writers of comedy about whom one could make such a claim. These comedies use and transform the conventions of tradition, both theory and practice; they reflect and question each other; and they constantly provoke us to question them.

My first debt of gratitude is to the contributors, who have maximized the pleasures of editorship while keeping its frustrations to a reasonable minimum. We have had some conversations that made e-mail seem almost a civilized medium. Richard Helgerson, Linda Hutcheon, and Alan Somerset have offered practical help and advice. At the Press, Sarah Stanton has provided wise, firm, and good-humored guidance from the very beginning, and Teresa Sheppard has been unfailingly helpful, often stepping into the breach before I knew there was one. The anonymous readers who commented on an early proposal gave valuable advice that helped shape the volume as it now stands. I am particularly grateful to my wife Anna Leggatt, who not only urged me to take this project on and offered practical help throughout, but was prepared to put up with me on those days when I felt the reality of the old story of the actor on his deathbed who, when asked how he felt, replied, "Dying is easy; comedy is hard."

CHRONOLOGY

Dates given for plays are of first performance unless otherwise specified; most of these dates are approximate.

1564   Shakespeare born at Stratford-upon-Avon
1566   George Gascoigne, *Supposes* (translation of Ariosto's *I Suppositi*, and source for the Bianca plot of *The Taming of the Shrew*)
1567   The Red Lion playhouse opens
1576   The Theatre opens
1577   The Curtain playhouse opens
1582   Shakespeare marries Anne Hathaway; the license is issued on November 27 and the first child (Susanna) is born six months later
c. 1584   Lyly, *Campaspe*, *Sappho and Phao*
1585   Shakespeare's twin son and daughter, Hamnet and Judith, born; Lyly, *Gallathea*
c. 1586   Shakespeare leaves Stratford; nothing is known for certain of his life between this date and 1592, by which time he is in London
1587   The Rose playhouse opens
1588   Lyly, *Endymion*
c. 1589   Greene, *Friar Bacon and Friar Bungay*; Lyly, *Mother Bombie*; Marlowe, *The Jew of Malta*; Anon., *The Taming of a Shrew*
c. 1590   Greene, *The Scottish History of James IV*; Peele, *The Old Wives' Tale*; Anon., *Mucedorus*
c. 1592   Shakespeare, *The Comedy of Errors*, *The Taming of the Shrew*
c. 1593   Lyly, *The Woman in the Moon*; Shakespeare, *The Two Gentlemen of Verona*
c. 1594   Around this time Shakespeare becomes a sharer in the Chamberlain's Men
c. 1595   Shakespeare, *Love's Labor's Lost*
c. 1596   Shakespeare, *A Midsummer Night's Dream*, *The Merchant of Venice*

I

Shakespeare and comic tradition

I

DAVID GALBRAITH

Theories of comedy

Comedy is notoriously resistant to theorization. There is, after all, something inescapably comic and self-defeating about the scholar, oblivious to comedy's charms, searching out its origins or trying to account for its effects. In Cicero's *De Oratore*, one of the interlocutors in the discussion of the comic notes that everyone "who tried to teach anything like a theory or art of this matter proved themselves so conspicuously silly that their very silliness is the only laughable thing about them."[1] Small wonder then, that at the conclusion of Umberto Eco's *The Name of the Rose* the sole manuscript of Aristotle's treatise on comedy, the counterpart to his discussion of tragedy in *The Poetics*, should perish and a fire destroy the monastery library in which the corpus of classical learning has been preserved. But the situation is, of course, more complicated than Eco's fable suggests, both because of widely known alternate accounts of comedy in the classical tradition and of the presence of the outlines of a theory of the genre in *The Poetics* itself. Any discussion of theories of comedy in the Renaissance will inevitably emphasize the importance of these resources in sixteenth-century discussions of the issue.

This approach runs certain risks: there were, after all, sometimes divergent conceptions of comedy in the period. Moreover, Shakespeare's comedies in particular resist theoretical and generic pigeonholing. In fact, Shakespeare seems to take up the language of Renaissance genre theory only to parody it: Polonius catalogues the dramatic range of the players, considering them "the best actors in the world either for tragedy, comedy, history, pastoral, pastoral-comical, historical-pastoral, tragical-historical, tragical-comical-historical-pastoral, scene indivisible, or poem unlimited" (*Hamlet*, 2.2.396–400).[2] Bottom is equally confident of his ability to make generic distinctions: "What is Pyramus?" he asks Peter Quince, "a lover, or a tyrant?," echoing the distinction between comic and tragic protagonists which the classical tradition had put into place and which is parodied in the generic confusion of Quince's title, "*The most lamentable comedy, and most cruel death of Pyramus and*

Thisbe" (1.2.11–22). The principal justification, though, for emphasizing the classical tradition and its subsequent elaborations is simply that it is in these sources that we find the most sustained accounts of the genre at the level of conceptual generality that we associate with the idea of theory. Shakespeare's parodies would make no sense if these ideas of the genre were not firmly in place.

Even if comedy has sometimes seemed to lack its theorists, it has hardly ever lacked its critics. In 1579, one of the latter, the reformed playwright and aspiring divine, Stephen Gosson, published *The School of Abuse*, "a pleasant invective against poets, pipers, players, jesters, and such like caterpillars of a commonwealth."[3] Gosson's tract, issued only three years after James Burbage had built his theatre, was one of the opening blasts in a controversy over the stage that would flare up repeatedly until the theatres were closed in 1642. It provoked a response from the young Thomas Lodge, best known to Shakespeareans subsequently as the author of *Rosalynde*, Shakespeare's source for *As You Like It*. Modern readers might wonder, though, about their use of classical citation. Both insist that the theatre has immediate social consequences for their contemporaries yet rely on definitions and examples drawn from classical sources. Gosson draws on a long tradition of classical and early Christian opposition to the stage. Lodge begins his discussion of dramatic genres by citing the account provided by the late Roman grammarian and commentator on Terence, Aelius Donatus, of the origins of both tragedy and comedy in the desire "by the learned fathers of the old time to no other purpose but to yield praise unto God for a happy harvest or plentiful year."[4] He goes on to quote a definition attributed to Cicero of comedy as "imitatio vitae, speculum consuetudinis, & imago veritatis" (an imitation of life, a mirror of custom, and an image of truth) (*Reply*, 1, 36), a definition which many readers have found echoed in Hamlet's advice to the players "to hold as 'twere the mirror up to nature; to show virtue her feature, scorn her own image, and the very age and body of the time his form and pressure" (*Hamlet*, 3.2.21–24). In foregrounding these sources, Lodge is directing his readers to a tradition which was familiar to any of them who had absorbed the humanist educational curriculum.[5] Prior to the widespread adaptation and elaboration of Aristotle's arguments from *The Poetics* in the second half of the sixteenth century, the authority of Donatus and Cicero in discussions of comedy and of the comic passed almost unchallenged.

In order to bring this tradition into focus, I shall turn first to some accounts of laughter and of the comic and comedy itself in the classical world, and then consider the Renaissance elaborations of these ideas in the early years of the sixteenth century and in the period following the reemergence of Aristotle's arguments. What will become clear in surveying this material, however, is that the anxieties that prompted Gosson's attack on the stage were not newly coined in the sixteenth century. In a sense, his repudiation of the theatre stems from the same concerns which typically engender comic theory. Critics of the theatre fear the consequences of depicting misbehavior on the stage; theorists of comedy attempt to account for the relationship between the violations of social decorum which provide comedy's material, and the pleasure produced by its dramatic representation.

Classical arguments

The ancients recognized both the opposition and the proximity of laughter and tears. Both were subject to physiological and psychological explanations. The classical medical tradition, inaugurated by Hippocrates and consolidated by Galen and his followers, attempted to provide physiological explanations of the phenomena, often emphasizing in the case of laughter the role of contractions of the diaphragm. But in the Galenic tradition, the predisposition to laugh stemmed from an imbalance of the humors, the four elements whose combination shaped the human personality. The author of a text ascribed to Meletius, believed in the sixteenth century to have been a fourth-century AD. doctor, combined etymology and humoral psychology in his account of laughter in the treatise *On Human Nature*: "Laughter is called *gelos* by the Greeks, and *gelos* comes from *hele*, which means heat. For those who are hot are considered to be very inclined to laugh. And elsewhere *haema* (which signifies blood), said to be from *aetho* which means 'I am burning.' For it is the hottest of all the humors made in our body; and those in whom blood abounds, their mind is more joyous."[6]

The most famous classical commonplace on the topic of laughter was Aristotle's claim, in *The Parts of Animals*, that "no animal but man ever laughs."[7] Rabelais recalls these words at the beginning of *Gargantua*; they were also frequently cited in sixteenth-century medical texts.[8] Aristotle's argument is physiological: he discusses in the same paragraph the claim that wounds to the midriff can produce laughter in their victims because of the heat produced by the injury. Not all later commentators, however, accepted the potential implication of this assertion, that laughter might even be constitutive of humanity. Many viewed laughter and the comic as potentially dangerous. The early Church father Lactantius responded to Aristotle that "the chief good in man is religion only," noting that other animals also "have a kind of smile."[9] Moreover, Aristotle elsewhere distances himself from some of the implications of his claim. In Book IV of his *Nichomachean Ethics*, for example, he warns of the dangers of an excess of laughter, and of the importance of a "middle state" in dealing with the humorous, one which avoids the excesses of "vulgar buffoons, striving after humor at all costs" (*Nichomachean Ethics*, II, 1780 [1128a]). This insistence on a mean differentiates him from Plato, however, who in Book III of *The Republic* cautioned that the guardians of the commonwealth "must not be prone to laughter. For ordinarily when one abandons himself to violent laughter his condition provokes a violent reaction." Plato goes on to suggest that "if anyone represents men of worth as overpowered by laughter we must not accept it."[10]

The principal reason for the suspicion of laughter and of the comic derived from their association with the vulgar or the base. In the Galenic tradition an imbalance in the humors shapes the personal predisposition to laugh; but what provokes laughter is often ridiculous or excessive. In Book X of *The Republic*, Plato worried that comedy led its spectators to accept what they would otherwise repudiate, arguing that "in comic representations, or for that matter in private talk, you take intense pleasure in buffooneries that you would blush to practice yourself, and do not detest them as base" (*The Republic*, 831 [606c]). Aristotle refines this argument in the *Nichomachean Ethics*. His attempt to posit a "middle state" allows him to distinguish between the buffoon and "the ready-witted man." The former "is the slave of his sense of humor, and spares neither himself or others if he can raise a laugh"; the latter displays the sense of tact and "jokes well by his saying what is not unbecoming to a well-bred man, or by his not giving pain, or even giving delight, to the hearer" (*Nichomachean Ethics*, II, 1780 [1128a]). He extrapolates from this distinction an analogy to the history of Greek theatre, and suggests a progression from the Old Comedy of Aristophanes to the New Comedy of which Menander would become the most important practitioner: "to the authors of the former indecency of language was amusing, to those of the latter innuendo is more so; and these differ in no small degree in respect of propriety" (*Nichomachean Ethics*, II, 1780 [1128a]).

Aristotle's brief account of comedy in *The Poetics* elaborates on these ideas. Unlike tragedy, whose protagonists are men of stature, comedy, he argues, is "an imitation of men worse than the average; worse, however, not as regards any and every sort of fault, but only as regards one particular kind, the ridiculous, which is a species of the ugly." He goes on to specify that, "The ridiculous may be defined as a mistake or deformity not productive of pain or harm to others" (*The Poetics*, II, 2319 [1449a]). He speculates on its origins, suggesting that, like tragedy, it evolved from preexisting poetic forms. Poets gravitated toward one of the two kinds of verse depending on their nature: "the graver among them would represent noble actions, and those of noble personages; and the meaner sort the actions of the ignoble. The latter class produced invectives at first, just as others did hymns and panegyrics" (*The Poetics*, II, 2318 [1448b]). Homer provides the precedent for both: his epics (particularly *The Iliad*) point to tragedy; *The Margites*, a burlesque poem ascribed to him in antiquity, to comedy, since it provided, according to Aristotle, "not a dramatic invective, but a dramatic picture of the ridiculous" (*The Poetics*, II, 2318 [1448a]). From their origins in improvised forms, each type of poetry, in turn, acquired characteristic and appropriate verse forms. Ultimately, he suggests, the dithyramb evolved toward tragedy and the phallic songs associated with the cult of Dionysus toward comedy.

Aristotle's ideas about comedy exist only in outline in *The Poetics*. Moreover, the text appears not to have been widely influential until the mid-sixteenth century.[11] Until this time, along with the pervasive influence of Horace's so-called *Ars Poetica*, the most important classical sources for the theory of comedy were Cicero's discussion of laughter and the comic in the second book of *De Oratore*, and the essays attributed to the fourth-century grammarian Aelius Donatus. In Cicero's dialogue on the question of the ideal orator, Julius Caesar Strabo Vopiscus divides the topic of laughter into five sections: "first, its nature; second, its source; third, whether willingness to produce it becomes an orator; fourth, the limits of his license; fifth, the classification of things laughable" (*De Oratore*, 373). The first three of these topics receive only slight consideration. After concluding that "it clearly becomes an orator to raise laughter," he explores both the appropriate limits of humor for the orator, and the varieties of wit. Like Aristotle's "ready-witted man," the orator must exercise caution in provoking laughter. Certain topics are clearly inappropriate: "neither outstanding wickedness, such as involves crime, nor, on the other hand, outstanding wretchedness is assailed by ridicule." The orator must be governed by restraint. Cicero emphasizes that "the things most easily ridiculed are those which call neither for strong disgust nor the deepest sympathy. This is why all laughing-matters are found among those blemishes noticeable in the conduct of people who are neither objects of general esteem nor yet full of misery" (*De Oratore*, 375).

Cicero's speaker then goes on to elaborate at considerable length the varieties of wit. Initially, he distinguishes "two types of wit, one employed upon facts, the other upon words." The latter, wit "upon words," which produces laughter through "something pointed in a phrase or reflection," will later be elaborated extensively, in a long passage that bears comparison to Freud's account of humor in *Jokes and their Relation to the Unconscious* (*De Oratore*, 379). The former, wit "upon facts," is of two types: the anecdotal narrative, in which "the character, the manner of speaking and all the facial expressions of the hero of your tale, are so presented that these incidents seem to your audience to take place and to be transacted concurrently with your description of them"; and the technique of impersonation derived

7

from "vulgar mimicry," in which the orator must "borrow merely a suspicion of mimicry, so that his hearer may imagine more than meets his eye" (*De Oratore*, 377–79).

Cicero's dialogue does not, to be sure, engage the question of comic drama directly. Nonetheless, the stage is never far from his mind. The orator must above all, in his use of laughter, avoid "buffoonery or mere mimicking" (*De Oratore*, 375). These are real dangers because the orator relies, in the techniques he uses to provoke laughter, on strategies that he shares with the comic actor. Both varieties of wit "upon facts" depend on forms of representation closely akin to the drama: in the first case on "continuous irony, wherein the characters and individuals are sketched and so portrayed" and in the second on "the infusion of a trifle of mimicry" (*De Oratore*, 379). In the case of wit "upon words" the orator risks "buffoonish raillery" of the type that Cicero associates with characters in pantomimes (*De Oratore*, 379). The task of Cicero's ideal orator is then, to adapt comic techniques while preserving his distance from the contaminating excesses of the comic stage.

During the early phases of the Renaissance, the most important classical treatments of comic drama itself were the essays ascribed to Aelius Donatus. The latter was a figure of considerable cultural authority in medieval Europe, a status facilitated by his role as the teacher of Saint Jerome. Apart from these essays, attached to a sixth-century adaptation of his commentary on the plays of Terence, he was also the author of the *Ars Major* and *Ars Minor*, two of the most important Latin grammars used in the schools. There are two essays on the theatre: one, "On Drama," was considered by early scholars to be by Donatus but is now usually attributed to another contemporary grammarian, Euanthius; the other, "On Comedy," is still ascribed to Donatus.[12] Both were widely cited, and often included in editions of Terence throughout the sixteenth century.

Euanthius locates the origins of both tragedy and comedy "in religious ceremonies which the ancients held to give thanks for a good harvest" ("On Drama," 41). The name *comedy* (*comoedia* in Latin) is derived, he suggests, from the Greek terms "villages" (*komai*) and "song" (*oide*), and refers to the songs sung to Apollo, "the guardian of shepherds and villages" ("On Drama," 41). At first a song performed by a chorus, it later acquired characters speaking in turn. Euanthius emphasizes the complex social dynamics of "Old Comedy." Originally it was not a fiction, for its authors wrote openly about the conduct of members of its audience. But the abuses to which this license gave rise led to the emergence of a new form, the satyr play, which "through the device of crude and, as it were, rustic jesting, attacked the vices of citizens without mentioning specific names" ("On Drama," 42). But this form too was subject to abuse and was ultimately replaced by "New

Comedy." Aristotle had pointed to the greater propriety of this form; with its Roman adaptation and particularly the achievement of Terence in mind, Euanthius stresses its more elaborately wrought fiction and artifice: "This kind of poem was concerned with more typical situations and in general terms with men who live a middle-class life. It gave the spectator less bitterness and more pleasure, being close-knit in plot, true to life in characterization, useful in its sentiments, delightful for its wit, and apt in its prosody" ("On Drama," 42).

Both Euanthius and Donatus discuss the structural elements of Terentian comedy, using a set of terms which would pass from these essays into common use in Renaissance Europe. In the *Ars Poetica*, Horace had insisted that "no play be shorter or longer than five acts."[13] But comedies, Donatus notes, "are divided into four parts: prologue, protasis, epitasis, and catastrophe" ("On Comedy," 47). The prologue is "the first speech"; the protasis "the first action of the drama, where part of the story is explained, part held back to arouse suspense among the audience"; the epitasis "the complication of the story, by excellence of which its elements are intertwined"; and the catastrophe "the unravelling of the story, through which the outcome is demonstrated" ("On Comedy," 47–48). Euanthius' definitions are similar: he emphasizes that the prologue is "a kind of preface to the drama" and that "in this part only is it permissible to say something extrinsic to the argument, addressed to the audience and for the benefit of the poet or the drama or an actor." In addition, he augments Donatus' accounts of the epitasis and the catastrophe, defining the former as "the development and the enlargement of the conflict and, as it were, the knot of all error," and the latter as "the resolution of the course of events so that there is a happy ending which is made evident to all by the recognition of past events" ("On Drama," 45). These definitions of the components of a comic plot, together with the parallel insistence that a comedy be comprised of five acts, provided Renaissance Europe with the essential vocabulary and the structural understanding of the genre which would inform the theory of comedy throughout most of the sixteenth century.

Euanthius concludes his treatment of the development of comedy with a comparison to tragedy which summarizes succinctly the differences between the two forms:

Of the many differences between tragedy and comedy, the foremost are these: in comedy the fortunes of men are middle-class, the dangers are slight, and the ends of the action are happy; but in tragedy everything is the opposite – the characters are great men, the fears are intense, and the ends disastrous. In comedy the beginning is troubled, the end tranquil; in tragedy events follow the reverse order. And in tragedy the kind of life is shown that is to be shunned; while in comedy the kind is shown that is to be sought after. Finally in comedy the story is always fictitious; while tragedy often has a basis in historical truth.

("On Drama," 45)

This account implies a suggestive itinerary for the development of the genre: moving from its earlier, more socially problematic representations of vice and folly, comedy suppresses both the particularity of its reference and the range of behavior that it will accommodate on the stage. Unlike tragic protagonists, to be sure, comic characters will often be closer in social position to members of the audience. Moreover, particularly in New Comedy they had evolved toward stock comic types. But the comic dramatist will avoid, as much as possible, directly engaging excesses of behavior which might undermine the stability and coherence of the "tranquil" resolution which resolves the action.

Renaissance elaborations

For modern scholars, as for European writers from Petrarch onward, what came to be known as the "Renaissance" was intimately linked to the idea of a revival of classical learning.[14] Such learning had, of course, never disappeared. But the humanist intellectuals of the period saw themselves as agents in a process of cultural renewal and of the restoration of (in Erasmus' famous phrase) "bonae literae" – good letters. One crucial aspect of this process was a reform of the school curriculum. The imitation of the style of classical authors became a central aim. New textbooks, such as William Lily and John Colet's *Short Introduction of Grammar* (*c.* 1510) and Erasmus' *De Copia* (1512) (first prepared for St. Paul's School in London) taught the student the foundations of classical Latin and fitted him with a good prose style. This cannot always have been easy, either for the teacher or the student, as Shakespeare's comic Latin lesson and recitation in *The Merry Wives of Windsor* (4.1) suggests.

Comedy, and particularly the plays of Terence, played an important role in the school curriculum. As Erasmus explained in *On the Method of Study* (1512), "[A]mong Latin writers who is more valuable as a standard of language than Terence? He is pure, concise, and closest to everyday speech and then, by the very nature of his subject-matter, is also congenial to the young." [15] Terence offered the additional advantage that his subject matter could rarely provoke moral objections. [16] For Erasmus, comedy was particularly valuable for its techniques of characterization and its observance of decorum. He notes that the teacher "should show that decorum especially is studied, not only in its universal aspect, I mean that youths should fall in love, that pimps should perjure themselves, that the prostitute should allure, the old man scold, the slave deceive, the soldier boast and so on, but also in the particular delineation of individual characters as developed by the poet" (*On the Method of Study*, 687). This insistence on decorum – the "fit" of speech and conduct to character – is one of the most pervasive themes of classical and Renaissance rhetorical theory. Comedy, especially the plays of Terence, simultaneously illustrates and validates these principles. Although comedy tends to rely on comic types and conventional plots, the successful comic poet ought nonetheless to aim to impart "individual characteristics even within these general types."[17]

In the early Renaissance, most criticism of Terence, and of comedy in general, derived much of its material from Donatus and Euanthius.[18] Several sets of annotations to his comedies appeared in the years following the first printed edition of 1470. The lengthy prologue to Terence prepared by the French humanist printer Badius Ascensius reflects these developments. Badius' *Praenotamenta* was first printed in 1502 and continued to preface editions of Terence throughout the first part of the century.[19] He begins by discussing the character and dignity of the poet's art. This defence of poetry, which incorporates ideas from a wide variety of classical, early Christian, and contemporary sources, is followed by a brief account of the history of tragedy and comedy based, in its essentials, on the essays of Donatus and Euanthius. These sources also provide Badius with the material for his account of the structure of comedy. Like Erasmus, he is particularly concerned with the issue of decorum, for which he elaborates principles governing characters, things, words, and the totality of the artistic work. Of these, the first receives the most detailed attention: age (as Horace had examined) sex, social position, country of origin, and temperament are cited as components of character (*Praenotamenta*, 106–09).

During the first half of the sixteenth century, then, rhetorical models of decorum informed discussions of comedy and of the comic, whether in arguments over the aims and methods of using drama in the classroom, or in the elaboration of Cicero's account of the orator's uses of humor in Baldassare Castiglione's *Book of the Courtier*.[20] What though of *Aristotle's Poetics*? To be sure, the text had not been lost entirely to Western scholars during the medieval period. It survived in paraphrases and commentaries, most notably by the twelfth-century Arab philosopher Averroes (Ibn Rushd). However, *The Poetics* was the last of Aristotle's texts to be made available in print, either in Greek or in a reliable Latin translation. It was not found in Aldus Manutius' first "complete" edition of his work in Greek printed in Venice between 1495 and 1498. It was included, however, in a collection of Greek rhetorical texts which Aldus printed in 1508. Until mid-century, however, its impact was relatively slight. The emerging prominence of *The Poetics* is both a response to what Daniel Javitch calls "the new need to classify and define poetry according to its genres," and an indication of an increasing separation of poetics from rhetorical theory.[21] Neither development was abrupt nor definitive. Throughout the century many critics aimed for syncretic conflations of Aristotelian-influenced genre theory and rhetorical models which looked to Horace. In addition, an important current of Platonic theory had emerged in Italy at the end of the fifteenth century.[22] This theoretical diversity and even eclecticism is analogous in some respects to the diversity of comic form and techniques which is so central to Shakespearean comedy.

Of the many commentaries and elaborations on *The Poetics*, two merit special mention both because of their general significance and their attention to issues of comic form: Francesco Robortello's *De Arte Poetica Explicationes*, with its companion essay, "On Comedy," and Lodovico Castelvetro's *Poetica d'Aristotele Vulgarizzata et Sposta*. In 1548 Robortello published the first major commentary on Aristotle's text.[23] The volume also included a series of appended essays, in which he attempted to apply Aristotelian principles to genres which the philosopher had not examined, such as comedy, satire, the epigram, and the elegy. Drawing on Aristotle's account of the components of tragedy, Robortello attempts to formulate an analogous model of the parts of comedy in his essay on the genre. He argues that "it is first necessary to invent the matter which is to be written; this comprises the Plot" ("On Comedy," 231). He goes on to note that "the Plot, because it imitates, must bring out Character and accurately express the manners of diverse people" ("On Comedy," 231). Comic plots are distinguished from tragic plots by their matter. But they are subject to analogous rules of construction:

> The plot ought not to be episodic, for such a plot is faulty. I call that plot episodic in which many things are inserted over and above the one action that was set up in the beginning . . . Since the imitation of Comedy is not only of low and trifling affairs, such as take place in the private actions of people, but also of disturbances, there should also be present that which is taken from the nature and custom of human actions, which always have in them something troublesome or distressing. ("Of Comedy," 232)

Robortello's treatment of comic character combines Aristotelian concepts with elements of the earlier tradition. "Four things," he argues, "should be considered": "that goodness and badness are presented in several kinds of people"; that "appropriateness" be maintained; that characters be "'like the reality' . . . that is to say, the imitation of character in any role should be expressed according to his traditional reputation and the common opinion of mankind"; and that characters "be consistent throughout the poem" ("On Comedy," 234–35). Robortello's analysis is poised between the old and the new: the Aristotelian emphasis on the primacy of plot coexists with an account of comic character that incorporates many ideas from the earlier tradition of Terentian commentary.

Lodovico Castelvetro's *Poetica d'Aristotele Vulgarizzata et Sposta* (1570) was the first major commentary on *The Poetics* published in a European vernacular language.[24] It is here that Aristotle's theory of dramatic action begins its transformation into the prescriptive "unities" of time, place, and action.[25] But this formal rigidity represents only one aspect of his recasting of *The Poetics*. He also reworks Aristotle's ideas about the spectator's relationship to the drama in a manner which leads Bernard Weinberg to argue that "Castelvetro transposes the whole of the analysis from the world of art to the world of reality" (*History of Literary Criticism*, I, 503). In doing so, he ruptures the dialectical relationship between text and world that informs Aristotle's concept of mimesis. This is particularly clear in his account of the causes of laughter, which tends to conflate the dramatic action of comedy with the sources of humor in everyday life. There are, he argues, four classes of phenomena which provoke laughter: "everything that becomes ours after we have desired it long or ardently"; "[d]eceptions, as when a person is made to say, do, or suffer what he would not say, do, or suffer unless he were deceived"; "wickedness of the soul and physical deformities"; "all the things to do with carnal pleasure, like the privy parts, sexual intercourse, and the memories and representations of both" (*Castelvetro on the Art of Poetry*, 214–18). The contrast with Robortello is suggestive: while the former had attempted to coordinate Aristotelian-influenced ideas about comic character with theories derived from Donatus and the rhetorical tradition, Castelvetro seems to bring back into the purview of the dramatist whole classes of material which had been excluded from the stage in earlier accounts of comedy.

Conclusion

In his reply to *The School of Abuse*, Stephen Gosson's attack on the theatre, Thomas Lodge emphasized the traditional accounts of comedy derived from Donatus and the earlier tradition. These ideas would continue to exert considerable influence in England. As late as 1612, Thomas Heywood's *Apology for Actors* continues to cite these sources; Ben Jonson's Prologue to *Every Man in his Humour* brings together a series of related critical commonplaces in promising "deedes, and language, such as men doe vse, / And persons, such as *Comoedie* would chuse, / When she would shew an Image of the times, / And sport with humane follies, not with crimes."[26]

But this critical tradition also came under pressure, both from alternative theoretical paradigms and from the practice of the stage. *The School of Abuse* was dedicated to Sir Philip Sidney. While it is unlikely that Sidney's *Defence of Poetry* was conceived as a response to Gosson, it is instructive to compare his account of comedy to Lodge's very traditional defense of the comic stage.[27] Writing only approximately ten years after Castelvetro, Sidney takes up some of the tenets of the contemporary elaborations of Aristotle, insisting that "the stage should always represent but one place, and the uttermost time presupposed in it should be, both by Aristotle's precept and common reason, but one day" (*Defence of Poetry*, 65). He goes on to criticize contemporary English dramatists for their violations of decorum and mixing of genres: "all their plays be neither right tragedies, nor right comedies, mingling kings and clowns, not because the matter so carrieth it . . . so as neither the admiration and commiseration, nor the right sportfulness, is by their mongrel tragi-comedy obtainde" (*Defence of Poetry*, 67). In contrast to Castelvetro's account of the comic, however, Sidney insists that "the end of the comical part be not upon such scornful matters as stir laughter only," but that comedy ought to provoke "delightful laughter, and teaching delightfulness" (*Defence of Poetry*, 68–69).

Sidney's own discussion of comedy, however, is difficult to reconcile with the dramatic practice that emerged in the public theatres in the years after his death in 1586. In *Every Man out of his Humour*, Jonson has Cordatus, a character "[o]f a discreet, and vnderstanding iudgement" who occupies "the place of a Moderator," summarize the evolution of the genre in antiquity and then argue that "we should enjoy the same license, or free power, to illustrate and heighten our inuention, as they did; and not bee tyed to those strict and regular formes, which the nicenesse of a few (who are nothing but forme) would thrust vpon us."[28] Shakespeare's comic practice provides a compelling illustration of this license. "[T]he mingling of kings and clowns" in *A Midsummer Night's Dream*; the *deus ex machina* of Hymen at the end of *As You Like It*; the real threat of violent death in *The Merchant of Venice*; let alone the systematic violation of "the unities" in *The Winter's Tale*: each seems inconsistent with much of the comic theory I have described; each though throws more light on the limitations of that theory than on its own dramatic flaws. But simply to dismiss the relevance of this theoretical tradition would be too hasty. Shakespeare's art assumes a system of genres. Many of his most striking effects involve the exploitation of (in Rosalie Colie's phrase) "the resources of kind."[29] Compare his plays to Erasmus' enumeration of the stock characters of comedy. That "the old man scold" might bring to mind Egeus in *A Midsummer Night's Dream*; that "the soldier boast" Parolles in *All's Well That Ends Well*. Or recall Castelvetro on the sources of laughter. That we laugh "when a person is made to say, do, or suffer what he would not say, do, or suffer unless he were deceived" throws light on the gulling of Malvolio in *Twelfth Night*; that we are amused by "all the things to do with carnal pleasure" the bawdy repartee of *Love's Labor's Lost* or *Much Ado About Nothing*. Shakespeare's art is at the same time embedded in the traditions of the comic stage and engaged in a continual transformation and renewal of its sources. Any assessment of his relationship to early theories of comedy must come to terms with both aspects of this relationship.

NOTES

1 Cicero, *De Oratore*, trans. E. W. Sutton and H. Rackham, 2 vols. (Cambridge, Mass.: Harvard University Press, 1942) I, 359 (2.54.217).

2 G. Blakemore Evans *et al.* (eds.), *The Riverside Shakespeare*, 2nd edn (Boston and New York: Houghton Mifflin Company, 1997). All subsequent quotations from Shakespeare will be taken from this edition.

3 Stephen Gosson, *The shoole [sic] of abuse*, The English Experience 523 (1579; reprinted Amsterdam: Theatrum Orbis Terrarum, 1972), title page. For larger aspects of the controversy over the stage, see Jonas Barish, *The Antitheatrical Prejudice* (Berkeley: University of California Press, 1981), particularly pp. 80–131 and the account of opposition to the stage by E. K. Chambers in *The Elizabethan Stage* (Oxford: Clarendon Press, 1923), I, 236–68.

4 Thomas Lodge, *Reply to Gosson's "Schoole of Abuse,"* in *The Complete Works of Thomas Lodge* (1883; reprinted New York: Russell and Russell, 1963), I, 35.

5 The standard account of this curriculum in England is T. W. Baldwin, *William Shakspere's Small Latine & Lesse Greeke*, 2 vols. (Urbana: University of Illinois Press, 1944). Its impact on Shakespeare's imagination has been examined in Emrys Jones, *The Origins of Shakespeare* (Oxford: Oxford University Press, 1977).

6 Cited in Laurent Joubert, *Treatise on Laughter*, trans. David de Rocher (Alabama: University of Alabama Press, 1980), p. 105. This is a translation of the 1579 *Traité du Ris*, one of the most sustained accounts of the physiological and psychological elements of laughter produced in the sixteenth century. For an account of classical medical theory, emphasizing its relevance to Shakespeare, see F. David Hoeniger, *Medicine and Shakespeare in the English Renaissance* (Newark: University of Delaware Press, 1992), pp. 71–116.

7 Aristotle, *Parts of Animals*, in *The Complete Works of Aristotle*, ed. Jonathan Barnes (Princeton: Princeton University Press, 1984), I, 1049 (673a). All subsequent quotations from Aristotle will be taken from this edition.

8 The opening poem "Aux Lecteurs" concludes: "Mieulx est de ris que de larmes escrire, / Pource que rire est le propre de l'homme." François Rabelais, *Gargantua*, ed. Ruth Calder and M. A. Screech (Geneva: Librairie Droz, 1970), p. 7. For an important discussion of this commonplace in relation to larger issues in Renaissance literary and scientific theory see M. A. Screech and Ruth

DAVID GALBRAITH

Calder, "Some Renaissance Attitudes to Laughter," in *Humanism in France*, ed. A. H. T. Levi (Manchester: Manchester University Press, 1970), pp. 216–28.

9 Lactantius, *The Divine Institutes*, in *The Ante-Nicene Fathers*, ed. Alexander Roberts and John Donaldson (Buffalo: Christian Literature Company, 1886), VII, 77 (III.10).

10 Plato, *The Republic*, in *The Complete Dialogues of Plato*, ed. Edith Hamilton and Huntington Cairns (Princeton: Princeton University Press, 1963), 633 (388e). All subsequent quotations from Plato will be taken from this edition. There is also an interesting discussion of "the mixture of pleasure and pain" provoked by comedy in the *Philebus*. Socrates defines the ridiculous as "that species of the genus 'badness' which is differentiated by the opposite of the inscription at Delphi." Rather than "Know thyself," "the opposite of that would be for the inscription to read, 'By no means know thyself'" (*Philebus*, 1129 [48c]).

11 D. A. Russell, *Criticism in Antiquity* (London: Duckworth, 1981), pp. 29–31 contrasts the influence of Aristotle's *Rhetoric* to the relative neglect accorded *The Poetics* in antiquity.

12 Both essays are translated in *Medieval Literary Criticism*, ed. O. B. Hardison, Jr. et al. (New York: Frederick Ungar Publishing, 1974), pp. 39–49. All quotations from these texts will be from Hardison's edition.

13 Horace, *Ars Poetica or Epistle to the Pisos*, trans. H. R. Fairclough (Cambridge, Mass.: Harvard University Press, 1966), p. 467.

14 See Wallace Ferguson, *The Renaissance in Historical Thought* (Cambridge, Mass.: Houghton Mifflin Company, 1948) for the history of the idea of the Renaissance, and Jill Kraye (ed.), *The Cambridge Companion to Renaissance Humanism* (Cambridge: Cambridge University Press, 1996) for a recent survey of European humanism.

15 Erasmus, *On the Method of Study*, in *Collected Works of Erasmus* (Toronto: University of Toronto Press, 1978), XXIV, 669.

16 In his discussion of Virgil's homoerotic "Second Eclogue," ("On the Method of Study," 683–87) Erasmus demonstrates how the teacher can ensure that "the minds of his audience will suffer no ill effects, unless someone comes to the work who has already been corrupted" (687).

17 Erasmus, *De Copia*, in *Collected Works of Erasmus*, XXIV, 584. Erasmus further elaborates upon these ideas in his discussion of "prosopopoeia," "dramatization" or "the realistic presentation of persons" in this work.

18 See Marvin T. Herrick, *Comic Theory in the Sixteenth Century* (1950; reprinted Urbana: University of Illinois Press, 1964) for a detailed account of the Terentian tradition in the sixteenth century.

19 See for example Terence, *Comedie a Guidone Juvenale explanate: et a Jodoco Badio Ascensio annotate* (Lyons: I. Huguetan, 1511). The *Praenotamenta* is translated into French in *Préfaces de Josse Bade (1462–1535)*, trans. Maurice Lebel (Louvain: Peeters, 1988), pp. 49–119. In the absence of a modern edition, I refer to this source. Sixteenth-century folio editions of Terence typically contained an extensive apparatus including the essays by Donatus and Euanthius, the short biography of Terence by Donatus and his annotations to the comedies. More recent sources often included Badius' annotations, and essays or notes by such scholars as Erasmus, Melanchthon, and Julius Caesar Scaliger.

16

20 Baldassare Castiglione, *The Book of the Courtier*, trans. Sir Thomas Hoby (London: Everyman's Library, 1928), pp. 133–82. This discussion revolves around a speech assigned to Bernardo Dovizi, who examines "matters that cause laughter, which is so proper to us, that to describe a man, the common saying is, He is a living creature that can laughe" (137). He emphasizes that "In case therefore the Courtier in jesting and speaking merry conceites have a respect to the time, to the persons, to his degree, and not to use it too often . . . hee may be called pleasant and feate conceited" (168).

21 Daniel Javitch, "The Assimilation of Aristotle's *Poetics* in Sixteenth-Century Italy," in *The Cambridge History of Literary Criticism*, vol. III, *The Renaissance*, ed. Glyn P. Norton (Cambridge: Cambridge University Press, 1999). The standard account of the impact of *The Poetics* on literary theory in this period is Bernard Weinberg, *A History of Literary Criticism in the Italian Renaissance*, 2 vols. (Chicago: University of Chicago Press, 1961), I, 349–423. Excerpts from some of the most important primary sources can be found in translation in Allen H. Gilbert, *Literary Criticism: Plato to Dryden* (Detroit: Wayne State University Press, 1962).

    Some important aspects of Renaissance genre theory are discussed in Rosalie L. Colie, *The Resources of Kind: Genre Theory in the Renaissance* (Berkeley: University of California Press, 1973) and Barbara K. Lewlaski (ed.), *Renaissance Genres: Essays on Theory, History, and Interpretation*, Harvard English Studies 14 (Cambridge, Mass.: Harvard University Press, 1986). See also Jill Levenson, "Comedy," in *The Cambridge Companion to English Renaissance Drama*, ed. A. R. Braunmuller and Michael Hattaway (Cambridge: Cambridge University Press, 1990), pp. 263–301 for a discussion of English Renaissance comedy which emphasizes questions of genre.

22 For a survey of literary theory in the period see Danilo Aguzzi-Barbagli, "Humanism and Poetics," in *Renaissance Humanism*, ed. Albert Rabil, Jr., 3 vols. (Philadelphia: University of Pennsylvania Press, 1988), III, 85–169.

23 Francesco Robortello, *In librum Aristotelis De Arte Poetica Explicationes* (1548; reprinted. Munich: Wilhelm Fink Verlag, 1968). Although the commentary has never been translated, the appended essay "On Comedy" ("Explicatio eorum omnium quae ad Comoediae artificium pertinent") is included in Herrick's *Comic Theory in the Sixteenth Century*, pp. 227–39. I quote from this source. The essays are also discussed in Weinberg, *History of Literary Criticism*, I, 399–404.

24 Lodovico Castelvetro, *Castelvetro on the Art of Poetry*, trans. Andrew Bongiorno (Binghamton: Medieval and Renaissance Texts and Studies, 1984).

25 Although Castelvetro does not use the term, the idea is clearly articulated. See *Castelvetro on the Art of Poetry*, p. 33.

26 Thomas Heywood, *An Apology for Actors*, ed. Richard H. Perkinson (New York: Scholars' Facsimiles and Reprints, 1941); Ben Jonson, *Every Man in his Humour* (1616 text), in *Ben Jonson*, ed. C. H. Herford and Percy and Evelyn Simpson, 11 vols. (Oxford: Clarendon Press, 1929–52), III, Prologue 21–24.

27 Philip Sidney, *A Defence of Poetry*, ed. Jan Van Dorsten (Oxford: Oxford University Press, 1966).

28 Ben Jonson, *Every Man out of his Humour*, in *Ben Jonson*, III, 1.1.266–70.

29 See the elaboration of this understanding of the uses of genre in Rosalie Colie, *Shakespeare's Living Art* (Princeton: Princeton University Press, 1974).

2

ROBERT S. MIOLA

Roman comedy

Romans laughed at a rich variety of comic entertainments, some surviving today only in fragments: scurrilous Fescennine verse, coarse, improvisational farce (*fabula Atellana*), mime (*fabula planipedia* or *riciniata*), drama featuring Italian characters in Italian settings (*fabula togata*). They also enjoyed the *fabula palliata* (a play dressed in a Greek cloak), in other words, a play set in Greece featuring Greek characters in Greek costumes.[1] Deriving from Menander (fourth century BC) and other Greek writers, this kind of play also became known as New Comedy, in contradistinction to Old Comedy, the satirical, political, fantastic, obscene, and profound romps of the earlier Aristophanes (fifth century BC). Both Greek and Roman New Comedy featured stock characters like the old man (*senex*), young girl (*virgo*), and clever slave (*servus callidus*); the action generally involved forbidden love affairs, misunderstandings, and confusions of identity.

The works of two playwrights – Plautus and Terence – largely constitute the extant corpus of Roman comedy. Inventive and exuberant, Plautus (c. 205–184 BC) emphasizes musical elements and verbal jokes. His twenty-one surviving plays include a mythological travesty (*Amphitruo*), deceptions (*Pseudolus, Epidicus*), confusions of identity (*Menaechmi, Casina*), a revels (*Stichus*), and a moral fable (*Captivi*). The six surviving plays of Terence (c. 160 BC) thoughtfully adapt conventions to explore human relations. *Adelphoe* depicts rival theories of raising children, *Hecyra*, the ironies of love and self-delusion. Like their great predecessor Menander, both Plautus and Terence exhibit everywhere a restlessness with received tradition and a willingness to experiment. These authors created a rich treasury of dramatic character and situation, as well as a dense, flexible, and expressive set of codes and conventions. Their descendants include the tenth-century nun, Hrosvit of Gandersheim, the ingenious playwrights of the *commedia erudita* in Italy (Ariosto, Dolce, Della Porta, Machiavelli), the neoclassicists in France (Grévin, La Taille, Molière) and Spain (Molina, Vega, Calderón). From these two fertile Roman ancestors, early modern

English playwrights, no less than their European counterparts, took life and breath, especially Thomas Heywood, William Shakespeare, Ben Jonson, and Thomas Middleton.

London playwrights such as these came to Roman comedy by various routes. They first encountered Plautus and Terence in grammar school, where teachers and commentators ransacked the plays for grammatical illustrations, rhetorical figures, and moral sententiae. Such aggressive management aimed to improve the students' Latin and to protect them from the vicious examples on abundant display – the gleeful liars, lusty youths, and disobedient sons. To these ends Renaissance editions of Plautus and Terence often contained extensive grammatical and moral commentary. Published translations of Roman comedy likewise fretted about the potential moral danger to readers. W. B.'s English version of *Menaechmi* (1595), for example, advertised itself on the title page as "Chosen purposely from out the rest, as least harmful and yet most delightful." Similarly, R. B.'s *Terence in English* (1598) glossed scenes with a moral exposition (*moralis expositio*) and an enumeration of the edifying lessons found therein (*theses*). *Eunuchus* 4.5, for example, a vignette of about twelve lines featuring the tipsy Chremes, teaches that "drunkenness takes away the memory, dissipates the sense, confuses the intellect, arouses lust, weakens all the limbs, and extinguishes life" (ebrietas aufert memoriam, dissipat sensum, confudit intellectum, incitat libidinem, membraque debilitat omnia, atque vitam exterminat).[2] Fortunately, audiences and playwrights felt free to ignore such stern finger-wagging. But this didactic presentation ultimately bore rich fruit as later playwrights adapted Roman comedy to accommodate Christian values. In one common variation, for example, New Comedy's amoral young man (*adulescens*) became a later version of the Prodigal Son.[3] To early modern Europe, Plautus and Terence presented comedy as a range of dramatic possibilities rather than as a series of moral lessons, exclusive options, or rigid formulas.

Language and style

Written entirely in verse, Roman comedy provided ancient audiences with lively stage musicals. About half (48 percent) of both Plautus and Terence appears in recitative, in long lines meant to be chanted or declaimed to instrumental accompaniment. The remaining verse consists of the iambic senarius (a line of six iambic feet) to represent ordinary speech, and songs in various meters, those special musical numbers much more frequent in Plautus (14 percent) than in Terence (less than thirty lines in total).[4] Renaissance editions of Roman comedy, the great *Terentius* (Lyons, 1560), for example, often begin with detailed discussion of meter and verse form. The pervasive musicality of Roman comedy entertained audiences and lightened the action to facilitate certain kinds of laughter, especially ridicule. It created a style and sound for comedy that shaped the genre, even in plays not specifically Plautine or Terentian.

Drawn from many other sources, *Love's Labor's Lost*, for example, features a dazzling array of linguistic music and sonic effects. Characters talk largely in verse of various measures and line lengths, often (about one-third of the time) in rhymes, consecutive or alternating. Holofernes speaks a pedantic sputter of Latinate definitions and distinctions; Constable Dull cannot tell the difference between "allusion," "collusion," and "pollution" (4.2.41–6). The witty Moth punctures the pretensions of Armado's fantastic metaphors and periphrases. The lords write sonnets to their ladies; Costard delights in the discovery that "remuneration" means actually payment of "three farthings" (3.1.136). Music sounds in the scene of the Muscovite masque (5.2) and in the opposing songs of spring and winter that end the play. In its varieties of verse style and music, this play shows throughout the formative influence of New Comedy.

More specifically, Roman comedy, especially Plautus, bequeathed to later writers interest in wordplay, puns, dialect, and comic neologisms. In *Menaechmi*, Messenio puns on the *damnum* (263–4), "loss," that threatens travelers to Epidamnium; a joke in *Curculio* (314ff.) turns on the two meanings of *ventum*, past participle of *venire*, "to come," and accusative of *ventus*, "wind." Hanno in *Poenulus* speaks Persian. And Plautus loves creating new words, usually mixing Greek and Latin forms in cacophonous mouthfuls: *sicilicissitare* (to affect the Sicilian manner) (*Menaechmi*, 12), *ferritribax* (iron-rubbed) (*Mostellaria*, 356), *oculicrepidae, cruricrepidae* (clatter-eyed and clatter-shinned) (*Trinummus*, 1021).⁵ Wordplay and punning, of course, characterize Shakespeare's comic language, early and late. Antipholus and Dromio jest about bald Time and hairs (*Comedy of Errors*, 2.2.68ff.); Dogberry tells Borachio that he will be "condemned into everlasting redemption" (*Much Ado About Nothing*, 4.2.56–57); Sir Andrew interprets "accost" as a proper noun; Sir Toby puns incessantly (*Twelfth Night*, 1.3.51, 94ff.). Interest in foreign languages animates many scenes, including the Latin lesson in *The Merry Wives of Windsor* (4.1), and the English lesson of *Henry V* (3.4). Shakespeare shows occasionally a Plautine flair for Latinate inventions: Costard mouths the longest word in Shakespeare, *honorificabilitudinitatibus* (*Love's Labor's Lost*, 5.1.41), and the phrase *ad dunghill* (74); Sir Andrew compliments Feste's talk "of Pigrogromitus, of the Vapians passing the equinoctial of Queubus" (*Twelfth Night*, 2.3.23–24). Shakespeare shows on-going indebtedness to his Roman origins in these particulars of language and style.

Roman comedy also bequeathed to later generations specific lines and passages for imitation. Elizabethan grammar school students worked to memorize speeches; anthologies collected extracts from the plays under various rhetorical or thematic headings. Nicholas Udall published in many editions a popular conversation handbook, *Flowers for Latin Speaking Selected and Gathered out of Terence* (1533), which provided selections with explication and translation. Playwrights like Shakespeare grew up with Latin lines, monologues, and conversations in mind. Sometimes a swatch of Plautus or Terence supplied a scene directly or indirectly. The quarrel of Face and Subtle that opens Jonson's *Alchemist* echoes that of Tranio and Grumio in Plautus' *Mostellaria* (1.1). Young Lionel in Heywood's *The English Traveller* refashions a set-piece from the same play, the extended comparison of the speaker to a house.[6] Both Jonson and Heywood adapt incidents as well as language from Plautus' play.

Conversation in New Comedy also supplies a moment in Shakespeare's *The Taming of the Shrew*. The lovelorn Lucentio complains to his servant, "Tranio, I burn, I pine, I perish, Tranio, / If I achieve not this young modest girl"; Tranio replies: "Redime te captum quam queas minimo" (Ransom yourself out of captivity as cheaply as you can) (1.1.156–57, 163). They replay here the dialogue between the lovelorn Phaedria and his slave Parmeno. Phaedria complains, "et taedet et amore ardeo, et prudens sciens, / vivos videnque pereo, nec quid agam scio" (I'm both tired of her and burn in love for her; and deliberately and knowingly, fully alive and awake, I perish and don't know what I should do) (72–73); Parmeno replies: "quid agas? Nisi ut te redimas captum quam queas / minumo" (What you should do? Nothing but ransom yourself out of captivity as cheaply as you can) (74–75). Terence's *Eunuchus*, through the intermediary of a popular grammar book, shapes the complaint of the hapless, burning, perishing lover and the snappy response of the resourceful servant. In Shakespeare's play this dialogue sets up the exchange of identity between master and servant, which allows exploration of social role-playing as well as the paradoxes of power.

Plautus and Terence contribute to other, more complicated linguistic conventions, including overheard conversations. Ubiquitous in Roman comedy, eavesdropping scenes take many forms. In Plautus' *Miles Gloriosus*, for example, Milphidippa and Acroteleutium intentionally mislead the concealed eavesdropper with the tale of Acroteleutium's unrequited love (4.2, 4.6). Shakespeare stages two scenes of such disinformative eavesdropping in *Much Ado About Nothing*: there (2.3, 3.1) interlocutors deceive the hidden Benedick, and then the hidden Beatrice, with similar stories of their undeclared affections for each other. Shakespeare uses the Plautine convention to his own ends; the scenes work not to the exposure of the concealed and conceited fool, who thinks that he is cleverly spying out the truth. Instead, they work to the good of the reluctant lovers, who drop their defenses and take a chance on each other. Plautine ridicule here turns into romantic comedy.

Locality and stage action

The design of the ancient stage shaped Roman comedy and its descendants. The action took place on the *proscaenium* or stage, a wooden platform about 5 feet high, with an altar. Between the stage and front row the semicircular *orchestra*, originally a dancing place, provided room for special spectators. At the back of the stage loomed the *scaena*, the actors' dressing room, its front wall providing a permanent backdrop. This wall normally had columns, niches, and three doors in its façade.[7]

Devoid of painted scenery, the open stage promoted fast-paced and fluid action. Its architecture and symbolism joined to create a predominantly urban comedy. The stage normally represents a street in Athens or some other Greek city; the action moves rapidly back and forth between the doors, which lead into houses. Sometimes the middle door represents the entrance to a main house or temple. In such a playing space Roman comedy evolved to depict the ordinary lives of ordinary people. Its citizens bustle about their daily business: husbands and wives bicker, neighbors commiserate and quarrel, slaves scheme and shirk, elders preach and reminisce, children rebel against parents, young people fall in love, merchants, cooks, slave-dealers, and pimps ply their trades. Shakespearean comedy (and much other comedy in the West), brisk in action, urban in character, and populated with ordinary folk, bears the distinguishing marks of these Roman origins.

The Roman stage shaped comic action in other, more specific ways. In addition to providing for entrances and exits, the stage doors of Roman comedy often represent opposite sides of conflict. In Terence's *Adelphoe*, for example, one door houses Micio, who practices gentleness and lenity in raising Aeschinus; behind the other lives his brother Demea, who uses harshness and punishment on Ctesipho. Sometimes the doors suggest larger oppositions. The doors identifying the houses of the Citizen and Courtesan in Plautus' *Menaechmi* symbolize as well the opposed worlds of work and pleasure (*industria* and *voluptas*). Moreover, in this play, the Citizen's side of the stage (probably the right, from the audience's viewpoint) leads to the forum, the economic center of the city; the Courtesan's side (probably the left) leads to the harbor, to the wide world and the foreign shores outside.[8] Such suggestive contrasts inspired, or at least encouraged, those locality oppositions pervasive in Shakespearean comedy: Syracuse and Ephesus, Athens and the enchanted wood, Venice and Belmont, Orsino's and Olivia's homes, city and country or forest, land and sea.

Moreover, the doors of Roman comedy produce much later stage action. Throughout Plautus and Terence doors creak, crack, open, stay ajar, stay closed, and slam shut. Scenes of door-knocking and lock-outs abound. Plautus' much-imitated *Amphitruo*, for example, features the lock-out as a central structural device. First, Sosia, the slave, returns home from accompanying his master Amphitruo to war, only to meet Mercury, disguised as Sosia himself. Sosia suffers repulse. Later, the master Amphitruo comes home and suffers similar repulse from his divine double, Jupiter, who has been making love to the wife within. "But they have locked up the house!" (sed aedis occluserunt, 1018), Amphitruo exclaims; "I'll knock on the door" (feriam foris, 1019). Mercury-as-Sosia scolds Amphitruo for almost breaking the doors down (paene effregisti, fatue, foribus cardines, 1026). The exasperated Amphitruo remains outside until Jupiter appears as a god to resolve the mystery.

The Plautine door-knocking and lock-out in *Amphitruo* inspired many later adaptations. In *Geta* (twelfth century), Vitalis of Blois turned the play into a satire on scholastic logic: Amphitruo becomes a philosophy student, not a soldier, and the hapless locked-out servant tries to parse his predicament by means of chop-logic and humorous syllogisms. *Jack Juggler* (1555) largely drops the master and the illicit sexual activity and focuses on the lock-out of the servant, one Jenkin Caraway, by the tricky impersonator, Jack Juggler. It adds to the story the frustrations of Dame Coy, who misses her supper because of the trickery, and a moralizing ending, which laments the prevalence of deceit in the world. The added emphasis on the role of wife forecasts future developments. In the loose translation of *Amphitruo* entitled *The Birth of Hercules* (1604), Alcmena laments the lot of women with an added character, her servant Thessala. Another added servant, Dromio, provides low comedy and joins the disguised Mercury within to mock the returning master knocking on the door (1765ff.). Thomas Heywood retells the story as one of the plots in his mythological sequence, *The Silver Age* (1611). He stages two lock-outs, that of the servant and the master, and adds some slapstick comedy as the enraged Amphitruo beats his men. The irate Juno appears at the end searching for her adulterous husband.

Like these Renaissance adaptations of Plautus, Shakespeare's *The Comedy of Errors* emphasizes the rambunctious fun of the lock-out, expands the role of women, and develops moral implications. Based on another Plautine play, *Menaechmi, The Comedy of Errors* adapts *Amphitruo* in 3.1, where Antipholus of Ephesus and his servant Dromio return home to the locked door, behind which the wife Adriana entertains her husband's long-lost identical twin and his servant, Dromio's identical twin. Antipholus pounds on the door and demands his right of entry: the Dromio within abuses the Dromio without in gleeful rhyme:

> Mome, malt-horse, capon, coxcomb, idiot, patch!
> Either get thee from the door or sit down at the hatch.
> Dost thou conjure for wenches, that thou call'st for such store
> When one is one too many? Go, get thee from the door.

> (3.1.32–35)

The long-lined rhymes give pace and humor to the scene, organizing the voices into an energetic musical number. As Antipholus sizzles in frustration outside, a servant (Luce) and Adriana add to the melee from above and provide opportunities for slammed windows or sashes. In Trevor Nunn's musical production (1976) the irate, exasperated master finally ripped off the wall the offending intercom conveying Dromio's insults; it kept right on talking.

Shakespeare's addition of Adriana to this scene signals her expanded role in the Plautine action. Adriana rises beyond her original in *Menaechmi*, the unnamed *matrona* or wife who merely nags and scolds. She discusses the place of women in marriage with her sister (another Shakespearean invention), suffers from jealousy, invokes the great conjugal vow and bond (to the wrong twin, as it happens), and takes a larger role in the final revelation. Pursuing the wrong Antipholus to the abbey in the conclusion, Adriana herself experiences an embarrassing lock-out. Then the Abbess publicly rebukes her for jealousy: "The venom clamors of a jealous woman / Poisons more deadly than a mad dog's tooth" (5.1.69–70). These reversals tilt the farcical action into a deeper play of self-discovery. The lock-outs here, moreover, can betoken fundamental displacements and suggest a disquieting loss of self and sanity. The final revelations and reconciliations, consequently, can play as spiritual and social, as well as merely physical, recognitions.

Playing and playing against the mask

Classical theory and practice advocated the presentation of recognizable character types – the old man (*senex*), wife (*matrona*), young man (*adulescens*), young girl (*virgo*), slave (*servus*), soldier (*miles*), and others. To identify and classify characters, comic dramatists employed appropriate or speaking names. R. B.'s English Terence, for example, explains names by recalling Greek etymologies. The girl's name, Glycerium, for example, comes from a diminutive form of *glukeros*, "sweet," and means "little sweet thing." The slave Dromos gets his name from the irregular perfect formations of *to trexein*, "to run," because he is always running to carry out orders.[9] Roman comic dramatists also used readily identifiable costumes and, probably, acting masks. All externals together raised a set of expectations about the character types on stage and their behaviors. And like their Greek predecessors, especially Menander, Plautus and Terence always delight in upsetting these expectations, in creating characters who variously play against their names, costumes, and masks. The usually silent or absent *virgo* stars in Plautus' *Persa*, for example, where she impersonates a Persian captive. In Plautus' *Captivi*, Tyndarus steps beyond the conventional role of the clever slave when he nobly risks his life to free his master. Unlike the shrewish *matrona*, Terence's Sostrata in *Hecyra* responds to unjust accusation by offering to make any sacrifice for her son's happiness.

Plautus and Terence's artful characterization includes the braggart soldier, who swaggers across many stages in various incarnations.[10] The Plautine name Pyrgopolynices (Victor over many cities) (*Miles Gloriosus*) constitutes a roaring self-advertisement as does the Terentian Thraso (the Bold) (*Eunuchus*). Clad in a tunic, short cloak, and military cap, the soldier on the ancient stage carried a sword and often referred to his shield. His hair was thick and heavy, probably curled and perfumed. He probably wore a mask with heavy stylized features – a beetling brow and open mouth. Accompanied by a flattering parasite, the soldier typically boasts of his military and amatory prowess but comes at last to some sort of exposure. Pyrgopolynices, for example, suffers a humiliating stripping and beating. Thraso mounts an attack on a courtesan's house but stations himself safely away from the action.

The braggart soldier (*miles gloriosus*) experienced many transformations in European theatres. The Italians often cast him as a Spaniard, usually a beggar, and added conventional situations like the mock duel, wherein the soldier makes excuses to avoid a fight. In the English interlude *Thersites* (1537) the titular character ceremoniously arms himself for combat with a snail and gets beaten by a real soldier, Miles. The swaggering Ralph Roister Doister, in the play of the same name (1552), unsuccessfully besieges his love, Dame Custance. John Lyly's mythological *Endymion* (1588) features in a subplot Sir Thopas, who wants to triumph over sheep, wrens, and fish, and who woos two crones, Dipsas and Bagoa. An early comedy of Ben Jonson, *Every Man in his Humour* (1598) features Bobadilla, who affects great experience in combat and great skill in the new science of fencing. Bragging, Bobadilla vows to beat the choleric Giuliano, who suddenly appears on stage and cudgels the cowardly soldier. Jonson here portrays the ancient character type as a humor, a ruling folly of self-love that requires comic exposure.

Shakespeare experiments with the *miles gloriosus* in the Spanish Don Adriano de Armado of *Love's Labor's Lost*. The name evokes the Armada, the formidable Spanish fleet that sailed against England in 1588, only to be dispersed by a storm. Like his classical prototypes, Armado swaggers throughout the action, here rounding out the gallery of fools that includes the pedant Holofernes and the four academic Lords of Navarre. But Armado can acquire a surprising dignity at the end of the play, when he excuses himself before the jeering nobles and resolves to make amends for his wrong-doing, the impregnation of Jaquenetta: "For mine own part, I breathe free breath. I have seen the day of wrong through the little hole of discretion, and I will right myself like a soldier" (5.2.719–21). He dedicates himself to the humble, hard work of farming, vowing to "hold the plough" for Jaquenetta's love for three years (873–74), and introduces the dialogue between Spring and Winter that closes the play.

In *All's Well That Ends Well* Shakespeare more fully develops the braggart soldier. Parolles, whose name appropriately means "words," boasts of past exploits, like the wounding of one Captain Spurio (2.1.43–44) (also appropriately named). Like Bobadilla, he threatens terrible reprisals just before he confronts his suddenly appearing adversary, Lafew, who administers a tongue-lashing. Uncowed by the humiliation, Parolles blusters on about a lost drum, symbol of his noisy vanity, until he endures captivity and imprisonment by his own men, disguised as the enemy. They blindfold him, mutter foreign-sounding mumbo-jumbo (e.g., *Oscorbidulchos volivorco*, 4.1.81), and threaten him with death. Begging for mercy, Parolles sings like a lark, enthusiastically slandering his friends and betraying his fellow soldiers. The ordeal and exposure recall Plautus' *Miles Gloriosus*, where Pyrgopolynices likewise ends up amidst a hostile, jeering crowd and begs for mercy; the tormentors strip both soldiers of their fine clothing and leave them in shame. Again the braggart surprises us at the end of the play, this time self-consciously repudiating his mask, "Captain I'll be no more" (4.3.333). Realizing that "every braggart shall be found an ass," Parolles resolves to live on anyway, "Being fooled, by foolery thrive!" (338, 340). In *All's Well That Ends Well* the exposure of Parolles illuminates that of his friend, the proud, lusty, deceitful Bertram, who shows other varieties of self-love. Parolles' false capture parallels Bertram's public humiliation. Exposed as boasters and liars, both come to hard realizations about themselves and their follies.

The bragging soldier appears variously in the history plays as well as the comedies. In *2 Henry IV* and *Henry V*, Pistol, whose name "sorts well" with his fierceness (*Henry V*, 4.1.64), discharges volley after volley of boasting threats. He speaks a strange, bombastic language, filled with classical allusion and garbled echoes of contemporary plays:

> Shall packhorses
> And hollow pampered jades of Asia,
> Which cannot go but thirty mile a day,
> Compare with Caesars, and with cannibals,
> And Troiant Greeks? Nay, rather damn them with
> King Cerberus, and let the welkin roar.
>
> (2 *Henry IV*, 2.4.162–67)

Here literary reminiscence (the "pampered jades" derive from Marlowe's 2 *Tamburlaine* 4.4.1–2), classical allusion, and theatrical posturing substitute for courageous action. Pistol and his gang of rag-tag tavern buddies bicker throughout the plays. Despite the pretentious swagger, they live like paupers and adopt any shift to survive. In *Henry V* Pistol leads his fellow roisterers to the war in France to steal and scavenge, "like horseleeches, my boys, / To suck, to suck, the very blood to suck!" (2.3.54–55). One of them, Bardolph, gets hanged for robbing a church. Pistol himself suffers humiliating exposure: he gets publicly beaten and must eat a leek for insulting a true soldier, Fluellen. After, he vows to turn bawd and cutpurse (*Henry V*, 5.1.79–88).

Falstaff of the history plays represents Shakespeare's most complex adaptation of the braggart soldier. Part Plautine parasite, folk Lord of Misrule, and medieval Vice from the moral play, Falstaff raises bluster to the level of theatrical art. He covers his cowardice at Gadshill by inventing a tale of combat against an ever-expanding number of phantom men in buckram (*1 Henry IV*, 2.4.113ff.). Quick with colorful insult, he eats, drinks, and makes merry, displaying a genius for extemporaneous performance and for creating excuses. "Thou knowest in the state of innocency Adam fell; and what should poor Jack Falstaff do in the days of villainy? Thou seest I have more flesh than another man, and therefore more frailty" (3.3.165–69). Falstaff also has excellent instincts for survival. He plays dead to avoid fighting; "The better part of valor is discretion" (5.4.119–20). In *1 Henry IV* he misuses the king's press to draft wealthy men so that he can collect bribes for exemptions from service. He winds up with an army of sick paupers who die in battle. Finally, anticipating royal favor, Falstaff receives instead from the new King public rebuke and humiliation. Poor and alone, Falstaff dies, we hear in *Henry V*, partly of a broken heart.

Pistol and Falstaff have always entertained audiences and set into relief the courage of the true soldiers around them. The rebel Hotspur from *1 Henry IV*, for example, boasts, but also dares to "pluck bright honor from the pale-faced moon" (1.3.202); he dies valiantly and movingly on the battlefield. Prince Hal enjoys the tavern world also but rises to face his responsibilities and enemies with deadly competence. Pistol and Falstaff, however, have another, more subversive, function in the history plays: together they undercut the values of nationalism and heroism on display. Pistol goes to France to steal but so too does King Henry, we uneasily realize, his claims to that throne spuriously justified by the self-serving prelates Ely and Canterbury in the first scene. Is the English invasion noble imperialism or grand theft? Falstaff pointedly challenges the entire ethos of military honor. "What is honor? A word. What is in that word, 'honor'? What is that 'honor'? Air" (1 Henry IV, 5.1.133–35). Looking at a fallen comrade, he says, "I like not such grinning honor as Sir Walter hath. Give me life" (5.3.58–59). In these plays classical stereotypes raise searching questions about the nature of fame and heroism.

Plot tangling and untangling

A monk's discovery of Aristotle's lost treatise on comedy causes death and destruction in Umberto Eco's brilliant *The Name of the Rose*. That teasing fantasy notwithstanding, posterity has rested content with Aristotle's random observations and the *Tractatus Coislinianus*, a series of notes presumably derived from his lectures. These materials rank plot (*muthos*), or the arrangement of incidents, as the most important element of drama. Accordingly, Greek playwrights like Menander devised intricate patterns of comic action – including mistaken identities, deceits, and conflicts between parents and children – which served as models for Plautus, Terence, and their followers.

Plautus and Terence arranged these incidents into a sequence consisting of *protasis* (exposition), *epitasis* (complication), and *catastrophe* (resolution). Later commentators on Terence perceived a five-act structure in his works.[11] This sequence and structure of action became standard in early modern comedy. Inheriting a drama played in masks, Plautus and Terence often wrote plots with parallel characters in parallel situations: *Bacchides* features two young men, two old men, and two courtesans, for example; *Andria*, two young men, two young women, and two love affairs. The Roman penchant for parallels bore fruit in the rich varieties of plot doubling, repetition, contrast, and counterpoint in Shakespearean comedy – the two gentlemen of Verona and their loves, for example, the two sets of twins in *The Comedy of Errors*, the two sisters and courtships in *The Taming of the Shrew*, the two love affairs in *Much Ado About Nothing*, and the two households in *The Merry Wives of Windsor*.

Later playwrights, of course, raided individual plays for action and story. Both Jonson and Shakespeare, for example, adapted Plautus' *Aulularia*, particularly the story of Euclio, an old miser. Euclio wants the fires extinguished lest someone borrow a light (90–92); he is so cheap, the slaves joke, that he closes his mouth when he sleeps so as not to lose air; he saves his bathwater and clipped nails (302ff.). On stage he frets about his nubile daughter, Phaedria, whom he has deprived of a dowry. He worries much more, however, about a pot of gold which he carts around and tries to hide. When Strobilus, a slave, steals the gold, Euclio howls in frantic desperation: "heu me miserum, misere perii, / male perditus" (Alas, O wretched me! I am done for in the worst way! Ruined horribly!) (721–72). Euclio recovers his gold finally but, the fragments of the end suggest, hands it over to his daughter and her fiancé as a wedding present.

Ben Jonson combines *Aulularia* and another Plautine play, *Casina*, to create *The Case is Altered* (1597), his earliest surviving comedy. Euclio becomes Jaques de Prie, who also keeps a cold hearth, "Put out the fire, kill the chimney's heart / . . . / The more we spare, my child, the more we gain" (2.1.64, 66). He too frets about his treasure, collars a nosey onlooker, buries the gold, and loses it to some spying servants. Like Euclio, he cares more for his gold than for his daughter. Despite these similarities, Jonson radically adapts the Plautine plot. Jaques (actually Melun) a long time ago stole the girl, Rachel, and the gold from his master Lord Chamont. Jonson has Jaques praise his money lyrically for its power to create "Elysium," where blessed ghosts walk in the glorious palace of the God of gold (5.4.1ff.). The raptures show moral depravity and set up the reversal when the thief strikes: "Rachel call help! Come forth, / I'll rip thy entrails but I'll have my gold!" (5.5.10–11). Here comic obsession displays also sinful avarice. Jonson clearly signals Jaques' culpable inversion of values: "My gold, my gold, my life, my soul, my heaven!" (5.11.1). Rachel, meanwhile, has many suitors, endures an attempted rape, discovers her true identity and family, and winds up with the money and her beloved Paulo. The mute Phaedria moves center stage.

Shakespeare continues such adaptation in *The Merchant of Venice*. Like his prototypes, Shylock worries about his wealth, even dreaming anxiously of his moneybags (2.5.19). He too tries to lock up his daughter, Jessica, in the house, away from dangerous outsiders: "Shut doors after you. / Fast bind, fast find" (2.5.54–55). Losing Jessica and his money, he rages in the familiar frenzy, as Solanio reports: "My daughter! O, my ducats! O, my daughter!" (2.8.15). Like Euclio and Jaques but under compulsion, Shylock gives his fortune over to his daughter in the end. And like Rachel de Prie, Jessica takes on a larger role than Phaedria; she cheerfully steals her father's money, converts to Christianity, and elopes with her lover.

Not merely a miser and blocking father, Shylock embodies other comic stereotypes including the moneylender and the Jew. And, of course, he transcends all of them as Shakespeare endows him with a personal history, including the sentimental reminiscence of a turquoise ring he gave to one Leah. Shylock also has a keen, if literalist, sense of justice. In the celebrated "Hath not a Jew eyes" (3.1.55ff.) speech, he exposes Christian hypocrisy and hatred toward Jews; while asserting his right to revenge, he, paradoxically, asserts his common humanity. Once again, Shakespeare creates a classical character who plays and plays against the conventional expectations of the mask. The moral issues raised by the story of this reformulated Plautine miser can be difficult and disturbing, as the history of twentieth-century productions, particularly those in Israel, amply demonstrate.

The untangling of plot in Roman comedy often results in a discovery of identity (*anagnorisis*) that enables a wedding. Characters finally throw off their disguises (*Pseudolus*); long-lost daughters (*Cistellaria, Andria*) or sons (*Captivi*) suddenly get recognized, often by tokens like necklaces or rings. This discovery of identity becomes central to later comedy, particularly to Shakespeare. In *The Two Gentlemen of Verona* Julia climactically produces two rings (her own and Sylvia's) before stepping out of her disguise as a page. The revelation shames her astonished and unfaithful lover, Proteus, and effects a reconciliation. Similarly, Rosalind's doffing of her disguise as Ganymed enables the final harmonies and weddings of *As You Like It*. She pairs with Orlando, and leads three other couples to marital celebration. Often the discovery resonates with moral and spiritual significance. Hero's unveiling in *Much Ado About Nothing* rewards (perhaps excessively) Claudio, who unjustly spurned her as unfaithful. Rumored dead from grief, Hero restored to life strikes up wonder on stage and turns tragedy to comedy.

This turning of tragedy to comedy leads audiences beyond the farcical terrain of confusion into the marvelous region of romance. Plautus and Terence also supplied this genre of sea voyage, shipwreck, tried heroines, and miraculous restoration. Such elements recur throughout Roman comedy, especially in Plautus' *Rudens*, an important play for Heywood's *The Captives*. Refiguring the imperiled heroines and evil pimp, Heywood emphasizes the immorality of slavery and the girls' virtue and patience. *Rudens* directly or indirectly inspires Shakespeare's romances as well, those magical sea plays he wrote late in his career. The virtuous maid in *Pericles*, for example, Marina, maintains her chastity in the brothel and comes at last to moving reunion with her father, whom she saves from lethargy and despair. The classical *virgo*, often mute and off-stage, finally becomes a chaste healer, graceful and mysterious.

Such transformation shows how far later playwrights could go in adapting Roman comedy to different audiences and cultures. Their use of rhetoric, staging, character, and plot furnished later comedies, histories, romances, and even tragedies. Capulet plays the blocking father to Juliet, Polonius to Ophelia. Othello, at times, struts like a bragging soldier, and King Lear experiences a tragic version of the lock-out. The comic types and situations in these plays, evoked then shattered, augment their power to shock and disturb. Plautus and Terence created the essential theatrical vocabulary of comedy in the West, which Shakespeare, along with many others, variously deployed.

NOTES

For citations to Shakespeare I have used David Bevington (ed.), *The Complete Works of Shakespeare*, updated 4th edn (New York: Longman, 1997); for Plautus and Terence, the Loeb editions, *Plautus with an English Translation*, trans. Paul Nixon, 5 vols. (1916–38), and *Terence with an English Translation*, trans. John Sargeaunt, 2 vols. (1912; reprinted 1979).

1 See *The Oxford Classical Dictionary*, ed. Simon Hornblower and Anthony Spawforth (New York and Oxford: Oxford University Press, 1996).

2 R. B., *Terence in English* (Cambridge, 1598), p. 162.

3 See Ervin Beck, "Terence Improved: the Paradigm of the Prodigal Son in English Renaissance Comedy," *Renaissance Drama* 6 (1973): 107–22.

4 See George E. Duckworth, *The Nature of Roman Comedy* (Princeton: Princeton University Press, 1952), pp. 361–83; John Barsby (ed.), *Eunuchus* (Cambridge: Cambridge University Press, 1999), pp. 27–29.

5 For these and other examples see Duckworth, *Nature of Roman Comedy*, pp. 345–46.

6 I cite Ben Jonson from the C. H. Herford and Percy and Evelyn Simpson edition, 11 vols. (Oxford: Clarendon, 1929–52); Thomas Heywood from *Three Marriage Plays*, ed. Paul Merchant (Manchester: Manchester University Press, 1996). For Lionel's speech see 1.2.92–129; *Most.* 84–156.

7 W. Beare, *The Roman Stage*, 3rd edn (New York: Barnes and Noble, 1965), pp. 176ff.

8 Erich Segal, *Roman Laughter*, 2nd edn (New York and Oxford: Oxford University Press, 1987).

9 *Terence in English*, pp. 2, 107.

10 See Daniel C. Boughner, *The Braggart in Renaissance Comedy* (Minneapolis: University of Minnesota Press, 1954).

11 See T. W. Baldwin, *Shakspere's Five-Act Structure* (Urbana: University of Illinois Press, 1947).

3

LOUISE GEORGE CLUBB

Italian stories on the stage

Stephen Gosson might treble and intensify his famous antitheatrical malediction could he know what a cliché of theatre history one sentence of it has become:

> I have seen it that the *Palace of Pleasure*, the *Golden Ass*, the *Ethiopian History*, *Amadis of France*, the *Round Table*, bawdy comedies in Latin, French, Italian and Spanish have been thoroughly ransacked to furnish the playhouses in London.[1]

It is time to take Gosson seriously, to identify Shakespeare as one of the ransackers and to treat his Italian stories as a chapter in the history of ransacking, which also entails treating ransacking itself as a first premise of Renaissance dramaturgy.

Ever since Chaucer's Clerk and Franklin told tales from the *Decameron*, English literature has borne traces of Italian stories, though to call them "Italian" is to dismiss their remote origins, in many cases lost in the distance of antiquity and Indo-European folklore. It was the Renaissance versions, however, the "mery bookes of *Italie*" that delighted sixteenth-century English readers and, according to Roger Ascham, undermined their faith and morals. Playwrights in those times before copyright laws were under no pressure to invent original stories and instead valued new presentation of old material. Italy was the contemporary crucible of dramatic theory and Tasso, foremost among theorists, wrote that originality in dramatic composition should consist in form rather than in matter. Shakespeare took his plots wherever he found them, and he makes Hamlet explicit about his play-within-the-play: "The story is extant, and writ in choice Italian" (3.2.240).[2]

Shakespeare's Italianate plays, broadly classified, comprise five comedies and two tragedies entirely or partly set in Italy and for which ultimate sources of plot have been identified in Italian *novelle*: *The Two Gentlemen of Verona*, *The Taming of the Shrew*, *The Merchant of Venice*, *Much Ado About Nothing*, *All's Well That Ends Well*, *Romeo and Juliet* and

32

Othello, not counting the Rome of *Titus Andronicus, Julius Caesar, Antony and Cleopatra* and *Coriolanus*; two "romances," better described as tragicomedies, *The Winter's Tale*, with its beginning and ending in Sicily, and *Cymbeline*, in which Jachimo's name and ruse belong to the Boccaccian *novella* tradition and to the Rome of the Renaissance rather than to the Empire of the play's time setting; two comedies not set in Italy but based on Italian stories that circulated both in *novella* and dramatic form, *Twelfth Night* and *Measure for Measure*; and six that either came principally from the Italian theatre, *The Tempest* and *A Midsummer Night's Dream*, or contain some characters or scenes typical of its repertory, *The Comedy of Errors, Love's Labor's Lost, As You Like It*, and *The Merry Wives of Windsor*.

The method traditionally employed to account for Shakespeare's Italophilia is a long and instructive, but now exhausted, practice of source study that has pursued specific parallels in innumerable Italian texts, especially in narrative genres such as *novelle*, a number of which were "Englished" from French translations, chivalric *romanzi*, histories and such dialogues as Castiglione's *Libro del cortegiano*. Scrutiny of Painter's *Palace of Pleasure* and other compilations has revealed ultimate sources of various Shakespearean plays in Italian prose fiction from the fourteenth through the sixteenth centuries, flowering particularly in Boccaccio's collection of *novelle* and its abundant progeny:

1. *The Two Gentlemen of Verona* has sometimes been connected with Boccaccio's *novella* of Tito and Gisippo, *Decameron* (c. 1352), x, 8, through Elyot's *Boke named the Governour* (1531) and other English versions. The complete *Decameron* was not translated into English until 1620.

2. *Romeo and Juliet* is related to a story in Masuccio Salernitano, *Il Novellino* (1476) 33, retold in Luigi Da Porto's *Historia novellamente ritrovata di due nobili amanti*, "Romeo e Giulietta" (1530), again in Matteo Bandello's *Novelle* (1554–73), II, 19, translated by Pierre Boaistuau and appended to François de Belleforest, *Histoires Tragiques Extraictes des Oeuvres Italiennes de Bandel* (1559), by William Painter, *Palace of Pleasure* (1566–67), II, 25, and into verse by Arthur Brooke, "The Tragicall Historye of Romeus and Juliet" (1562).

3. *The Merchant of Venice* fuses several sources, including Masuccio's *Novellino* 14, and Ser Giovanni Fiorentino, *Il Pecorone* (c. 1390), IV, 1, not translated in Shakespeare's time.

4. *The Merry Wives of Windsor* has been thought to owe something to *Pecorone* II, 2.

5. *Much Ado About Nothing* is indebted to Bandello's *novella* 1, 22, of Timbreo and Fenicia.

6. *Twelfth Night* comes from a plot also used in Bandello II, 36, and Barnabe Riche, *Farewell to the Militarie Profession*, the tale of Apolonius and Silla (1581).

7. *Measure for Measure* is based on Giovanni Battista Giraldi's *Ecatommiti* 8, 5, the *novella* of Iuriste and Epitia (1565), the whole collection translated into French by Gabriel Chappuys (1584); the same story was adapted by George Whetstone as a play *Promos and Cassandra* (1578) and in *Heptameron of Civil Discourse* (1582).

8. *Othello* also is from the *Ecatommiti* 3, 7, the tale of the Moor of Venice.

9. *All's Well That Ends Well* follows *Decameron* III, 9, the tale of Giletta, translated by William Painter, *Palace of Pleasure* (1566–67), 1, 38.

10. *Cymbeline* contains elements suggesting that Shakespeare knew both *Decameron* II, 9, the tale of Zinevra, and an anonymous English version *Frederyke of Jennen* (1516).

More Italian stories than these were known and adapted in England, but the best known were the complete *novelle* collections available in French: Boccaccio's, Bandello's and Giraldi's; and the chivalric romance cycles, of which the crown jewel, Ariosto's *Orlando Furioso*, was translated by John Harington in 1591. All of these narratives were outgrowths of longer traditions, with roots in the classics – Homer, Ovid, Apuleius, Heliodorus, Achilles Tatius – and in folktales from as far away as India, transmitted in the *Gesta Romanorum*, hagiographies, and various other forms.

If, as Gosson said, English playwrights ransacked Italian narratives and comedies, it is equally true that Italian *novellieri* took their stories from anywhere and that Italian playwrights also ransacked *novelle*, *romanzi* and other narrative sources to make comedies, tragedies, and pastoral plays. Sometimes the playwright and the *novelliere* were the same person, as in the case of Giraldi, who dramatized one tale from his own *Ecatommiti* as *Orbecche, tragedia* and another as *Epitia, tragedia di fin lieto* (tragedy with happy ending). Indeed, the Italian sixteenth-century invention of a modern dramaturgy was based on the principle of staging mixed narrative sources within a five-act theatrical structure purposefully defined by imitating the classical comedies of Plautus and Terence, according to the latter's practice of *contaminatio* or commingling plots. Boccaccio, widely endorsed as the model for Italian prose, had a special status as a source for both comic and romantic matter. The theatrical receptacle into which the stories were poured was known as *commedia erudita* or *grave* because of its classical lineage; its regular plan of unified place, time, and action gave focus and climax to imbroglio plots and a variety of interchangeable structural units or "theatregrams" (characters, situations, actions, speeches, thematic patterns) which could be combined in dialogue and visual encounters to act out the fiction with verisimilitude.

The relation between Shakespeare and the *novella* and *romanzo* is a staple of Shakespeare studies, but the form in which these Italian narratives reached him is less commonly considered. Except for Giraldi's tale of the Moor of Venice, all the stories Shakespeare used had already been used in Italian drama, either whole or in pieces differently combined. The old method of source study also sifted some Italian plays, with modest results linking parts of Shakespeare's comedies to specific theatrical texts: *The Taming of the Shrew* to Ariosto's *Suppositi* through Gascoigne's *Supposes*, *Twelfth Night* to the Intronati Academy's collaborative *Gl'ingannati*, *The Tempest* to Rossi's *Fiammella* and analogous Arcadian scenarios, *Two Gentlemen of Verona* to Scala's fifth scenario, *Flavio tradito*, *Measure for Measure* to Giraldi's *Epitia*, and a few other like pairings.

A richer harvest of connections appears when general Italian theatrical practice and repertory, rather than specific sources, are surveyed. From the time of Ariosto's *La cassaria* (1508), Bibbiena's influential *Calandria* (1512) and Machiavelli's *La mandragola* (1518), the Plautine–Terentian form, modernized, Italianized, and amplified with Boccaccian or other *novella* content was established as the model of the new *commedia erudita*. Hundreds of plays flowing from competing courts and academies were printed during the course of the century. When Shakespeare began writing for the stage, the Italian comedy was in a state of full development and had produced different strains and styles, approaches to tragicomedy, romantic courtship plays of revelation, satirical adulterous farces of concealment, and double-plotted combinations of the two. The literary comedy also opened the way to a new "regular" third genre, the pastoral play, cultivated in the second half of the century with huge success.

Professional companies of what would eventually be called the *commedia dell'arte* were formed about mid-century, and the *comici* in turn ransacked the literary plays for materials for their improvised three-act scenarios or for their own occasional five-act scripted plays. On tour they disseminated theatregrams throughout Italy and abroad. In the 1570s they achieved lasting popularity in France and Spain. Shakespeare had access to printed plays; to accounts of the *commedia dell'arte* from Italians in London and Englishmen who traveled on the Continent, among them his colleague William Kempe; and to who knows how many actual performances. In whatever he encountered of the Italian theatre, whether literary plays, manuscript scenarios or performances, Shakespeare would have found narremes from *novelle* trimmed, shaped, and made stageworthy. Those in the scenarios would have been tailored specifically to the size and specialties of professional troupes.

The mass of such evidence, from printed and reprinted regular comedies and pastoral plays to fragmentary scenarios and dialogues for improvisation, yields no document more revealing than the actor Flaminio Scala's *Teatro delle favole rappresentative* (The Theatre of Stage Plots) (1611). These fifty "ideal" scenarios (forty "*comedie*" and ten pastoral or mixed "*opere*") memorialize several decades of experience in the Italian professional theatre and demonstrate much of its range. They attest to a continual mining of the kinds of fictive material also used by Shakespeare and to a method of selecting, combining and disposing stageworthy elements from a shared repertory.

Scala's scenarios are skeletal, a shorthand series of entrances, exits, disguises, and errors. They represent the kinds of plays improvised by Italian actors on plots appropriated from scripted *commedie erudite* that they read in print or memorized when invited to participate in court theatricals, ceaselessly augmenting their store with *novelle*, lyric poetry, classical compendia, and whatever else might serve for performing – and occasionally writing – new plays. Their immediate audiences heard what no scenario can show: the language that the *comici* brought to the blueprints of action. Our only knowledge of this comes from poems and dialogues that some published after retirement and from the regular five-act plays resembling *commedie erudite* written by a few. Nicolò Barbieri's famous defense of the players, *La supplica* (1634), refers to the many kinds of reading and writing necessary to their art. This exercise of the mind, like the constant practice in the dancing, singing and instrumental performances that were standard features of their plays, though invisible in most scenarios, was the discipline of the *commedia dell'arte*. Thus the best troupes prepared themselves for whatever occasions might arise; readiness was all.

Italian regular comedy and pastoral plays (what Polonius describes to Hamlet as the "writ"; 2.2.383) and the scenarios for improvising (the "liberty") all drew on the stage repertory accumulated in decades of ransacking and recombination, composed of pieces of stories, situations, speeches, moves, themes, and characters. The classical Plautine cast was updated and augmented in *commedia erudita*, the old man as the *vecchio*, the young lovers as *giovani innamorati*, with *servi* and freeloaders, the braggart *capitano* frequently Hispanized, the procurer as *ruffiano*, the prostitute as *cortegiana*, the nurse as *balia*, together with friars, pedants, alchemists, Moors, Jews, Germans and Ragusan seafarers, innkeepers, gypsies, comic hangmen, constables, and other additions from narrative sources, especially the *Decameron*.

A difference between the regular scripted *commedia erudita* and the improvised *commedia dell'arte* was that scenario plots were cut to fit a nuclear company of fixed roles with variable doubled parts. Scala's ideal company evokes his old friends the Andreini family and their stage names: thus the leading *innamorata* is always Isabella, the *capitano* always Spavento, one of the *innamorati* always Flavio (Scala's own role). The two *vecchi* are the universal *veneziano* Pantalone and *dottore* Graziano, the middle-aged *serva* is Franceschina, and the *servo* roles go to masked *zanni* with stable identities: Arlecchino, Burattino, Pedrolino. The plots in the bare-bones scenarios seem slapdash compared to regular comedies but indications of motion, music, comic turns, and dialects suggest the complex demands made on the actors. Essentially, however, the theatregrams of character and plot in the writ and the liberty come from the same repertory. Common among them are errors involving twins; the bed trick in a dark room; disguise of sex or social condition in order to serve a beloved, often entailing carrying messages to a new love and becoming the object of his or her affections; revelations of identity and reunions of separated families; tricks to fleece misers and to mock would-be seducers, presumptuous wooers and fortune hunters; madness and pretended madness; supposed death.

The fashionable pastoral play was invented by theorizing playwrights for court productions, adapting many features from comedy and a few from tragedy to an Arcadian setting. The compelling themes of love and providence had been staged increasingly in *commedia grave* as far as the rule of unity of place permitted, but a change of venue was needed for fully representing inner realities of emotion, psychological change, and supernatural providence, and so was born a new third genre, presided over by Amore. Unawakened or ill-assorted lovers learning to know their hearts constituted the primary cluster of types in the *favola pastorale*–their names and occupations came from classical and early Renaissance pastoral eclogues and narratives, their stage relationships, functions, and actions from comedy: *innamorati* and *innamorate* with assisting or competing friends, *servi* and *vecchi*, became shepherds and nymphs, principal and subordinate; the lustful importuning *capitano* and the more transgressive *zanni* were replaced by satyrs.

The best known of all pastoral plays, Tasso's *Aminta, favola boscareccia* (1573), is in its simple brevity the least representative exemplar of the genre. Experimentation with the stage pastoral was intense and produced imbroglio plots of several types, one of which allowed for magic, transformations and hybrid elements, while maintaining the unities of place, time, and action. Plays like Luigi Pasqualigo's *Gl'intricati, pastorale* (1575), Cristoforo Castelletti's *L'Amarilli, pastorale* (1580), and Orlando Pescetti's *La regia pastorella, favola boschereccia* (1589) contain some typical theatregrams: sorcerers with spirits at their command; visions and dreams, working toward a denouement revelation; cloddish rustics contrasting with the refined shepherds, like the bawdy servants of comedy – one of Castelletti's is temporarily turned into a tree; courtiers or citizens lost or shipwrecked in Arcadia, destined to figure in a recognition scene, like long-lost relations in comedy; even visitors from the *commedia dell'arte*, such as Pasqualigo's Gracian, who magically acquires an ass's head. Scala's scenarios accommodate theatregrams from the written pastoral drama to the personnel of an acting troupe: in *L'arbore incantato* (49) Arlecchino is turned into a crane and a nymph into a tree, finally restored by a magician with his book and rod. This type of pastoral plot, so well established that it had even been reexpanded into a full-length play by the actor Bartolomeo Rossi in *La Fiammella, pastorale* (1584), was repeated in the Arcadian scenarios from the Locatelli/Corsini manuscripts (1618–22), not printed until 1913.[3]

What Scala recorded was the high fashion of the *commedia dell'arte* repertory before 1611, just what William Kempe would have brought back from his Italian sojourn in 1601. His successor as clown in Shakespeare's company, Robert Armin, knew Italian well enough to translate a *novella* of Straparola and very likely read plays too. Many were available in England; Aretino's were even printed there in Italian in 1588, Guarini's and Tasso's in 1591. Knowing how writers of *commedia erudita* and players of *commedia dell'arte* made theatregrams from myriad stories and plays, Shakespeare could do the same with any source, mixing his own, proportioning them to his company's capacities and his audience's expectations. Whenever he takes up a story, he disposes it with boundless creativity and, even in the earliest plays, with the confidence of one whose methods and normative plots have been tested on stage. Even where Shakespeare unquestionably follows a specific *novella*, comparisons with *commedie erudite*, scenarios, and dialogues of *comici* suggest that the narrative has been processed for the theatre and belongs to the common repertory of playmakers. The more extensive the comparison the more unavoidable the conclusion that a primary object of Shakespeare's ransacking was Italian stage production, tradition, and technology.

The audience of his own day recognized as much. John Manningham noted in his diary a performance at the Inns of Court, 1602: "At our feast wee had a play called "Twelve Night, or What You Will," much like the *Commedy of Errores*, or *Menechmi* in Plautus, but most like and neere to that in Italian called *Inganni*."[4] The inexact reference is to the Sienese Intronati Academy's famous *Gl'ingannati* (The Deceived), produced as a sequel to their celebration of the opening of the carnival season on the twelfth night of Christmas, 1531/32. It was in this year that a literary fellowship of witty gentlemen in Siena was formally baptized "The Academy of the

Thunderstruck," inaugurating a series of elegant comedies that would continue into the next century, despite periodic prohibitions by municipal authorities. The plays were written and privately performed by the academicians, ostensibly in compliment to the ladies in their audience. Their first production became the single most imitated *commedia erudita* of the Renaissance, a point of departure for dozens of others throughout Europe. In the 1590s it was performed at Cambridge in Latin as *Laelia*.

Shakespeare's Viola is obviously sister to Lelia of *Gl'ingannati*. A courageous but sensitive girl with a troubled history, Lelia has survived the Sack of Rome in which her brother is believed to have perished. She disguises her sex to escape a marriage arranged by her impoverished father and takes service with a man who has forgotten her and now sends her to woo another, who in turn falls in love with the deputy wooer but finally is contented with the long-lost brother while Lelia recaptures her beloved's heart.

The Sienese play is a variation on Bibbiena's pioneering *commedia erudita Calandria*, itself a modern *contaminatio* of *Menaechmi* with comic tales from Boccaccio and a sex change for one twin. The plot of *Gl'ingannati* is disposed dramatically with theatregrams typical of the new well-made genre: disputes of the disguised girl with her *balia*, parents planning distasteful marriages for children, *servi* intriguing on behalf of their *padroni*, tricking and outwitting each other and mocking whatever is high-flown and solemn, from sententious pederastic tutors to strutting Spanish soldiers to ecstatic lovers. Competing innkeepers and rollicking feasters add to the various registers of style, love speeches are interspersed with fast-talking comic turns. The action flows constantly around the streets of Modena, complexity of motive and action given tension by a time frame and an interrelation of parts, the characters all tangled in a knot of deceits and errors arising from family separations, sex disguise, conflicting loves and lusts, hungers and greeds, most of them satisfied by the denouement. If its atmosphere lacks the lyricism and psychological delicacy of *Twelfth Night*, *Gl'ingannati* is markedly more romantic than its precursor *Calandria*.

Twelfth Night also inherits from Sienese comedy a history involving both narrative and drama, which illuminates the developing technology of Italian theatre and points to Shakespeare's grasp of it. The recent rediscovery of Giovanni Lappoli Pollastra's *Parthenio* (1516),[5] long lost because its only edition was so quickly sold out that too few copies survived to be noted in early bibliographies, reveals the theatrical origins of *Gl'ingannati* itself. *Parthenio* was a major carnival event, the first published play sponsored by the University of Siena, certainly witnessed and possibly acted in by some of the spirited young noblemen who would found the Academy of the Intronati fifteen years later.

Parthenio has characters and plot material enough to furnish forth several plays. In a disjointed episodic form and meter characteristic of the medieval *sacra rappresentazione* but demonstrating some knowledge of the new well-built and linguistically current *commedia erudita*, the Aretine schoolmaster Pollastra drew on Roman legend, medieval narrative romance, and Terentian comedy for his "commedia" about the resourceful Galicella (named from the chivalric romance cycles), who dons male disguise to follow Parthenio from her Greek pastoral retreat to Babylon and win back his love. He sends her to court his new love, who falls in love with the messenger, and at last, after redisguising herself as a servant girl and substituting herself for another woman in his bed, Galicella reclaims her husband and is crowned empress. Here, with a variety of low comedy scenes, are combined narremes from folktale, romance, and two *Decameron novelle*: that of the calumniated Zinevra (II, 9) who, in male disguise, serves a sultan and proves her innocence to her husband, and that of the repudiated Giletta di Narbona (III, 9) who, unrecognized in the dark, manages to conceive by her husband and so to gain his love.

When the Intronati winnowed this superabundance for materials to construct their up-to-date *commedia erudita*, catering to a feminine Sienese audience's stated preference for *Decameron* tales featuring resolute and loyal heroines, the narremes became theatregrams through which the seeds of romantic comedy would be sowed throughout Europe. The sequence demonstrates the evolution of modern comedy. Using the model of plotting represented by *Calandria*, the Intronati made selections from *Parthenio*, the momentous theatrical initiation of their adolescence. They tightened the action, concentrated on the primary love plot, and gave it unity of place and relevance to its audience by setting it in actual time in a real Italian city and discarding the antiquated verse for idiomatic modern prose.

Imitations of *Gl'ingannati* soon appeared on stage in Italy, France, Spain, and the coast of Illyria, where it was adapted in Ragusa by the Croatian playwright Marin Držiċ, who had studied in Siena. The story was also retold in *novella* form, by Giraldi, Bandello, Belleforest in his translation of Bandello, and by Barnabe Riche in his tale of Apolonius and Silla. Above all, its scattered members (themselves derived from scattered members) appear in dozens of scripted *commedie erudite* and in scenarios like Scala's. Details of the love plot of *Twelfth Night* suggest that Shakespeare had read Riche and probably Belleforest, but he disposed, cut, and augmented the narrative material according to the theatrical structures of the Italian comedy already widely disseminated as a repertory of combinable parts in printed texts and *commedia dell'arte* performances.

Many *commedie erudite* with different plots have clusters of the same theatregrams: that of the transvestite woman, disguised for safety and/or love; brotherless in *Parthenio* and numerous later comedies, she is sometimes joined by an identical male twin, as in *Gl'ingannati*, Niccolò Secchi's *Inganni* (1547), Curzio Gonzaga's *Inganni* (1592), Sforza Oddi's *Prigione d'amore* (1590), and many others, not counting the cases in pastoral plays and even in a *tragedia di fin lieto* like Giraldi's *Antivalomeni* (1548), where there are two sets of boy/girl twins; the disguise of sex may be linked to serving a lover or spouse and becoming the mistaken object of love to third or even fourth parties, as in Andrea Calmo's *Travaglia* (1556) and Della Porta's *Cintia* (1601); a witty dialogue on wooing between loved one and cross-dressed lover commonly occurs in connection with the situation of the unrecognized servant but also appears in exchanges like Rosalind's with Orlando in *As You Like It* (4.1); and *commedie erudite* with romantic disguise plots routinely contain interspersed scenes of below-stairs carousing of *servi*, altercations with comic suitors, and similar standard Plautine elements absent in the source *novelle*.

Conversely, there are theatregrams in *Parthenio* that are omitted from *Gl'ingannati* but present in scores of other comedies, such as the substitution of lovers in the dark. Although *Gl'ingannati* includes the tactic of locking two girls in a room and discovering that one is a boy, a variation on *Calandria*, in which shutting up a pair as proof of adultery backfires when they are discovered to be of the same sex, it lacks the Boccaccian bed trick found in *Parthenio*, Della Porta's *Cintia*, *Measure for Measure* and *All's Well That Ends Well*. For the latter Shakespeare probably read a French version of the *Decameron* tale of Giletta, but he structured the bed trick theatrically in the manner of *commedia erudita*, with apposite dialogues between Helena and the Widow, the Widow and her friends, Helena and Diana, Diana and Bertram and so forth. These scenes are also reminiscent of Girolamo Bargagli's *Pellegrina* (1563), the most renowned of the later Sienese *commedie erudite*; here the disguise is varied in the primary *innamorata's* disguise as a pilgrim and the secondary *innamorato's* as a tutor, while the secondary *innamorata* disguises her true state of mind by pretending to be insane. Most of these plays end with revelations of identity and reunions of families, a finale that was itself a repertorial setpiece.

Parthenio was a prophetic compendium of playwrights' and players' choices among narrative sources that would export the recipe for romantic comedy to the rest of Europe and to Shakespeare. Looking back in 1572 at the tastes of the founding members of the Intronati, Bargagli cited their preference for stories about greatness of spirit, especially in virtuous and long-suffering women like the patient Griselda (*Decameron* x, 10), or those who after persecution and calumny are found to be chaste and innocent, such as Giletta, who won her husband twice (*Decameron* III, 9), Ariosto's traduced Ginevra (*Orlando Furioso* v), and Boccaccio's Zinevra (*Decameron* II, 9), who was found alive and innocent when her husband thought her dead and guilty.[6] A predecessor of Imogen in *Cymbeline*, Zinevra's plight figures also in Luigi Groto's *Pentimento amoroso*, a pastoral play, its single set permitting the scene of the calumniated wife's escape from execution in the woods to be staged without loss of unity of place. One feature of *Parthenio* that could not have been transferred to a *commedia erudita* is the sojourn in the country; change of scene was regarded as sloppy and unverisimilar in the regular modern genres. A desire to use country settings and Arcadian themes was one of the forces behind the development of the pastoral play.

In eighteen of Scala's forty comedy scenarios the primary *innamorata* puts on boy's clothes, usually to seek the man she loves. *Li finti servi* (30) uses the boy/girl twins of the *Gl'ingannati* story (Isabella as *servo* to Orazio) but ends with three marriages, including that of the Capitano with the pregnant slave Ortensia, in reality long-lost sister to Flavio. In a different plot, *La gelosa Isabella* (25), Isabella dresses as a man and is taken for her missing brother Fabrizio: here she is not servant to Orazio, whom she believes faithless, her father Pantalone boozes with household cronies, like Sir Toby in *Twelfth Night*, and a *serva* Franceschina practices the deceit of imitating her mistress from a window, varying the familiar deceit used in *Much Ado About Nothing* and in Della Porta's regular comedy *Gli duoi fratelli rivali* (1601). The transvestite *innamorata* appears in another combination in *Il ritratto* (39) when "Silvia milanese," a name reminiscent of *The Two Gentlemen of Verona*, masquerades as the page Lesbino and performs the bed trick, substituting herself for the actress Vittoria in a dark room.

With *Twelfth Night*, Shakespeare was not just adapting *Gl'ingannati* for the English stage but rather participating in the ingenious and by then well-tried Italian way of making comedy by reshuffling pieces from the repertory and fusing them into an intrigue structure. He combined features of *The Comedy of Errors* with the new plot, this time using a single pair of twins but changing the sex of one, mixing in remembered details from *novelle* and Plautus, adding different theatregrams, such as the tricks played on Malvolio, typical of *commedia* subplots: in Della Porta's *Il moro* (1607) a presumptuous wooer is tricked into dressing like a parrot to please his lady and ridiculed for his pains, in his *La furiosa* (1609) a *capitano* bent on seduction is taken for a madman and shut up in a dark basement.

Another view of Shakespeare's dramatizing of Italian stories on the principles of *commedia* is obtained by comparing *Much Ado About Nothing* with the contemporaneous *Fratelli rivali*. The point of departure for both was Bandello's *novella* (I, 22) about a deceit practiced to discredit a lady, a traditional plot that had been used by Ariosto and others before him. Pieces of it turn up in Scala's scenarios and in the wake of the *comici dell'arte* traveling abroad. In Bandello's version, Timbreo di Cardona, arriving in thirteenth-century Messina in the train of Pedro of Aragon, falls in love and plights his troth with Fenicia, whose chastity a rival traduces with the help of a servant who poses as her mistress entertaining a lover from her window. Fenicia appears to die of shock, the wicked rival confesses, and when Timbreo keeps his pledge to marry as Fenicia's father decrees, he finds himself wed to the revived Fenicia herself.

Shakespeare takes his setting, Messina in the time of Pedro of Aragon, from Bandello, perhaps in French translation, but once again his manner of dramatizing the story shows his adherence to the *commedia* method and its repertory of movable parts. The parts he chooses, however, dramatize the *novella* differently from Della Porta's more melodramatic and tragicomic handling of it. Della Porta also uses details of action from Bandello not to be found in other versions, but he changes the names and brings the action closer to his audience by setting it in sixteenth-century Salerno, adding pieces of local history and making the plot turn on the rivalry of brothers in love and the moral dilemma of their uncle the viceroy who must see justice done. Both Della Porta and Shakespeare double the sets of characters, omit long gaps in time, add clowns and constables, clever and stupid servants, mocking speeches, malapropisms and puns, eavesdropping and mistakes, encounters contrasting the young men in love, sword play and lovers' dialogues, all in the established Italian way of fitting *novella* matter by *contaminatio* and redistribution into high-tech *commedia* form. But the contrast is as revealing as the resemblance, for the two dramatists vary and stage the story with different theatregrams from the same repertory. Della Porta makes much of the baroquely swaggering amorous Capitano Martebellonio; Shakespeare had used this theatregram in its basic form dear to both scripted and improvised *commedia* in *Love's Labor's Lost*, but thereafter preferred to perform variations on it for brilliantly diverse characterizations, Falstaff, Othello, and Parolles. In *Much Ado About Nothing* only the traces of the typical *capitano* may faintly be seen in some of Benedick's attitudes and speeches.

An effective mobile structure in the common repertory was the balcony or window scene combined with lyric evocation of the beloved as sunlight. It appears in scenarios for romantic or comic purposes, with the speech barely indicated, as in Scala's *La caccia* (37): "Isabella alla fenestra, invoca il sole" (Isabella at the window invokes the sun), and in *Fratelli rivali* (II, 2–3) it opens an impassioned love scene as Ignazio beholds Carizia at her window "Già fuggono le tenebre dell'aria, ecco l'aurora che precede la chiarezza del mio bel sole" (Now darkness flees from the air, here is the dawn preceding the brightness of my beautiful sun), and closes it "Ecco tramontata la sfera del mio bel sole" (There sets the sphere of my beautiful sun). Shakespeare does not use this theatregram in *Much Ado About Nothing*, perhaps because it had already figured in *Romeo and Juliet* (2.2) and with a difference in *Richard II* (3.3). The ceremoniously metaphorical love exchange between Ignazio and Carizia has no equivalent scene between Claudio and Hero in *Much Ado About Nothing*, and *Fratelli rivali* has no Beatrice and Benedick. But for them too the Italian theatre offered parallels. Although scenarios are by definition too sketchy to reveal more than the gist of scenes, dialogues like Francesco Andreini's *Bravure* (1607) and his late wife's "contrasti amorosi," which he published after retirement, display a range of dialogues actually used on stage, including both the lyrical wooing type of duet and the verbal fencing style that Shakespeare used in creating Beatrice and Benedick.

The balcony scene is not the only theatregram from *commedia* in *Romeo and Juliet*. Its plot is tragic in all the many narrative versions, of which Shakespeare seems to have known more than one. He principally follows Brooke's "Tragicall Historye of Romeus and Juliet," a 1562 verse translation of Boaistuau's translation of Bandello's novella (II, 19) based on Da Porto's version of a still older story. Brooke saw "the same argument lately set foorth on stage,"[7] but says neither where nor in what language. The details he added to his source in "Bandell" are Italianate comic theatregrams, Juliet's nurse for example. Whereas in the repertory of *tragedia* this role, labeled *nutrice*, customarily calls for moralizing or pathos, in *commedia* the speeches of the equivalent character of the *balia* (a lower domestic term for the same function) are bawdy, quarrelsome, garrulous, and tinged with greed (her function often conflated with that of the go-between *ruffiana*). In Italy the story had been staged in several formats. Groto's *Adriana* (1578) presents the narrative as unrelieved tragedy set in ancient times; Scala's scenarios *La creduta morta* (7) and *Li tragici successi* (18) show how improvised comedy could make various combinations from pieces of the tale; Raffaello Borghini's late *commedia grave La donna costante* (1578), in tone, mixture of comic and serious, and emphasis on the theme of Fortune, best exemplifies the theatrical genre on which *Romeo and Juliet* was built: Shakespeare used the blueprint but excised the last turn of Fortune. To Brooke's embellishment of the *novella* with movable parts from the theatrical repertory Shakespeare added more in the same vein and introduced Mercutio's mocking of the Nurse (2.4), a standard stage device of youth baiting age. The entire dramaturgical procedure, the encounters and skirmishes, the alternation of jesting and lovemaking in *Romeo and Juliet* belong to Borghini's and Della Porta's genre of comedy – until the denouement, when the disasters averted in *commedia grave* are allowed to run their tragic course.

Othello is another extraordinary Shakespearean variation on Italian theatrical structures. Giraldi's *novella* of the Moor of Venice (*Ecatommiti* III, 7) is too sordid to be called tragic, but uniformly dismal in its ending. A handsome but wicked Ensign importunes the Moor's wife in vain, concludes that she loves a subaltern and persuades her husband of this, attacks the subaltern in the dark as he comes from a prostitute's house, cuts off his leg and, with the Moor's connivance, bludgeons Disdemona to death with a sock filled with sand. Eventually the Moor is killed by his wife's relatives. The Ensign dies from damage done under torture for another crime, after which his wife tells all. The characters are sketchy types and only one of them has a name, "Disdemona." To stage this brutal tale Shakespeare employed the *dramatis personae* of a standard Italian scenario and a couple of themes varied in innumerable scenarios and *commedie erudite*: jealousy and optical illusion, presented in familiar comic actions and relationships. Desdemona and Emilia are placed in the rapport of *padrona* with *serva*. Brabantio is assigned the stage function of the Pantalone, father of the runaway bride, resembling Shylock in this, and his brother's name, "Gratiano," is that of the second *vecchio* in improvised comedy. Othello's stage lineage may be traced to the figure of the *capitano*, here transformed in that his eloquent female-fascinating stories of military prowess and exotic travels are all true. Cassio and Rodrigo belong to the range of suitors, worthy and foolish, who pursue the *innamorata*. Bianca is a *cortegiana*, and Iago a diabolic mutant of the clever scheming *servo* who creates the illusion in Othello's mind that his situation is a stereotypical comedy of adultery, complete with stock figures and himself as the cuckold. Shakespeare propels this farce into tragedy by means of the psychological power he gives his characters, by Othello's refusal to play the role, showing how a "real" captain and husband might act if he took the scenario seriously. Making tragedy of comedy, Shakespeare also makes his own play seem "real" by contrast with farcical theatregrams.

Although neither originated in a *novella*, *A Midsummer Night's Dream* and *The Tempest* must be counted among Shakespeare's Italianate plays because their sylvan settings, fantasy plots, magic, super- and subhuman beings link them with the popular pastoral play. *A Midsummer Night's Dream* was printed with the comedies in the first folio, but in Italy it would have been classified *favola boscareccia* or *pastorale*, like Pasqualigo's *Intricati*, in which mismatched shepherds and nymphs are properly paired off in love by means of sleep, dreams, and a potion administered by a sorceress and her Puck-like familiar. By magic she attaches animal heads to three clownish visitors to the woods. Shakespeare chose to use all of these theatregrams minus the pastoral trappings. Scala's *Rosalba incantatrice* (44) employs the sorceress and her spirits but sets her on an island and introduces wandering princes and princesses in episodes reminiscent of *Cymbeline, The Winter's Tale,* and *The Tempest.* Like *A Midsummer Night's Dream, The Tempest* has no single narrative source but is composed on the principles of the Arcadian scenarios from the Locatelli/Corsini manuscripts and Scala's hybrids, such as *Gli avvenimenti comici, pastorali e tragici, opera mista* (42). Like some of them, it is a maritime version of the pastoral plays in which clowns, nobles, magicians, and lovers meet in the wild to know themselves and their hearts and to right old wrongs.

Polonius' praise of the traveling players for their productions "pastoral, pastoral-comical, historical-pastoral, tragical-historical, tragical-comical-historical-pastoral" performed by both "the law of writ and the liberty" (2.2.380–83), inevitably sounds like Shakespeare's jesting acknowledgment of a range of possibilities and principles of playmaking that came from Italy and found a matchlessly creative exponent in London.

NOTES

1 *Plays Confuted in Five Actions,* 1582, London, D6v, quoted in E. K. Chambers, *The Elizabethan Stage* (Oxford: Clarendon Press, 1923), IV, 216.

2 *The Norton Shakespeare,* ed. Stephen Greenblatt, Walter Cohen, Jean E. Howard, and Katharine Eisaman Maus (New York and London: W. W. Norton, 1997).

3 Ferdinando Neri, *Scenari della maschere in Arcadia* (Città di Castello: Lapi, 1913; reprinted Torino: Bottega d'Erasmo, 1961).

4 Quoted in Geoffrey Bullough (ed.), *Narrative and Dramatic Sources of Shakespeare* (London: Routledge and Kegan Paul; New York: Columbia University Press, 1957–75), II, 269.

5 A critical and historical account of the play and its author appears with a transcription of the complete text of *Parthenio* and of Pollastra's unpublished poem *Triumphi* in Louise George Clubb and Robert Black, *Romance and Aretine Humanism in Sienese Comedy, 1516: Pollastra's "Parthenio" at the Studio di Siena* (Firenze: La Nuova Italia, 1993).

6 Girolamo Bargagli, *Dialogo de' giuochi,* ed. P. D'Incalzi Ermini (Siena: Accademia Senese degli Intronati, 1982), pp. 223–24.

7 *Romeo and Juliet,* ed. Brian Gibbons, Arden Shakespeare (London and New York: Methuen, 1980), appendix II, p. 240.

4

JANETTE DILLON

Elizabethan comedy

"And where does the dog come in?," the players in *Shakespeare in Love* keep asking. This is one of the film's running gags about setting supposed high art within the context of hard economic forces. Dogs pull the punters in, it is implied; so to be popular a play must have its dog and, by wider implication, its clown scenes. The joke is based on some truth. Several extant plays have scenes with dogs, and many more have their clowns. Some even incorporate bears. *Mucedorus* (1588–98), one of the most popular plays on the public stage, reprinted at least fifteen times over seventy years, has a scene early on in which Mouse, the clown, probably first played by the great Richard Tarlton, exits backwards tumbling over a bear, and Shakespeare's *The Winter's Tale* (1610) surely glances at this tradition in the famous stage direction that has Antigonus "*Exit pursued by a bear*" (3.3.58).[1] Bears would not be difficult to get hold of, particularly as some playhouses did double duty as bear pits, but a bear part might sometimes be taken by a man in a bear suit. Mouse jokes about the probability that the bear rumored to be on the loose "cannot be a Beare, but some Divell in a Beares Doublet" (1.2.3–4).[2] The joke could work either way, allowing for either a real bear or a man in a bear suit to collide with Mouse.

Sir Philip Sidney, speaking from the position of conscious high art, attacked the public stage in the 1580s on the grounds of this tendency to drag in comic by-play. "Naughty play-makers and stage-keepers," he writes, have made comedy "odious." Their plays "be neither right tragedies, nor right comedies, mingling kings and clowns, not because the matter so carrieth it, but thrust in clowns by head and shoulders, to play a part in majestical matters, with neither decency nor discretion."[3] It is certainly the case that many Elizabethan and earlier plays import comic routines as an add-on element, and that this is as true of every other genre as it is of anything we might structurally classify as comedy. The generic label of *comedy* is in fact quite difficult to apply to many plays before the 1580s, except those that consciously translate or imitate classical structures; and the term remains very broad and undefined in contemporary usage into the early seventeenth century. During the first half of Elizabeth's reign we might say that comedy in the generic sense is relatively undeveloped, while comedy in the sense of comic matter is alive and well, kicking its way into every possible dramatic shape. The Vice, a familiar and often dominant figure in medieval morality plays, lives on in all kinds of later plays with and without a strong didactic element, characteristically undermining the most serious concerns of the play; and comic elements intrude at even the most apparently solemn or climactic moments in the earlier Elizabethan drama. Thus, for example, in *The Rare Triumphs of Love and Fortune* (1582), at the point where the court hears that Armenio's dumbness can only be cured by blood taken from the tenderest part of his worst enemy, one of the clowns turns to the audience to ask them which part of a man they think is the tenderest; at the point in *Damon and Pythias* (1564–68) where the two friends are both saved from imminent execution by each other's faithfulness, the hangman has an aside in which he confides his intention to make an immediate exit before he loses his fee; and Ambidexter, the Vice in *King Cambises* (c. 1558–69), moves swiftly from weeping for the death of Lord Smirdis, an innocent slain by the tyranny of his own brother, to laughing at it, at the same time explicitly reminding the audience of the quality his name identifies, the capacity "with both hands to play" (line 744).[4]

Yet we should recognize that in none of these plays can the decision to incorporate clowning in this way be put down to economic imperatives. All three were court plays, and *Damon and Pythias* was also performed at Merton College, Oxford. Though clowns and dogs were undeniably popular, they were as popular with the elite as with less fashionable audiences. One of Tarlton's most famed routines was jousting with a little dog with sword and longstaff – but the venue was the court and the dog was the Queen's. The thrusting in of clowns and dogs taps a deeper root than pragmatic economics. Where it is part of wider structures that pull against it, such thrusting suggests an instinct for playing on the edge that is incompatible with classical notions of unified genre. Nor is it an instinct that disappears in the latter part of the period. Shakespeare still understood the risky pleasures of letting grave diggers joke about Ophelia's burial or having Cleopatra exchange bawdy innuendo with a clown in the moments before her death, as well as the more straightforward routines with Launce's dog (though even the dog is not wholly discrete from the main plot; his reported pissing on Silvia's farthingale [*Two Gentlemen of Verona*, 4.4.16–39] changes the audience's relationship with Silvia).

While the instinct for mixing comic elements into various kinds of dramatic structures persists into the seventeenth century, however, drama from about the 1580s does become more generically classifiable. In the earlier part of Elizabeth's reign, miscellaneity is almost a principle of construction in many plays, which may bring together comic, tragic, moral, biblical, political, topical, and romantic elements in ways that seem confusing to modern audiences familiar only with Shakespeare and later drama. In fact prologues and title pages from the earliest printed plays (*Fulgens and Lucres*, the first printed play in English, was printed by John Rastell *c*.1512–16) down to the 1580s not only regularly advise readers or prospective players that they contain a mixture of serious and frivolous matters, but sometimes advise them how to cut bits out to emphasize one over the other or simply to reduce performance time. Rastell's *Four Elements* (*c*. 1517–*c*. 1518), for example, states in a prefatory note that the whole play will take about an hour and a half to perform, but adds that "yf ye lyst ye may leve out muche of the sad [serious] mater . . . and than it wyll not be paste thre quarters of an hour of length."[5] *King Cambises*, although it incorporates several deaths, culminating in the death of King Cambises himself, has a title page describing it as "A Lamentable Tragedie, mixed full of plesant mirth," while the running heads call it "A Comedie of King Cambises." Richard Edwardes, in the prologue to *Damon and Pythias*, advises his audience that because his play contains "matter mix'd with mirth and care," he has decided to call it a "tragical comedy."[6] The only plays of early date that evidence care for a more unified comic structure are those in a consciously classical tradition, plays such as *Thersites* (1537), *Ralph Roister Doister* (1552–54?) and *Gammer Gurton's Needle* (*c*. 1552–63); and within this tradition the tendency toward unity predates even Elizabeth's accession.

A rather sudden change is apparently visible, however, in the Christmas season of 1583–84, when three innovative plays were performed at court: George Peele's *The Arraignment of Paris* and John Lyly's *Campaspe* and *Sappho and Phao*. Since so many plays from this early period do not survive, it is always risky to make pronouncements about seemingly sudden innovation, but Lyly and Peele are here producing a kind of drama unparalleled in extant texts. All three plays were performed by children's companies. Boy companies had been more popular than adult companies at court throughout the first half of the reign, and in 1575–76 the Chapel Children and the boys of St. Paul's choir school had both begun performing plays publicly and commercially at playhouses in the Blackfriars and Paul's respectively. The children who performed Peele's *Arraignment* were, according to the play's printed title page, the Queen's Chapel children, but these first two plays of Lyly's seem to have been performed by a merged group of Chapel and Paul's children under the patronage of the Earl of Oxford, possibly including boys from Oxford's own chapel. Lyly's plays were performed at the Blackfriars as well as at court, but *The Arraignment*, at least in its extant form, which is reliant on the Queen's presence to bring it to a close, cannot have been played outside the confines of the court. The play, though constructed as a sequence of formal shows based on classical mythology, is unified by its upward movement toward resolution in the person of the Queen. Its structure, in five acts, is also carefully symmetrical, radiating outward from a center in Act 3:[7] Act 3 presents a woman (Oenone) deserted by a man (Paris) and a man (Colin Clout) rejected by a woman (Thestylis); Acts 2 and 4 on either side play out the familiar myth of Paris's judgment of Venus as the fairest of the three goddesses, Juno, Pallas, and Venus; while the first and last acts are virtually free of narrative, with Act 1 showing the lesser gods presenting gifts to Juno, Pallas, and Venus and Act 5 resolving the unacceptability of Paris' judgment by unanimously agreeing with Diana's wise award of the golden apple to "*the Nymphe Eliza a figure of the Queene*," as the stage direction so explicitly announces (line 1137).[8] Diana is given a long speech in praise of "this renowned Queene so wise and fayre" (line 1199), and the speech then makes way for an apotheosis of spectacle and Latin song, "*the state*," as another stage direction says, "*being in place*" (line 1207). The Queen's throne, or "state," which has been "in place," centrally positioned in the hall, throughout the play, becomes quite literally the centerpiece of the play. The actors must move from the stage, or the part of the hall where the fictional representation has been enacted, to the center of the hall, within the spectating area, so that the furies can "*laye downe their properties at the Queenes feete*" (line 1213) and Diana can place the golden ball into "*the Queenes owne hands*" (line 1240). The specificity of the directions marks the play's forcefully focused unity and certainty of vision.

This unity, however, is a broad structure encompassing separate shows working toward a shared purpose. Peele, like his father, was to become a writer of city pageants, which typically build separate tableaux around a central theme, geared to honor a single person; and *The Arraignment of Paris*, with its slight plot, separate strands, and rich, free-standing spectacles is pageant-like to a degree. It is in this respect that Peele's *Arraignment* most differs from Lyly's plays. *Campaspe* and *Sappho and Phao*, while also built around fairly slight plots, do not proceed by way of self-contained spectacular moments. Where Peele's dramaturgy seems to work through a primarily visual imagination, Lyly's seems to start from a more cerebral base, constructing dramatic action around intellectual questions rather than around visual spectacle. Both *Campaspe* and *Sappho and Phao* ask questions about the relations between love and power and passion and reason, and about the proper place of love in the life of a ruler. And common to both plays, as to most of Lyly's other plays, is the strong focus on love itself as the motivating force of the drama. This is an area in which Lyly's contribution is both innovative and hugely influential, for though earlier comedies had often followed romance-style plots where knights or princes fought for the love of ladies, love in those plays was simply a given. It is with Lyly that the exploration of love and its effects on lovers begins. We find the musings of lovers on their own feelings, the mockery of their folly by others, the careful plotting of the game of love all very familiar in Shakespearean comedy; but it is Lyly who first introduces this kind of subject matter into English drama.

Lyly also anticipates Shakespeare in providing witty minor characters who indulge in extended repartee. Though there is also, of course, classical precedent for the tradition of the clever slave, Shakespeare surely learned a particular style of dialogue from Lyly's attendants, with their love of wordplay and chop-logic. To a post-Shakespearean audience, Lyly's chattering court ladies mocking lovers

> having nothing in their mouths but "Sweet mistress," wearing our hands out with courtly kissings when their wits fail in courtly discourses – now ruffling their hairs, now setting their ruffs, then gazing with their eyes, then sighing with a privy wring by the hand, thinking us like to be wooed by signs and ceremonies (*Sappho and Phao*, 1.4.39–45)[9]

are irresistibly reminiscent of Moth, Speed, or Benedick joking about lovers (*Love's Labor's Lost*, 3.1.11–25; *Two Gentlemen*, 2.1.17–32; *Much Ado*, 2.3.7–21); while the intellectual sparring of his pages:

> MANES   I will prove that my body was immortal because it was in prison.
> GRANICHUS   As how?
> MANES   Did your masters never teach you that the soul is immortal?
> GRANICHUS   Yes.
> MANES   And the body is the prison of the soul?
> GRANICHUS   True.
> MANES   Why then, thus: to make my body immortal I put it to prison.
>
> (*Campaspe*, 1.2.32–41)

calls to mind Feste's proof that Olivia is a fool, or the conversation between Proteus and Speed proving that Speed is a sheep and his master a shepherd (*Twelfth Night*, 1.5.57–72; *Two Gentlemen*, 1.1.72–100).

Critics often describe Lyly's comedy as "delicate" by comparison with a more slapstick tradition of comic horseplay in earlier English drama; and it is partly its intellectual element, together with the distanced and skeptical stance toward the main characters it brings with it, that leads to that choice of adjective. In going for this more sophisticated and intellectual tone, Lyly was quite consciously doing something different from earlier comedy, as his prologues make clear. His announcement of intent in the Blackfriars prologue to *Campaspe* may sound something like the characteristic printer's statement or title page advertising the mixing of earnest and game: "We have mixed mirth with counsel and discipline with delight, thinking it not amiss in the same garden to sow pot-herbs that we set flowers," but, as Marco Mincoff has argued, Lyly's innovation was to run together what his predecessors had merely intermingled.[10] The Blackfriars prologue to *Sappho and Phao* shows a more marked care to distance this play from supposedly vulgar mixtures of an earlier type. "Our intent," Lyly states rather solemnly, "was at this time to move inward delight, not outward lightness, and to breed (if it might be) soft smiling, not loud laughing." As numerous critics have remarked, Lyly seems to be responding directly to Sidney's precepts, which are based on a classicist scorn for vernacular dramatic tradition. English comedy is, according to Sidney,

> nothing but scurrility, unworthy of any chaste ears, or some extreme show of doltishness, indeed fit to lift up a loud laughter, and nothing else: where the whole tract of a comedy should be full of delight, as the tragedy should be still maintained in a well-raised admiration.
>
> But our comedians think there is no delight without laughter; which is very wrong . . . Delight hath a joy in it, either permanent or present, Laughter hath only a scornful tickling. (Sidney, *Apology for Poetry*, p. 136)

Peele and Lyly seem consciously to strive toward Sidney's conception of art as a "golden world," not only by substituting graceful wit for pratfall clowning, but also by creating exotic fictional worlds, commonly grounded in myth or pastoral, and tending toward epiphanic resolution. This visionary climax is often staged, especially in Lyly's later plays, via the descent of gods or goddesses. Shakespeare's plays, of course, often incorporate either a pastoral setting or a celestial descent, though by the time of his last plays this influence was also coming more immediately from court masque, itself partly indebted to the plays of Lyly and Peele.[11]

These early court plays are more concerned to create elegance and symmetry of shape than individuality or psychological depth, and, though Shakespeare's incorporation of subplots is probably indebted to Lyly, the overall impression of construction is very different in the two playwrights. Where Shakespeare's subplots often extend and complicate the audience's engagement with particular characters or ideas, in Lyly the emphasis is on what Peter Saccio has called the "lines of reticulation" rather than the elements they join (*Court Comedies*, p. 93). Even where Shakespeare is quite consciously imitating Lyly, the effect is different. Lyly's *Gallathea* (1583–85), for example, follows the fortunes of two cross-dressed girls who fall in love with each other, and whose guarded progress toward love is expressed in carefully symmetrical sequences of dialogue, rhetorically constructed along the lines illustrated below:

GALLATHEA   Unfortunate Gallathea, if this be Phyllida!
PHYLLIDA   Accursed Phyllida, if that be Gallathea!
GALLATHEA   And wast thou all this while enamoured of Phyllida, that sweet Phyllida?
PHYLLIDA   And couldst thou dote upon the face of a maiden, thyself being one, on the face of fair Gallathea.   (5.3.113–18)[12]

When the intrigues of Shakespeare's *As You Like It* are approaching resolution, the influence of *Gallathea* is clear in the symmetrical exchanges of Act 5 scene 2:

SILVIUS   If this be so, why blame you me to love you?
PHEBE   If this be so, why blame you me to love you?
ORLANDO   If this be so, why blame you me to love you?
ROSALIND   Why do you speak too, "Why blame you me to love you?"
                                                             (103–07)

but the effect is both more comic and more bitter. The fact that the line is precisely the same, rather than elegantly varied, for three of the characters, and that Rosalind questions it, and at the same time breaks the rhythm set up by the other speakers, sets her apart from the parallelism and characterizes her in a different way from the other speakers. Where Lyly demonstrates the parity and seriousness of his two lovers, Shakespeare puts one figure in a position of greater awareness, seriousness, and depth than the others, thereby exposing the others as absurd and anticipating the pointlessness of their misdirected love. And where Lyly solves the conundrum of same-sex love by having Venus descend and transform one of the girls into a man by their mutual agreement, Shakespeare keeps Rosalind true to her given sex, and makes her the beloved of both a man and a woman, so that frustration and absurdity are incorporated into the complex mix of feelings that the revelation of her true sex must inspire. Both Lyly and Shakespeare take drama into new spaces of feeling and being that problematize familiar ways of categorizing identity and sexuality, but the riskiness they cultivate is different in tone. Where Lyly uses grace, pattern, and measured pace to fix our engagement with the utterly serious strangeness of the encounter, Shakespeare shifts us between serious and comic affect so that we confront our own uncertainties with a degree of ironic distance. In Lyly we look at the shape of what we see with wonder and fascination, while in Shakespeare we seem to see the differences between the individuals on stage more clearly than the shapes they make.

The precedence of plotting and shape over character effects and shifting affect may be related to the fact that Lyly was writing for boy actors. Ensemble playing, a certain formality, and a cool dispersal of interest across an elegant, patterned surface provide an easier and more discreet focus for child actors than sexually or psychologically complex territory (though some later writers for the children's companies played on this uneasy edge). Yet we should guard against thinking of this concentration on surface as somehow a failure of depth. It should be understood as a particular and fashionable aesthetic, a conscious prioritizing of formal style and structure over other areas of theatrical interest. Besides its relation to the capacities of boy actors, this aesthetic is also closely tied to high fashion, namely the conspicuously fashionable rhetoric given huge impetus by Lyly himself in his earlier prose work, *Euphues* (1578). This was a great success, running into seven editions by 1582 (with five editions of its sequel, *Euphues and his England*), and it set the tone for lavish stylistic excess.[13] Lyly's first two plays were also a great success in print (not surprisingly, since Lyly's writing style constructed not only a play for performance but a written text as art object), with three editions of *Campaspe* and two of *Sappho and Phao* in one year, 1584. As Edward Blount remarked in his collected edition of Lyly's plays, published in 1632, "All our ladies were then his scholars, and that Beauty in court which could not parley Euphuism was as little regarded as she which now there speaks not French" (quoted in Hunter, *John Lyly*, p. 72). Peele and Lyly both seek to please the court through wit and variety of ornamentation: where Lyly's drama is in a patterned prose that revels in its own excesses, Peele is notable for the metrical range of his verse, and both intersperse songs widely. The pleasure of their drama is located in the richness of the moment, and in the combining of luxuriance of visual and verbal texture in a carefully measured formal development.

Where almost all of Lyly's plays were written with the court in mind, Peele wrote more extensively for the public stage, and is usually numbered among the so-called University Wits, a grouping which also included Robert Greene and Christopher Marlowe. Peele's writing for the public theatre is very different from his court piece. One play, *The Old Wives' Tale* (c.1588–94), has been read as a burlesque of the older style of romantic comedy that began with *Sir Clyomon and Sir Clamydes* (c.1570–83) and remained so popular in plays like *Mucedorus*, but none of his other plays is classifiable as comedy. Greene's work is more important in the development of comedy on the public stage. His motto from Horace, printed at the end of

Friar Bacon and Friar Bungay (1589–90), *Omne tulit punctum qui miscuit utile dulci* (He will win everybody's vote who blends what is instructive with what is delightful),[14] is reminiscent of the precepts of Lyly and Sidney, and it is clear from Greene's prose works that he knew Lyly's *Euphues*. His plays, however, are very different from the court drama of Lyly and Peele, and privilege miscellaneity over unity and fun over wit in the manner of the older drama on which Lyly turned his back (though Peele did so only when writing for the court). Whereas Lyly's plays were elitist in performance and fashionable in print, *Friar Bacon and Friar Bungay* was popular in performance and much less so in print (the edition of 1594 remained the sole issue until 1630). Though there is no evidence regarding its first performances, it was still being regularly played in 1592–93, when it was given by Lord Strange's Men at the Rose theatre and was jointly played the next year by the Queen's Men and Sussex's Men. The Admiral's Men considered it worth paying Middleton in 1602 to write a prologue and epilogue for a court performance; and the company continued to perform it into the reign of James I.[15] The play brings together romance, disguise, clowning, and, above all, magic, with the full range of special effects that that implies. Stylistically it looks both backward and forward, bringing in old favorite setpieces, as when Miles, the clown, is taken to Hell on the devil's back, and new elements that will become setpieces in the drama of the 1590s, such as the motif of the king in disguise (taken up early on by Peele's *Edward I*) and the on-stage conjuring tricks (though there is no critical agreement about whether Greene's *Friar Bacon* or Marlowe's *Dr. Faustus* came first). It is strongly nationalistic in tone, ending with a prophecy of England's future glory and anticipating the vogue for xenophobic English history plays in the next decade. *George a Greene*, which may be Greene's, is similarly nationalistic and similarly fascinated by the figure of the king in disguise, but pursues the relationship between the disguised king and his humble rural subjects in more detail, building the loyal bond between king and plain-speaking countryman against rebellious subjects that is to become so central to Shakespeare's history plays rather than his comedy.[16]

Greene's *James IV* (c. 1590) may sound like a history play, but is no more historical than *Friar Bacon* or *George a Greene*, both of which are set in a fictional English past. Like *Friar Bacon*'s Prince Edward, James IV has a roving eye, although in this play it is married status rather than social class that outlaws the relationship. And like *Friar Bacon* again, the play contains both an impossibly virtuous heroine (James' wife, Dorothea) and a conjurer (Ateukin). The connection with morality play tradition that is evident in Friar Bacon's renunciation of magic and in the stage picture of Miles riding on the devil's back is more deeply embedded in *James IV* through the relationship between the king and Ateukin, the Vice figure who tempts him to evil-doing. More interestingly, however, and quite unlike *Friar Bacon* or *George a Greene*, the play is structured within a framing device that Greene may perhaps have borrowed from Kyd's hugely popular *Spanish Tragedy* (1582–92), though it is not certain that *The Spanish Tragedy* preceded *James IV*. The framing device is added by Greene to his source material and allows him to do two apparently contradictory things: to impose a unifying perspective on diverse and multiple plot strands and to bring in all manner of extra thrills and spectacles to please the audience.

The word *jig* focuses the paradox. The jig, like the morality play, has medieval origins, and draws on popular traditions of song, dance, clowning, and mime. Before Greene's time the word can refer to song or dance alone; but the stage jig, typically staged after a full-length play, is an Elizabethan innovation. Thomas Platter, visiting the Globe in 1599, famously draws attention to it in expressing his admiration for "an excellent performance of the tragedy of the first Emperor Julius Caesar with a cast of some fifteen people; when the play was over, they danced very marvellously and gracefully together as is their wont, two dressed as men and two as women."[17] In Greene's play an induction beginning with music and dance introduces characters who do not belong to the play-world of the main plot: Oberon (the fairy king), an "antic" (a group of grotesque dancers), and Bohan (a Scot marked by his dialect speech as different from all the Scottish characters in the inner fiction). Similar insertions of further music, dance, or dumb-shows between the acts allow the play to appeal in the way jig appeals by definition, as a separate and self-contained entertainment; and both characters and author explicitly refer to these *divertissements* as "jigs." Bohan, in the induction, for example, instructs his sons to "dance me forthwith a jig worth the sight," and the stage direction says that "*The two dance a jig devised for the nonce*" (Induction 83, 90).[18] But Bohan also, and quite differently, conceives of the whole play as a "jig" offered to Oberon. He first uses the term in this sense at the end of Act 2, when his closing words warn that "this jig will prove no jest" (2, Chorus, 17), and the word is several times repeated in the closing exchange between Bohan and Oberon:

> BOHAN   Mark thou my jig, in mirkest terms that tells
> The loath of sins, and where corruption dwells.
> . . .
> Accept my jig guid king, and let me rest,
> The grave with guid men, is a gay built nest.
> OBERON   The rising sun doth call me hence away,
> Thanks for thy jig, I may no longer stay.
> (5, Chorus, 5–12)

Used in this latter sense, the term carries a charge that is in straightforward and ironic contradiction to the implications of the jig as a piece of free-standing entertainment with little or no meaning as content, tying it instead to an overall perspective that moralizes on pleasure and frivolity as sinful and corrupt. And it is this didactic perspective that provides the unifying structure for the play, in that it is the only element never absent from the inter-act choruses. Not every chorus has setpiece shows or dancing; but every chorus has Bohan speak against the treacheries and deceits of this world. Like Revenge and the ghost of Andrea in *The Spanish Tragedy*, Bohan and Oberon loom visibly over all the action of the main play. "Gang with me to the gallery," Bohan invites Oberon in the induction (106), and Oberon agrees to follow.

Shakespeare borrowed more than the name of Oberon from Greene's *James IV*. In particular his use of framing devices in comic structure may owe as much to Greene as to Kyd, whose use of framing occurs within tragedy. *A Midsummer Night's Dream*, in which Shakespeare's Oberon, like Greene's, is king of the fairies and an invisible spectator of framed action, resembles *James IV* insofar as it uses the fairies as an excuse for inserting song and dance, but is quite unlike it in tone. Shakespeare's fairies laugh at mortal folly but they hardly moralize it. Given the on-going quarrel between Oberon and Titania, the play's ironies derive from parallelism between the two sets of characters rather than the knowing superiority of one set over the other, and hence surround the fairies as well as the mortals. (The superiority of both lovers and fairies to the mechanicals is a separate question.) Shakespeare aims here at relatively light-hearted resolution of folly, not grim reflection on sinfulness. The play's epilogue, with its closing invitation to the audience to think that they "have but slumber'd here / While these visions did appear" (5.1.425–26), is reminiscent not of Greene's dark didacticism but of the court prologue to Lyly's *Sappho and Phao*, which entreats the queen to "imagine yourself to be in a deep dream that, staying the conclusion, in your rising your Majesty vouchsafe but to say, 'And so you awaked'" (16–18).

Perhaps the single most exciting, innovative, and influential play in the sphere of pre-Shakespearean comedy is, paradoxically, a tragedy. *The Jew of Malta*, attributed to the same year as *Friar Bacon and Friar Bungay* (c. 1589–90), was Henslowe's most popular money-spinner, playing thirty-six times at the Rose between 1592 and 1597, more often than any other play recorded in his diary over the same period. Tragic by virtue of plot definition, in that so many, including the central protagonist, die, it nevertheless knowingly refuses almost every other aspect of tragic form and tone by constantly turning toward farce. Yet it is not in the same category as those earlier plays that mingle comic and serious matter. Marlowe does not merely play on the edge in an occasional way, opening up a sudden and momentary double perspective on the action. Instead he makes farce the continuous ground-bass framing every potentially tragic moment and thereby throws the whole question of dramatic form in doubt. Thus, when Abigail, the loving and obedient daughter of Barabas, the Jew, dies, Marlowe has her make a true Christian confession, ending with a plea to her confessor to convert her father and a profession of her own faith:

> Convert my father that he may be saved,
> And witness that I die a Christian;

but, as she expires with these last words, Marlowe forces the audience out of any pity with the friar's quick-fire response:

> Ay, and a virgin too, that grieves me most.
> (3.6.39–41)[19]

The most comic moments are not extraneous, but deeply implicated in the working out of the main plot. When Barabas scores over both the friars competing for "his soul," comic irony is present at all levels: first, in the fact that the friars are really competing for the money he will bring and could not care less about his soul; second, in the absurdity of the dialogue ("Oh good Barabas come to our house" / "Oh no, good Barabas come to our house" [5.1.76–77]); and third, in the wonderfully grotesque plot Barabas devises to make one friar think he has killed the other (already strangled by Ithamore and Barabas) by propping up the corpse for him to strike. And at every point of this device, the dialogue comments on its own comic excess in a manner more evocative of *Pulp Fiction* than of *Shakespeare in Love*. "Pull hard" (4.1.149), Barabas instructs, as Ithamore strangles the second friar; "so, let him lean upon his staff; excellent, he stands as if he were begging of bacon" (153–54), Ithamore comments as he sets up the corpse; and, supposedly confirming that the first friar has killed the second, Ithamore surpasses himself: "Ay, master, he's slain; look how his brains drop out on's nose" (176).

This kind of dramaturgy steps well clear of the moralizing world of Greene and earlier interlude tradition into an amoral world where corruption is funny and its excesses are presented for the audience to revel in. Even the "tragic ending" is subverted by a mode of presentation which deliberately parodies the traditional descent of the wicked into Hell as Barabas falls into a stage cauldron of his own making. The opening of this death scene, which shows Barabas "*with a hammer above, very busy*" enquiring about the construction of the cranes and pulleys, openly foregrounds and demystifies the stage cranes and pulleys which customarily provide the mechanics for supernatural intervention and divine punishment; and Barabas' refusal to repent ("Die life, fly soul, tongue curse thy fill and die" [5.5.90]) is equally contemptuous of earlier Christian stage tradition.

The opening of the play marks a similar break with tradition by direct reference to it and open distortion of it. Prologues before this time were commonly spoken by a nameless "neutral" figure instructing the audience in how to judge the play. His utterance was entirely trustworthy and usually provided a moral perspective on the stage action. Even in *The Spanish Tragedy*, though Andrea is a named figure with a stake in the fictional world of the play proper, his words represent a true account of what has taken place and offer a view of it which is endorsed by the working out of the plot. In *The Jew of Malta*, however, the speaker of the prologue is "Machevill," understood by Elizabethan audiences as the epitome of deceitfulness. The opening mode of engagement is thus highly uncertain, since its speaker is precisely not to be trusted. Yet his framing of Barabas as one who "smiles to see how full his bags are crammed, / Which money was not got without my means" (31–32) corresponds with what is shown next, so that the status of that ensuing tableau, together with Machiavelli's promise to present "the tragedy of a Jew," are both highly suspect. The stage picture of Barabas in his counting house, surrounded by heaps of gold, looks remarkably like the morality play picture of Avarice demonstrating his own essence; but the words that are spoken demonstrate the yawning gulf between the presentational mode of morality and the developing representationalism of soliloquy. The opening of the play in mid-speech ("So that of thus much that return was made" [1.1.1]) is a notable innovation,[20] inviting immediate empathy with Barabas as a mind in process. Yet the rhetorical panache of this speech also works against the empathetic engagement of the realist mode by inviting an aesthetic point of entry through language as object, thus distracting attention from the potential interiority of the speaker to the sensuous appeal of words themselves. As Barabas goes on to describe his commercial enterprises, involving "Persian ships ... Samnites, and the men of Uz ... Spanish oils, and wines of Greece" (2–5), Marlowe increasingly offers the listening ear a catalogue of the exotic which commands attention to its own sounds and textures, luxuriating in the rhetorical excess of

> Bags of fiery opals, sapphires, amethysts,
> Jacinths, hard topaz, grass-green emeralds,
> Beauteous rubies, sparkling diamonds,
> And seld-seen costly stones of so great price,
> As one of them indifferently rated,

And of a caract of this quantity,
May serve in peril of calamity
To ransom great kings from captivity.
(25–32)

The syntax, rhythms and sheer length of this speech offer a pleasure that has nothing to do with Barabas' psyche or motivations. We are asked to hear and recognize a stunning dialectic between control and excess, offered up as a conscious demonstration of skill for our admiration. The control of the blank verse line, the carefully measured move away from regularity into emphatic and daring irregularity, and back into regularity, all within the syntax of the same sentence, present themselves as a virtuoso display that distracts from the awareness of these lines as tied to the interiority of any particular speaker. Like neatness of plotting (which Marlowe himself also comments on explicitly, through Ithamore: "Why, was there ever seen such villainy, / So neatly plotted, and so well performed?" [3.3.1–2]), the tools of rhetoric demand engagement with themselves as instruments of stagecraft, not merely as means to dramatic ends.

Despite the fact that the Jew is shown as persecuted and manipulated by hypocritical Christians and Turks alike, any empathy with him is strictly limited by the way the part is constructed as one that dips in and out of different modes of being from moment to moment. Barabas is an instrument for Marlowe to play on, used to develop kinds of dramatic language other than the lyrical-descriptive. Just as the opening soliloquy moves between realism and lyrical excess, so another moves into playing the stereotype of the wicked Jew in virtually standard medieval self-presentational form (2.3.178–205), except that again its very excessiveness seems to signal awareness of its own constructedness and hence parodic function. Even more excessive is the way in which the aside is developed as a comic rhetorical tool. Speaking simultaneously to the friar and his daughter as she pretends to convert in order to recover her father's gold, for example, Barabas' change of address is dizzying and attention-seeking in its absurd play with the convention that asides cannot be heard by those to whom they are not addressed. I print the speech with Craik's editorial stage directions for ease of understanding:

Blind friar, I reck not thy persuasions
(aside) The board is marked thus † that covers it,
For I had rather die, than see her thus.
Wilt thou forsake me too in my distress,
Seducèd daughter, (aside to her) Go forget not.–
Becomes it Jews to be so credulous?

(aside to her) Tomorrow early I'll be at the door.–
No, come not at me, if thou wilt be damned,
Forget me, see me not, and so be gone.
(aside) Farewell. Remember tomorrow morning.–
Out, out thou wretch.

(1.2.364–74)

Add to this the fact that the part was played by Edward Alleyn with a false nose, to which Ithamore repeatedly calls attention ("I worship your nose for this" [2.3.177]; "bottle-nosed knave" [3.3.10]; "God-a-mercy nose" [4.1.23]), and the deliberate refusal to make Barabas available as a tragic hero could not be plainer.

Despite the play's scorn for religious hypocrisy, exploitation, and corruption Barabas is never even momentarily tragic. Shakespeare's Shylock, though modeled in many details on Marlowe's Jew, is unlike Barabas in this respect. One of Marlowe's characteristic comic moments shows Barabas' language gradually failing to distinguish between his love for his daughter and his love for his money bags, as she throws them down to him:

Oh Abigail, Abigail, that I had thee here too,
Then my desires were fully satisfied,
But I will practise thy enlargement thence:
Oh girl, oh gold, oh beauty, oh my bliss!

(2.55–58)

As he hugs his bags to him, the rehearsal of his liberation and embrace of Abigail is ironically put in its place and mocked. Shakespeare evidently remembered this scene in writing *The Merchant of Venice*; yet his account of Shylock mixing up his daughter and his ducats (borrowing even the alliterative technique from Marlowe, though changing the alliterating letter) hovers on the edge of pathos, partly because it is not shown, but recounted by a hostile and sneering Christian, and partly because it is made the expression of distress rather than glee:

I never heard a passion so confus'd,
So strange, outrageous, and so variable
As the dog Jew did utter in the streets.
"My daughter! O my ducats! O my daughter!"

(2.7.12–15)

The alliterative alignment of "dog" with "daughter" and "ducats" invites derision alongside pity for the Jew, but rejects the sheer fun of Marlowe's representation. And Shakespeare's later incorporation of Shylock's lament for the loss of the ring his daughter has stolen in her elopement with a

Christian ("I had it of Leah when I was a bachelor. I would not have sold it for a wilderness of monkeys" [3.1.121–23]) no longer hovers, but demands pity as the audience's primary response.

Marlowe is nowhere interested in evoking pity for Barabas. Instead he allows Barabas to express vengeful wrath on Abigail in farcical mode by poisoning her with the porridge he sends to the convent to poison all the nuns and then applauding his own success:

> There is no music to a Christian's knell:
> How sweet the bells ring now the nuns are dead,
> That sound at other times like tinkers' pans!
>
> (4.1.1–3)

Shakespeare borrowed from this smiling villain mode too, of course, but not in constructing Shylock. It is in Richard III that Marlowe's Jew, and his progenitor, the medieval Vice, find their heir. But above all, Shakespeare learned general techniques from Marlowe: the use of the aside, the flexibility of the soliloquy, the mid-speech opening into an apparently real fictional world. And these techniques were not by definition comic, but usable in all dramatic forms. In terms of comic form Shakespeare could owe no debt to Marlowe, since Marlowe never wrote a play that could be generically classified as comedy. Yet it remains the case that in *The Jew of Malta* Marlowe developed a kind of tragedy that was more innovative and inventive in its comic daring than any other play of its time.

NOTES

1 Quotations from Shakespeare are taken from *The Riverside Shakespeare*, ed. G. Blakemore Evans *et al.*, 2nd edn (Boston and New York: Houghton Mifflin Company, 1997).

2 *The Shakespeare Apocrypha*, ed. C. F. Tucker Brooke (Oxford: Clarendon Press, 1908).

3 Sir Philip Sidney, *An Apology for Poetry*, ed. Geoffrey Shepherd (Manchester: Manchester University Press, 1973), pp. 117, 135.

4 *Chief Pre-Shakespearean Dramas*, ed. Joseph Quincy Adams (Cambridge, Mass.: Houghton Mifflin, 1924).

5 *Three Rastell Plays*, ed. Richard Axton (Cambridge: D. S. Brewer; Totowa, N.J.: Rowman and Littlefield, 1979).

6 *The Dramatic Writings of Richard Edwards, Thomas Norton and Thomas Sackville*, ed. John S. Farmer (1906; reprinted Guildford: Charles W. Traylen, 1966), p. 4.

7 See Peter Saccio, *The Court Comedies of John Lyly* (Princeton: Princeton University Press, 1969), p. 206.

8 *The Life and Works of George Peele*, general editor C. T. Prouty, 3 vols. (New Haven: Yale University Press, 1952–70), vol. III.

9 Quotations from *Campaspe* and *Sappho and Phao* are taken from the edition of these two plays in one volume edited by G. K. Hunter and David Bevington for the Revels Plays (Manchester: Manchester University Press, 1991).

10 Marco Mincoff, "Shakespeare and Lyly," *Shakespeare Survey* 14 (1961): 17.

11 On Shakespeare's borrowing from Peele and Lyly, see ibid.; G. K. Hunter, *John Lyly: the Humanist as Courtier* (Cambridge, Mass.: Harvard University Press; London: Routledge and Kegan Paul, 1962), pp. 298ff; and Prouty (ed.), *Life and Works of Peele*, pp. 50ff.

12 *Gallathea* and *Midas*, ed. Anne Begor Lancashire (London: Edward Arnold, 1969).

13 As Hunter has demonstrated, however, Lyly did not invent "Euphuism," despite the fact that his own popularity gave the style its name (*John Lyly*, pp. 257–59).

14 Robert Greene, *Friar Bacon and Friar Bungay*, ed. Daniel Seltzer (London: Edward Arnold, 1963). The translation is Seltzer's.

15 See Seltzer's introduction, pp. x–xi.

16 See Janette Dillon, *Language and Stage in Medieval and Renaissance England* (Cambridge: Cambridge University Press, 1998), ch. 8.

17 *Thomas Platter's Travels in England*, ed. Clare Williams (London: Jonathan Cape, 1937), p. 166.

18 *The Scottish History of James the Fourth*, ed. J. A. Lavin (London: Ernest Benn, 1967).

19 Christopher Marlowe, *The Jew of Malta*, ed. T. W. Craik (1979; London: A. and C. Black, 1990).

20 Craik's note cites F. P. Wilson: "Is there another English play before *The Jew of Malta* which opens in mid-speech?"

5

FRANÇOIS LAROQUE

Popular festivity

In Shakespeare's day, long after the Reformation, the calendar as established by the Church, with its series of days consecrated to saints and its fixed and movable feasts, still played a role of major importance. It constituted a matrix of time, the effect of which was to subordinate events of secular life to those of the sacred cycle of the year (the movable feasts of the Christian liturgy governed by the Easter cycle and ranging from Shrove Tuesday to Corpus Christi) and to commemorate a host of popular beliefs and folkloric traditions that had developed over centuries. The year was, by and large, divided into two halves: the winter or sacred half, ranging from Christmas to 24 June (which corresponded to Midsummer but also to the latest possible date for the feast of Corpus Christi); and the summer half, with its mainly agrarian feasts and host of local and occasional celebrations, which went from 25 June to Christmas.

Shakespeare, as a playwright, is unique in the place and importance he ascribes to popular festivity and holidays, thus giving what might have been regarded as "airy nothing" a "local habitation and a name" (*A Midsummer Night's Dream*, 5.1.16–17).[1] He indeed includes all and sundry, court and country, in his festive kaleidoscope firmly set on the fertile ground of the variegated traditions and customs of "Merry England," and this without nostalgia or satire. He imbues the spirit of holiday with mirth, making it akin to the freedom necessary for comedy while also representing it in darker colors as riot, revolution, or madness in the world upside down of popular rebellion or dreamer's utopia (in 2 *Henry VI* and *The Tempest*). Popular festivity, then, becomes a subtle and effective means of generic subversion and reconstruction as, in the grotesque or savage humor of *Richard III*, *Hamlet* or *King Lear*, a dissonant and simultaneously enlightening note is struck to produce what Berowne thought was impossible, namely "wild laughter in the throat of death" (*Love's Labor's Lost*, 5.2.851).

Court and folk festivals

The main source of rejoicings came from a number of court activities which gave the impression that royal festivals provided the general impulse and rhythm for all sorts of different rites and celebrations taking place in the provinces and at all social levels. In other words, the queen was regarded as the center, as the *primum mobile* of all types of merry-making and festivity. The queen's year was also divided into two halves. The season of the revels in winter used to begin on 17 November when, in a jolly atmosphere of bell-ringing, bonfires, and jousts, Queen Elizabeth I returned to Whitehall to celebrate the anniversary of her accession to the throne in 1558. During the twelve days of Christmas, the court was alive with all sorts of entertainments, including plays, organized by the Master of the Revels. On Candlemas or Shrove Tuesday, the court set off for Greenwich or Richmond, where the ceremony of the washing of the feet of twelve poor people took place on Maundy Thursday. The Garter ceremony was traditionally held at Windsor Castle on St. George's Day, 23 April. The summer was devoted to royal progresses through the provinces. The entertainments (Kenilworth, Elvetham, etc.) that were organized in honor of the queen were highly extravagant affairs, laid on by the great aristocratic families of the realm. The whole court followed, and the high favor which was then granted to one of the families to lavish princely hospitality on the sovereign and her train for several weeks certainly brought a great deal of national attention to the house and county upon which the expensive honor befell. Shakespeare probably followed these events closely, as it is often argued that Oberon's description of the magic flower called "love-in-idleness" in *A Midsummer Night's Dream* was inspired by the extraordinary festivities organized for Elizabeth at Elvetham in 1591:

OBERON My gentle Puck, come hither. Thou remembr'est
Since once I sat upon a promontory,
And heard a mermaid on a dolphin's back
Uttering such dulcet and harmonious breath
That the rude sea grew civil at her song
And certain stars shot madly from their spheres,
To hear the sea-maid's music.

PUCK   I remember.

OBERON That very time I saw, but thou couldst not,
Flying between the cold moon and the earth,
Cupid all arm'd. A certain aim he took
At a fair vestal throned by the west,

And loos'd his love-shaft smartly from his bow,
As it should pierce a hundred thousand hearts;
But I might see young Cupid's fiery shaft
Quench'd in the chaste beams of the wat'ry moon,
And the imperial vot'ress passed on,
In maiden meditation, fancy-free

(2.1.148–64)

The passage probably conflates memories of this particular entertainment, which had apparently been one of the most spectacular and lavish of the queen's reign, with its gorgeous water pageantry and mythological apparatus, with the cult of the chaste vestal identified with the "cold moon" Cynthia and the celebration of the "Virgin Queen."[2]

These seasonal festivities were complemented by occasional events, such as royal christenings, weddings, and funerals, all of them pretexts for displays of liberality and rejoicing such as we see at the end of *Henry VIII,* when the populace beats at the doors of the royal palace in London for the christening of the infant Elizabeth:

PORTER ...
You must be seeing for christenings? Do you look for ale and cakes here, you
  rude rascals?

MAN   Pray, sir be patient.'Tis as much impossible –
Unless we sweep 'em from the door with cannons –
To scatter 'em as it is to make 'em sleep
On May-day morning, which will never be.
We may as well push against Paul's as stir 'em
  ...

PORTER ...
What should we do, but knock 'em down by the dozens? Is this Moorfields to
  muster in? Or have we some strange Indian with the great tool come to court,
  the women so besiege us? Bless me, what a fry of fornication is at door! On
  my Christian conscience, this one christening will beget a thousand; here will
  be father, godfather, and all together.   (5.4.8–37)

The grotesque humor and light obscenity of the passage gives a good example of the style and manner in which aristocratic or royal entertainment could pave the way for popular enthusiasm since, in this farcical passage, Shakespeare introduces a parallel with the climax of seasonal festivity in the English Renaissance, namely the rejoicings and excesses associated with May Day.[3]

Indeed festivity, which had always provided an outlet for popular energies, became under Elizabeth and James I an instrument of government as well as a source of national amusement.

City and country festivals

The contrast between London and the provinces was to become increasingly important with the spectacular urban and commercial boom that took place in the last decades of the sixteenth century. The opposition between the city and the country lay at the heart of the whole phenomenon of festivity, for even if it was through the towns that festivals were developed, embellished, and enriched, the festival itself was more often than not the product of a rural, popular culture whose seasonal rhythms and pre-Christian beliefs were linked with the mysteries and magic of natural fertility. To Shakespeare's contemporaries, the countryside lying outside the city walls was still the object of superstition and deep-rooted fears. The forest associated with royal privileges was the domain of hunting, of wildness and the sacred and this appears quite prominently in the frightening apparition of the "angry, chafing boar" in *Venus and Adonis* (line 662). There was also the world of folklore and the ballads of "old Robin Hood," as well as the iconography of the *homo sylvarum* or Wild Man echoed in texts as different as Spenser's *The Fairie Queene* and the anonymous play *Mucedorus* (1590), which was performed by Shakespeare's troupe, the Chamberlain's Men.

As Elizabethan England was gradually shifting from a ritualistic and relatively static system to a more secular one, the themes and images of popular festivals were being disseminated at the very moment when their existence was being questioned by Puritan pamphleteers such as Philip Stubbes.[4] It is quite possible that Puritan attacks made them better known, as they drew attention to them when University Wits like Thomas Nashe stood up in the defense of popular pastimes, a tradition later continued by Ben Jonson, Robert Dover with his Cotswold Games,[5] and by such remote disciples of the Tribe of Ben as Robert Herrick, the genial, nostalgic poet of *Hesperides* (1648). The defense of the traditions of "Merry England" led to what Leah Marcus has called "the politics of mirth,"[6] thus arousing a preethnological interest as it were in the forgotten games, customs, and festivals in the most remote corners of the land. A famous letter by Robert Laneham, giving an account of the royal progress at Kenilworth, tells of a local craftsman and colorful figure called "Captain Cox" and of his efforts to ask Queen Elizabeth to stand in defense of the local "Hocktide" games, which had been banned by the local Puritans.[7]

Shakespeare, whose rural childhood in Warwickshire and possible Catholic background[8] made him particularly alive to the importance of ritual and festivity, proved a genius at making dramatic use of all the flotsam and jetsam of myth and of the vestiges of folklore. He might be defined as an inspired "bricoleur" (in Lévi-Strauss' sense of the term),[9] who had the flair and vision to see what uses he could make in his comedies and drama at large of these generally despised bits and pieces of local "blue apron culture," to borrow Peter Burke's beautiful phrase to designate early modern popular culture.[10] Indeed, as more and more critics now acknowledge, various basic dramatic structures emerge from seasonal mimes and dramas like the folk plays and the morris dance, and it is quite likely that Shakespeare incorporated these as part of his plots or subplots or imagery networks.[11]

The green world and the calendar of popular festivals

The forest of Arden in *As You Like It*, the pastoral "shores" of Bohemia in *The Winter's Tale*, and Portia's enchanted place at Belmont in *The Merchant of Venice* were all Shakespearean versions of the pagan, ritualized vision of a traditional green world with its hunting rites and grounds, chance or sporting games, and its utopian or topsy-turvy scenarios. The green world was regarded as a place of escape from the constraints of the law and from everyday life, a place of change (of gender or of identity or both) and deep interior transformation where the contact with nature and "old custom" provided a form of content and fulfillment, as Duke Senior says in *As You Like It*:

> Now, my co-mates and brothers in exile,
> Hath not old custom made this life more sweet
> Than that of painted pomp? Are not these woods
> More free from peril than the envious court?
> ...
> And this our life, exempt from public haunt,
> Finds tongues in trees, books in the running brooks,
> Sermons in stones, and good in everything.
>
> (2.1.1–17)

But the green world is not just limited to forest and green pastures. It also corresponds to Portia's home in Belmont where Lorenzo and Jessica listen to the harmonies of celestial music at night (5.1.1–88) or to the scenes in the Boar's Head tavern in Eastcheap where Falstaff indulges in carnivalesque games and extempore witticisms to justify his licentious behavior:

> Let not us that are squires of the night's body be call'd thieves of the day's beauty. Let us be Diana's foresters, gentlemen of shade, minions of the moon
> ...
>
> (*1 Henry IV*, 1.2.24–26)

In *The Taming of the Shrew,* Shakespeare explores the theme of comic sexual warfare between men and women, a theme to which he will return in a more sophisticated way in *Much Ado About Nothing*. The taming of Katherina by Petruchio may indeed be taken as a dramatic variation on the traditional Hocktide games that playfully opposed the sexes in Warwickshire at Eastertide.[12] In *Much Ado*, the theme of sexual warfare leading to marriage is verbalized in the witty sparring between Beatrice and her cousin Benedick:

> LEONATO   You must not, sir, mistake my niece. There is a kind of merry war betwixt Signor Benedick and her. They never meet but there's a skirmish of wit between them.   (1.1.157–60)

The merry interlude at Messina represents the equivalent of a carnival period when the local court indulges in a hectic bout of laughter, alcohol, and dancing after the trials and dangers of the war that has just come to an end. In these "weak piping times of peace" (*Richard III*, 1.1.24), love games also form "dangerous liaisons" beset with all sorts of risks even when they are pursued amid the rowdiness of the ball and the carefree festive intrigues of the governor's palace. Shakespeare, then, associates the popular May Day festival with a disordering of the senses.[13] In *A Midsummer Night's Dream*, he plays on the similarities between the festive customs of May Day and Midsummer to add to the overall confusion.

After the summer, essentially marked by open air, pastoral rejoicings (harvest home, Lammas or sheep-shearing) in the country and fairs and wakes in the towns and parishes, came the autumn festivals. Martinmas, on 11 November, was one of them. Ageing, gouty Falstaff is identified with it by Poins, when the latter asks Bardolph "And how doth the martlemas your master?" (*2 Henry IV*, 2.2.95–96). But the fat knight is a calendar in his own right for the various parts of this body symbolize a whole string of the year's festive traditions. Now a "Manningtree ox," now a "wassail candle," Falstaff indeed flaunts the stigmata of his debauchery, which have been etched upon his grotesque physique.

At the end of the year, the most important festival was of course Christmas, with its train of twelve happy days, a long parenthesis that had been originally devised to bridge the gap between the solar and the lunar calendars. In two of his early comedies, *Love's Labor's Lost* and *The Taming of the Shrew*, Shakespeare associates the feast of Christmas with the performances of the minstrels or mummers who were all vaguely associated with the spirit of comedy and mirth (*LLL*, 5.2.461–63 and *Shrew*, induction, 2.133–34).

Clowns and jigs

In the London playhouses that attracted increasing numbers in the 1590s, due in part to the establishment of fixed and professional stages but also to the fierce competition between them, the upholder of the popular tradition was the stage clown. He was to become significant for the whole atmosphere, life, and structure of Shakespearean comedy (from Launce and his dog in *The Two Gentlemen of Verona* to Feste in *Twelfth Night*).[14] Yet Hamlet, in a famous passage, openly disapproves of him, of his idle jests as well as of his scurrilous jigs, often used to conclude a performance:[15]

> And let those that play your clowns speak no more than is set down for them; for there be of them that will themselves laugh, to set on some quantity of barren spectators to laugh too, though in the mean time some necessary question of the play be then to be consider'd. That's villainous and shows a most pitiful ambition in the fool that uses it.   (3.2.38–45)

The function of the clown was thus to cut down intellectual pretension and to draw attention to what Mikhail Bakhtin has called "the material bodily lower stratum,"[16] that is, the world below the belt and the sphere of human appetite, thus allowing the spectator to distance himself/herself from high-minded activity and discourse. The opposition functions particularly well in *Love's Labor's Lost*, where Costard and Jaquenetta unabashedly express their bodily needs against the high-flown, far-reaching, and pretentious aspirations of the courtiers, and in *A Midsummer Night's Dream*, where the myth of romantic love is subverted through the debunking and the bungling of "Pyramus and Thisbe" by the mechanicals. In *Much Ado About Nothing*, the "shallow wits," Dogberry and his hilariously inefficient watch, find the simple truth that the wiser characters could not discover, while in *The Merchant of Venice* the clown Gobbo gives us a farcical version of the "serious" plot and of family relations inside the Christian and Jewish communities. Strangely enough, Shakespeare's most extraordinary clown and expert in all tricks – carnivalesque jokes, theatrical ad-libbing, bibulous word games or superb comic monologues to obfuscate his lies or cover his bad faith – namely Sir John Falstaff, is mostly present in *1* and *2 Henry IV* and appears in one comedy only, *The Merry Wives of Windsor*. An adaptation of the Plautine parasite and glutton of Roman New Comedy, he becomes a fascinating lord of misrule whose headquarters at the Boar's Head tavern are an upside down image of a kingdom depleted and degraded by riot, dissension, and civil strife. In *2 Henry IV*, Falstaff loses some of his geniality and good spirits (the Lord Chief Justice calls him "a candle, the better part burnt out" [1.2.155–56]), while in *The Merry Wives of Windsor* Falstaff is turned into a rather pathetic, farcical figure.

Shakespeare's uses of the main popular festivals

In *Shakespeare's Festive World*, I have shown that, in his plays, Shakespeare was highly aware of and most attentive to the importance of folklore, high days, and holidays, and that calendrical allusions, without being systematic or even accurate, since not all of these customs were consistently observed, serve a great variety of purposes and dramatic effects in his plays.[17] In *A Midsummer Night's Dream*, there is as much confusion of festival dates (the night of the comedy could be situated any time between St. Valentine's Day and Midsummer) as there is in the phases of the moon; this, in spite of a number of sophisticated scholarly explanations,[18] is probably deliberate on the part of a playwright who always seems to have refused to follow a strict, rigid series of rules. This muddle over the calendar is analogous to his wonted disruption of the unities of space, time, and action in Aristotelian, classical dramaturgy, except for a few, highly visible exceptions like *The Comedy of Errors* or *The Tempest*. Shakespeare's point is to use festivity as a means of abolishing continuous time altogether and to make it the equivalent of sleep or a means of "recreation" as in *The Winter's Tale*; there, the long sheep-shearing scene in Bohemia (4.4) simultaneously serves to compensate for the sixteen-year gap of time between the two halves of the play and to restore what was lost, leading to a form of spiritual healing of the Sicilian king and kingdom and to the happy reunion of a family broken by the tragedy of sexual jealousy.

In popular memories, Midsummer was still linked to the London parades. The famous Midsummer Watch, suppressed in 1539, was replaced by the Lord Mayor's Show on St. Simon and St. Jude's Day on 28 October, usually staged at nightfall with torches, with the presence of St. George and the dragon (popularly referred to as 'Old Snap'), of giants and of Wild Men ("woodwoses"), all equipped with candles, lanterns, or "cressets."[19] These figures created a very special tinge of delight and fear, analogous to the ambivalent reactions prompted on contemporary English stages by fairies' magic as well as by demonic or ghostly apparitions. "Why, this is very midsummer madness" (*Twelfth Night*, 3.4.58), Olivia exclaims when she sees her besotted steward sporting yellow stockings cross-gartered with a large conniving smile, suggesting that Malvolio has been "moon-struck" and now behaves like a lunatic or like one of these fantastic midsummer dreams or apparitions. The whole moment is steeped in a sort of crazy topsy-turvydom, like much of what happens in this somber comedy of eros and errors. This is not just an innocent or chance proverbial saying on the part of Olivia in a comedy that takes its title from an allusion to the winter solstice, or rather from the twelfth night that follows, but looks ahead to its summer counterpart or calendrical antipodes, six months later.

If we are to take a contrary example and examine a festival more rarely mentioned by Shakespeare, it is interesting that the feast of Hallowmas and that of the day before, All Hallows' Eve or Hallowe'en, figures in a puzzling passage in *The Merry Wives of Windsor*, when Simple asks a rather astounding and apparently nonsensical question about a book of riddles: "Book of riddles? Why, did you not lend it to Alice Shortcake upon Allhallowmas last, a fortnight afore Michaelmas?" (1.1.187–89). By putting the order of festivals upside down (Michaelmas corresponds to 29 September and Hallowmas to 1 November), Simple provokes hilarity among the audience. Time seems to be running backward in this Saturnalian festive comedy. But there may be another meaning to this passage, as Jeanne Addison Roberts suggests, confirming that Shakespeare's one English, citizen comedy is in fact steeped in an autumnal background as well as a number of connections with carnival and charivari customs.[20] As far as *The Tempest* is concerned, John Bender has shown that Shakespeare's last "comedy" might also be placed in resonance with autumnal rites and the festival of Hallowmas.[21] But the most amazing, almost subterranean connection with Hallowmas is to be found in *Romeo and Juliet*, when the Nurse insists on Juliet's age and repeats that "On Lammas-eve at night shall she be fourteen" (1.3.22). As I have shown elsewhere,[22] the then popular method of backward reckoning used by judges and nurses to compute the exact time when the child was conceived, takes us back in that particular case to the night of Hallowe'en, since Lammas-eve is situated exactly nine months away from All Hallows' Eve on 31 October. This combination of birth day and death day, of light and darkness, of eros and thanatos fits the play's oxymoronic combination of contraries and adds an ironical calendrical comment to the theme of "star-crossed" love.

Memory and celebration

Love's Labor's Lost ends with a "Song of the cuckoo and the owl" in which the two birds respectively stand for spring and winter and compete with rival themes. This final song echoes and encapsulates the main topic of the comedy, which could be interpreted as a long struggle between the forces of Lenten meditation and study on the one hand and those of Carnival, love-making, and marriage on the other. Contrary to all the other comedies, marriage is finally postponed as the death of the French king is announced and the play, which had begun with a vow of asceticism and penance, ends in frustration, atypically and ironically confronting the young men with their antifestive pledge:

PRINCESS   go with speed
To some forlorn and naked hermitage,
Remote from all the pleasures of the world;
There stay until twelve celestial signs
Have brought about the annual reckoning.
If this austere insociable life
Change not your offer made in heat of blood;
If frosts and fasts, hard lodging and thin weeds
Nip not the gaudy blossoms of your love
. . .
Come challenge me, challenge me by these deserts,
And by this virgin palm now kissing thine
I will be thine
. . .
BEROWNE   Our wooing doth not end like an old play;
Jack hath not Jill. These ladies' courtesy
Might well have made our sport a comedy.

                    (5.2.790–872)

Contrary to this form of aborted or protracted festivity, 2 Henry IV ends with nostalgic memories of "the chimes at midnight" in Master Shallow's Gloucestershire orchard, just before Falstaff is banished by the new king. These chimes toll the knell of festivity because the recorded time of history now takes precedence over the dissipated time of holiday misrule. In Henry V, the feast of St. Crispin is turned into a remembrance for the high deeds of the English nation on foreign territory and anticipates the future celebration of the Agincourt victory over the French Army. The conversion of a guild holiday (that of the shoemakers) into a national red-letter day is facilitated by the magic of warrior valor, but also by the phonetic proximity of the words "feats" and "feast," since each word works as an anagram of the other:

KING HENRY   This day is called the feast of Crispian.
He that outlives this day and comes safe home
Will stand a-tiptoe when this day is named
And rouse him at the name of Crispian.

He that shall see this day and live old age
Will yearly on the vigil feast his neighbours
And say, "Tomorrow is Saint Crispian."
Then he will strip his sleeve and show his scars
And say, "These wounds I had on Crispin's day."
Old men forget; yet all shall be forgot,
But he'll remember with advantages,
What feats he did that day ...

(4.3.40–51)

The coincidence of popular festival with national commemoration makes this passage a unique one. What is more, the king buoyantly and brilliantly looks ahead to the significance that this particular date is to have for the English nation, thus creating a fraternity and bonding of blood that almost transcends the traditional feudal hierarchical links.

So, throughout the canon, Shakespeare reveals a surprising ability to appropriate both the religious and secular calendars and to establish a number of echoes and symbolic resonances in his festive comedies, but also in some of his histories and tragedies. Shakespeare's method is not that of a ritualist, as he never shows literal respect for the order of calendar customs. He has just as much interest in deviance from and exceptions to the rule, thus remaining free to upset or subvert the routines of long-established tradition in order to draw attention to other ways in which the calendar could work and to create new associations within it.

The function(s) of popular festivity in Shakespearian comedy

According to C. L. Barber, the pioneering author of *Shakespeare's Festive Comedy*, the main function of festive elements in Shakespearian drama is to trigger an emotional release and help create an atmosphere of joyful liberation in the face of an archaic moral order or tyranny. This, according to his optimistic view, is bound to produce a movement of clarification in the characters themselves, but also in the various complications or entanglements of the play:

> The *clarification* achieved by the festive comedies is concomitant to the release they dramatize: a heightened awareness of the relation between man and "nature" – the nature celebrated on holiday. The process of translating festive experience into drama involved extending the sort of awareness traditionally associated with holiday, and also becoming conscious of holiday itself in a new way.[23]

Barber's analysis sounds on the whole more Freudian than historical or political and it seems linked with the thesis that the presence of a popular festival miraculously provides the younger characters in the comedy with a possibility to reach a form of freedom or emancipation from patriarchy and to express their own desires against the mutilating or castrating nature of the "law of the father." In this connection, carnival provides the occasion or the welcome detour as well as the masks and the music that allow the young to get away with transgression and abuse (e.g. when Jessica elopes from old Shylock's house and "gilds" herself with her father's ducats) in a jolly atmosphere of revelry and almost innocent revolt.

For Marxist critics like Mikhail Bakhtin, Robert Weimann, and Michael Bristol, on the other hand, festive license is deeply indebted and fundamentally allied to popular culture. For these critics, carnival grotesqueries in Shakespeare are indeed endowed with a truly subversive power and with a desire to destabilize authority and its serious, official, one-sided, vertical vision of the world. Popular festivals and charivaris thus contributed to the expression of dissent, to the simultaneous presence of multiple voices, including those of children and women (through the rites of inversion of the Boy-Bishop or cross-dressing or witchcraft). So, the grotesque language and imagery of the lower parts of the body were given pride of place, just as the *platea* suddenly became more significant or thrilling than the *sedes*.[24]

It would seem that popular festivity, even when it is staged in a play, cannot be reduced to the function of a simple interval or "safety valve." But it all depends on the context, moment, and atmosphere and it seems quite difficult or dangerous to generalize in these matters. If it is true to say that popular festivals are more easily associated with the comedies and the romances, they also turn out to play a very important role in the histories and tragedies. In this particular background, festivity seems to produce improvidence, prodigality, and blindness that propel individuals toward their downfall (we could find examples in Falstaff, Antony, and Timon). The context of a network of communal obligations might suggest that it was not indispensable for each individual to take responsibility for his own destiny, while Shakespeare's entire work lays stress on the promotion of self-knowledge rather than on any particular action or mode of behavior recommended within some ritualized system.

Traditionally, popular festivals held a place of importance in the calendar and were so deeply rooted in people's imaginary representations of the world that they could resurface in the most unexpected places and times. But a dramatist's use of popular festivity could not be limited simply to transferring them to the stage or to superimposing them upon the structure of such or such a play. No doubt a minimum of fidelity to the forms of traditional festive customs was necessary to enable the audience to recognize the general references and allusions. It was also indispensable to mask those allusions, to introduce ellipses and eclipses, shortened or disguised versions of rituals and to develop correspondences and a system of metaphorical echoes. They could also be used with more somber implications and turn surface or momentary pleasures into forms of vanity or bitterly ironical reminders. In 2 *Henry VI* (4.6.3–4) the Pissing Conduit running with claret wine or the "fountain with an hundred spouts / [Running] pure blood" in *Julius Caesar* (2.2.77–78), both have somewhat sinister connotations as they are the presages of murder, bloodshed, and a long, painful civil war that will drain both the Roman and the English nation (both are more or less reversible metaphors in Shakespeare's Roman and English history plays). They remind us that commemoration is linked to sacrifice and they expose a common subtext of savage violence. They also show that the most exuberant rejoicings often take place at the door of annihilation.

Conclusion

At a time when Puritan ministers and pamphleteers repeatedly attacked the abuses and excesses of "Papist" rejoicings and popular festivals that were taken to be pagan remnants and forms of superstitious or licentious idolatry, Shakespeare stood in the defense of "old holiday pastimes" in his work, as these seemed to him to anchor his writing in tradition while allowing him a considerable amount of flexibility and a world of phrases, images, symbols all chiming together to create a tightly woven network of associations and resonances. In his green world comedies, and later romances, he chose festivity and mirth rather than city intrigue and satire, while in many of his histories and tragedies the same images serve him as landmarks in the calendar to lace a deeply felt sense of time with the belated and somewhat bitter ironies of retributive justice (as in *Richard III*, *Hamlet*, or *King Lear*), even if the overall pattern can never be said to be a providential one, especially in the last two examples. This is probably because he invested the celebration of calendar days and of old festivals with a fundamental ambivalence to illustrate the links between "clowns and kings," "mirth and funerals."[25]

So, popular festivals were for Shakespeare the linchpin that allowed him to transgress and transcend the usual generic borders and to endow his drama with some of the versatilities and surprises of life.

NOTES

1 All references to Shakespeare are to David Bevington (ed.), *The Complete Works of Shakespeare* (Glenview, Ill.: Scott, Foresman and Co., 1980).
2 See Roy Strong, *The Cult of Elizabeth* (London: Thames and Hudson, 1977), p. 16.

3 See my *Shakespeare's Festive World: Elizabethan Seasonal Entertainment and the Professional Stage* (Cambridge: Cambridge University Press, 1991; reprinted paperback, 1993), pp. 111–14.

4 Philip Stubbes, *Philip Stubbes' Anatomy of Abuses in England in Shakespeare's Youth, AD 1583*, ed. Frederick J. Furnivall, 2 vols. (London: New Shakspere Society, 1877–79).

5 See Laroque, *Shakespeare's Festive World*, pp. 163–64. See also Bruce Smith, *The Acoustic World of Early Modern England* (Chicago and London: University of Chicago Press, 1999).

6 See Leah Marcus, *Politics of Mirth: Jonson, Herrick, Milton, Marvel and the Defense of Old Holiday Pastimes* (Chicago and London: University of Chicago Press, 1986).

7 Laroque, *Shakespeare's Festive World*, p. 337, notes 97 and 99.

8 On this, see E. A. J. Honigmann, *Shakespeare: the "Lost Years"* (Manchester: Manchester University Press, 1985), pp. 8–30. See also Richard Wilson's "Shakespeare and the Jesuits," *TLS* (19 December 1997), 11–13.

9 Lévi-Strauss, *The Savage Mind* (Chicago: University of Chicago Press, 1966), p. 21.

10 Peter Burke, "Popular Culture in Seventeenth Century London," in Barry Read (ed.), *Popular Culture in Seventeenth Century England* (London: Routledge, 1988), p. 32.

11 One of the first was certainly E. K. Chambers in his monumental *The Mediaeval Stage*, 2 vols. (Oxford: Oxford University Press, 1903), while the pioneers of this type of critical approach to Shakespearean comedy were Northrop Frye ("The Argument of Comedy," in *English Institute Essays 1948* [New York: Columbia University Press, 1949], pp. 58–73) and C. L. Barber (*Shakespeare's Festive Comedy: a Study of Dramatic Form and its Relation to Social Custom* [Princeton: Princeton University Press, 1959; reprinted 1972]).

12 Laroque, *Shakespeare's Festive World*, pp. 108–09.

13 In this connection see the quotation from *Henry VIII* above.

14 In this connection see David Wiles, *Shakespeare's Clown: Actor and Text in the Elizabethan Playhouse* (Cambridge: Cambridge University Press, 1987).

15 See Thomas Platter's description of a jig at the end of a performance of *Julius Caesar* at the Globe in 1599: "After lunch, at about two o'clock, I and my party crossed the river, and there in the house with the thatched roof we saw an excellent performance of the tragedy of the first emperor Julius Caesar, with about fifteen characters; and after the play, according to their custom, they did a most elegant and curious dance, two dressed in men's clothes and two in women's." *Travels in England* (1599), p. 166, translated into English and quoted by T. S. Dorsch, *Julius Caesar*, Arden Shakespeare (London, 1955; reprinted 1977), p. vii.

16 Mikhail Bakhtin *Rabelais and his World*, trans. Hélène Iswolsky (Cambridge, Mass.: MIT Press, 1968), ch. 6, pp. 368–436.

17 Laroque, *Shakespeare's Festive World*, pp. 228–35.

18 See, for instance, David Wiles, *Shakespeare's Almanac: "A Midsummer Night's Dream," Marriage and the Elizabethan Calendar* (Cambridge: D. S. Brewer, 1993).

19 See Laroque, *Shakespeare's Festive World*, pp. 344–46, notes 238–42.

20 Jeanne Addison Roberts, *The Merry Wives of Windsor* as a Hallowe'en Play," *Shakespeare Survey* 25 (1972): 107–12. On carnival and other festive traditions, see Christiane Gallenca, "Ritual and Folk-Customs in *The Merry Wives of Windsor*," *Cahiers Elisabéthains* 27 (April 1985): 27–41.

21 John Bender, "The Day of *The Tempest*," *ELH* 47 (1980).

22 François Laroque, "Tradition and Subversion in *Romeo and Juliet*," in Jay L. Halio (ed), "*Romeo and Juliet*": *Texts, Contexts, and Interpretation* (Cranbury, N.J., London and Misissauga, Ontario: Associated University Presses, 1995), pp. 26–27.

23 Barber, *Shakespeare's Festive Comedy*, p. 8.

24 Bakhtin, *Rabelais and his World*; Michael Bristol, *Carnival and Theater: Plebeian Culture and the Structure of Authority in Renaissance England* (London: Methuen, 1985; reprinted (paperback) New York and London: Routledge, 1989); Robert Weimann, *Shakespeare and the Popular Tradition in the Theater* (Berlin, 1967; Baltimore: Johns Hopkins University Press, 1978). The two Latin terms, *platea* and *sedes*, are borrowed from Weimann's approach and represent the opposition he introduces in medieval and Tudor drama between the characters and plays situated on a platform above and representing the serious voices of authority (*sedes* or throne) and the low or "common" characters who descend on to the marketplace (*platea*) and move among the spectators with their subversive, scurrilous or seriocomic voices (Vices, devils, and clowns).

25 Philip Sidney, *The Defence of Poesie* (London, 1595; reprinted Menston: Scolar Press Facsimile, 1968), sig. l.v.

2

Shakespearean comedy

6

JOHN CREASER

Forms of confusion

Drama makes a ceremony out of a muddle. Much of the world's theatre originated in seasonal festivals, rites of fertility and initiation, and forms of liturgy. It still retains a ceremonious quality, with performers and audience responsive to conventions of conduct. Yet the subject of drama is confusion: whether evoking horror or hope, drama gives shape to the disarray and precariousness of our lives. Accordingly, the word *confusion* is one which Shakespeare explores. While he uses it most often in the root meaning of ruin or perdition (*OED*, sense 1), he also employs most of the other senses then current: putting to shame (sense 2); mental perturbation, embarrassment (3); the 'confusion of tongues' at the tower of Babel (4); the now standard meaning of disorder (5); tumult and commotion (6); and finally conflation, or the 'con-fusion' of intimate mingling and blending (7). He also delights in the possibilities of the word. When Launcelot Gobbo is teasing his old father, he says, "I will try confusions with him" instead of "try conclusions" or make an experiment (*The Merchant of Venice*, 2.2.37).[1] When out hunting, Theseus and Hippolyta relish "the musical confusion / Of hounds and echo in conjunction" (*A Midsummer Night's Dream*, 4.1.110–11), an echoing con-fusion of senses 5, 6, and 7. When Hymen comes to resolve the enigmas of Rosalind with "Peace ho! I bar confusion" (*As You Like It*, 5.4.125), he gives his statement a comprehensive finality by blending senses 3, 5, and 6. Friar Lawrence insists on the irrelevance of histrionic outpourings of grief at Juliet's apparent death by juxtaposing senses 1 and 6: "Peace ho, for shame! Confusion's [cure] lives not / In these confusions" (*Romeo and Juliet*, 4.5.65–66).

Confusion, being essential to drama, is not essentially comic, not even in comedy. There is cruel wit but no humor when Feste bewilders Malvolio in the guise of Sir Topas the curate: it is unmitigated persecution, at least until the self-serving Toby Belch intervenes (*Twelfth Night*, 4.2.66–71). Nevertheless, there is a primitive humor in simple confusions of word or deed that Shakespeare never tired of exploiting. Nothing in his earliest plays is funnier than the laments of Launce, the clownish servant of *The Two Gentlemen of Verona*, as he deplores the failures of the stubbornly canine Crab to live by human standards:

> I think Crab my dog be the sourest-natur'd dog that lives: my mother weeping, my father wailing, my sister crying, our maid howling, our cat wringing her hands, and all our house in a great perplexity, yet did not this cruel-hearted cur shed one tear. He ... has no more pity in him than a dog ... Nay, I'll show you the manner of it. This shoe is my father; no, this left shoe is my father; no, no, this left shoe is my mother; nay, that cannot be so neither; yes, it is so, it is so – it hath the worser sole. This shoe, with the hole in it, is my mother, and this my father ... Now, sir, this staff is my sister ... This hat is Nan, our maid. I am the dog – no, the dog is himself, and I am the dog – O! the dog is me, and I am myself; ay, so, so. (2.3.5–23)

Such timeless theatricality survives throughout Shakespeare's career, for example when Caliban hides from Trinculo, and Trinculo – despite the "very ancient and fish-like smell" (*The Tempest* 2.2.26) – creeps under Caliban's gabardine for protection from the storm, and Stephano comes upon a beast with four legs and two voices. When the invisible Ariel joins in the threesome's next scene (3.2) and gets Trinculo into trouble, we are not far from Christmas pantomime. There is a lot of Puck in any audience: "And those things do best please me / That befall prepost'rously" (*Dream*, 3.2.120–21).

There is, it is true, more to such episodes than mere drollery. Launce's doleful devotion is an ironic echo of the love of his master Proteus and Julia, while the absurd reactions of Trinculo and Stephano to the "strange fish" (2.2.27) continue to be a central issue in *The Tempest*: what it is to be human. Moreover, though we laugh *at* Launce, we laugh *with* the actor performing the role beside his unpredictable stooge. His soliloquies are star turns; bumbling becomes virtuosity. Nevertheless, the core of the humor is the simple confusion of the characters. It is the same in the dominant tradition inherited by Shakespeare: the "New Comedy" of ancient Rome (discussed by Robert Miola in chapter 2 of this volume) and its imitators in Renaissance Italy. Many of the Latin plays of Plautus and especially of Terence, and their late classical and Renaissance commentators, were then known to every schoolboy. Their plots, models of how to organize chaos and crisis, normally lead to the sexual gratification of a young man of no great abilities or character, thanks to the inspired improvizations of a crafty household servant, the *servus delusus*. The hero desires a girl who seems inaccessible, usually because she is not freeborn (she may also be pregnant or in the hands of a pimp). He has a rival or some other "blocking figure" to overcome – often his own father. There is a complicated plot of intrigue and deception, with the knots of confusion often untied only when the girl turns out to be freeborn after all and a suitable partner for the hero.

Over twenty of the surviving twenty-seven plays by Plautus and Terence are on formulaic lines like these; likewise, the young men and their slaves are virtually interchangeable from play to play. There is no interest in the development of character; the speedy, condensed plots mean that the plays anticipate the unities of time, place, and action which Renaissance scholars sought to make obligatory. The plays exist for their local inventiveness, and the star role is the slave's, since this is a saturnalian world, where anyone who obstructs the hero's desires is fair game, but where everyone except the despised pimp is eventually reconciled to the trickery. The plays are farces: orthodox virtues are relevant only intermittently, and the principal vice is to lack a robust sense of humor. The simplified characters are scarcely touched by moral or even physical pain, so that the audience enjoys a moral holiday, laughing without restraint at predicaments which in reality or even in comedy would be brutal or mortifying. Farce goes for the maximum complication of action with the minimum complexity of response. Although ancient and Renaissance commentators labored to turn the works of Plautus and especially Terence into treatises on morality, theirs is in essentials the simplified world of Tom and Jerry, as a few scholars were prepared to acknowledge. Nevertheless, these ancient farces remain fundamental to European comedy, and later writers have developed their simplicity of effect into drama of unprecedented resource and diversity.

Shakespeare and the learnedly neoclassical Ben Jonson, for example, fill a void at the center of New Comedy plotting in revealingly diverse ways. The love promoted by the farcical intrigues cannot usually be shown, because a respectable young woman could not be represented on the Roman stage, so in the plays leading to marriage the heroine is at most a fleeting presence. Jonson's reaction, at least in his major plays, is to write loveless, satirical comedies of deception, without heroines. He created in reality the satiric and didactic comedy that most commentators imagined in Plautus and Terence, but with the dramatic power of the *servus delusus* now given over to villains and tricksters. Jonson's episodes are often farcical, but his plays are never simply farces. Our moral judgment is continually, though rather teasingly, evoked, while pain and punishment can be realities. No threat to punish a Roman *servus* is ever carried out, whereas in *Volpone* Mosca is condemned to lifelong servitude in the galleys.

Jonson's art remains neoclassical not only in its adoption of the unities but also in being a comedy of intrigue, based therefore on deception. For his characters with strong dramatic presence, deception is the means to power, survival and self-esteem in the plays' competitive urban world, reflecting the new sense of the individual's anonymity in the metropolitan London of Jonson's lifetime. Until the more Shakespearean work of his later years, Jonson celebrates the values of a supportive community only by their absence. His characters are self-obsessed; there is no trust, let alone honor, among thieves. His plays remain classical at base because their plots are driven by a single ruling passion, though it tends to be desire for gold, or self-esteem through gold, rather than sexual desire. So the modes of confusion which his comedies generate are, however inventive, limited in range.

Shakespeare's crucial reaction to the empty center of New Comedy is to give the heroines all the prominence in the drama which is latent in the motivation of the comic stories – taking a lead from simply but vividly sketched heroines such as Campaspe and Gallathea in the distinctive comic art of John Lyly. Moreover, this prominence is not only in the action: through their love and resilience, the heroines embody the positive values of their plays and help to transform a society into a community. Inevitably, even these comedies also present a simplified world. Despite the abrupt ending of *Love's Labor's Lost*, the unrequited devotion to their young men of the Antonios in *The Merchant of Venice* and *Twelfth Night*, and deep uncertainties at the outcome of the dark comedies *Measure for Measure* and *All's Well That Ends Well*, the norm is clear: genuine love is fulfilled. Illicit sex is joked about and aimed at, but rarely committed during the plays.[2] Apart from Shylock, a figure of tragedy trapped in comedy, evil characters are little more than plot mechanisms. Shakespeare is not here concerned with the psychology of evil deception; it would be futile to read Don John as envious of Claudio just as Iago is of the "daily beauty" of Cassio (*Othello*, 5.1.19). Malice is brushed aside by abrupt conversions or the promise of "brave punishments" (*Much Ado About Nothing*, 5.4.128). Yet by including malign characters at all, Shakespeare transcends the generic limits of New Comedy – one sign of the unprecedented expansiveness of his work. This enables him to elaborate the central comic experience of confusion while diminishing the role of deception, making it incidental rather than the mainspring of the plot. There is no role for the *servus delusus*.

Consequently, Shakespeare devises a new kind of exposition or, as late classical and Renaissance scholars termed it, *protasis* (normally Acts 1 and 2). Whereas a New Comedy is organized around a single impulse, Shakespeare mediates the predominant impulse of love through processes of more variety and import, making for less predictable modes of action and confusion. Fundamentally, two forces set a Shakespeare comedy in motion. The first is a conflict between law and justice: an abuse of law or power creates tremors in an apparently stable society or household.[3] The second is the arrival of one or more travelers or strangers with grounds for discontent or insecurity. The result is a state of confusion with consequences which, ultimately, are benign. The first of these drives follows from the paradox that Shakespeare's comedies, though fanciful and romantic in setting and story, are more open to the variety of social experience than are the superficially more realistic and urban plays of New Comedy, confined as these are to the lives of citizens and their servants. Shakespeare is prepared to sketch relations within a much wider social group, "mingling kings and clowns" without the fastidious reserve of neoclassical theorizing.[4]

The dual impetus of the plotting is there from the start. In *The Comedy of Errors*, Shakespeare demonstrates his mastery of New Comedy and outdoes his primary source, the *Menaechmi* of Plautus, in farcical confusion, notably by adding a second pair of separated twins. But already he complicates and deepens this confusion by adding a clash between law and justice: the punitive law recently passed in Ephesus which demands the life of the innocent and ignorant Egeon merely because he comes from Syracuse. The Duke of Ephesus himself is trapped between natural justice and the letter of the law, sympathetic toward Egeon but legally unable to free him from state tyranny. Egeon's desperate plight looms over the farcical muddles of the central acts. Meanwhile, the outsider, Antipholus of Syracuse, feels himself painfully incomplete without the twin he has scarcely known: "I to the world am like a drop of water, / That in the ocean seeks another drop, / Who, falling there to find his fellow forth / (Unseen, inquisitive), confounds himself" (1.2.35–38). To Antipholus, the bizarre chaos of the day further undermines a sense of self already under duress. In *The Taming of the Shrew*, the domestic injustice of Baptista the rich Paduan whose favoritism toward his younger daughter Bianca has encouraged an aggressive but essentially self-defensive shrewishness in her elder sister Katherina, is complicated by his arbitrary ruling that the lovely and sought-after Bianca cannot marry before the formidable Kate. Into this volatile situation come Lucentio of Pisa, an intending student who at once falls for Bianca, and Petruchio of Verona, in search of wealth through marriage.

The action of every one of the comedies is driven in this dual way. (Even in *Measure for Measure*, where all the characters and locations are Viennese, Duke Vincentio is a virtual outsider, partly through his disguise as a foreign priest and partly because he moves from the court to an alien milieu, the underbelly of the city.) Nevertheless, the plays' situations come in such variety that there is no sense of a formula being applied. In New Comedy, for example, tensions between father and son are predictable. While there are some "heavy fathers" in Shakespeare, families are much more varied in their insecurities. The only norm is the abnormal absence of that traditional root of social stability, the settled household of two parents and their children.[5] There is a remarkable lack of mothering. Instead, the initial instabilities arise from such varied causes as the misplaced enthusiasms of independent youth (*Love's Labor's Lost*), a vindictive response to a lifetime of prejudice (*The Merchant of Venice*), rivalries within a small-town community (*The Merry Wives of Windsor*), or grave acts of tyranny (*As You Like It, Measure for Measure, Pericles, The Winter's Tale, The Tempest*). Similarly, the newcomers include rogues, fortune-hunters, exiles, victims of shipwreck, and even the itinerant King of the Fairies, unhappy about a little Indian boy. Shakespeare's outsiders can be seen as the greatly enriched equivalent of the "alazon" of New Comedy, who adds variety to the citizen cast. The alazon is the braggart and pretender, such as a boastful soldier, but the original meaning of the word is a vagabond. There are such traditional figures in Shakespeare – Falstaff and Don Armado are magnificent specimens – but his outsiders bring a much greater social and emotional range.

To motivate his major plays, Ben Jonson devised the comic technique of the "magnetic center": the wealth in Volpone's bedroom or the laboratory of Subtle draws in a clutch of victims; the ostentatious misanthropy of Morose brings a crowd of tormentors around him; citizens gather in Bartholomew Fair like flies around carrion. It is an invention of genius, but it generates less rich possibilities of both confusion and vision than Shakespeare, whose methods encourage varied levels of seriousness and depths of disorder. For example, Jonson's pattern creates a rigorous division between insiders and visitors, while the fertile possibilities of confusion in Shakespeare mean that both groups soon, while still within the *protasis*, find themselves changing position and role in almost every play. Petruchio makes himself very much at home, while Katherina becomes an internal exile. Lovers and artisans at home in Athens become bemused aliens in the wood nearby. In *As You Like It*, Adam leaves his home of almost sixty years and nearly dies; Duke Senior is more at home among his "sermons in stones" (2.1.17) than Duke Frederick on the throne. Much confusion in depth is generated by concentrating on characters who may seem to have an established place but are inwardly ill at ease. Shylock, with his acknowledged although disdained social role, is the most potent figure, but his enemy Antonio is almost as alienated, since the social esteem he enjoys as a merchant is undermined by the love for Bassanio which he never can enjoy. The venom he habitually utters against the Jew as an obvious scapegoat may be a projection of the intuitive self-dismay which is to surface when he describes himself as "a tainted wether [castrated ram] of the flock / Meetest for death" (4.1.114–15). *Much Ado About Nothing* brings together two related little communities – the Governor of Messina's household and Don Pedro's senior officers – in holiday mood. The ensuing tensions are generated not only by the stupidly persistent disaffection of the bastard brother but also by those who in more subtle ways do not quite belong: the diffident and itinerant Claudio who seeks an establishment, the witty Benedick who fears he may be no more than "the Prince's fool" (2.1.204), and Beatrice, the orphan poor relation, who, though loving and beloved, is marginal to the household. In such ways, the plays dramatize a need to belong, a yearning for community. Both the established household or society and the itinerant characters have their vulnerabilities and sense of incompleteness. While Jonson engenders dramatic energies out of obviously antisocial conduct, Shakespeare multiplies and varies instability by tracing it even within the established leaders of society as well as the outsiders.

As a result, actions and confusions of great complexity become possible. The desire to belong can be subjected to abnormal stress, as becomes all the clearer when we move from the *protasis* to the complication, climax, and then resolution of the action – technically known as the *epitasis* (normally Acts 3 and 4) and *catastrophe* or *dénouement* (Act 5). New Comedy is an art of concentration: character is simplified; time, place, and action are unified. Shakespeare's is an art of expansiveness, and this is epitomized by his readiness to abandon the neoclassical unities. New Comedy locates itself in the familiar, in a conventionalized urban setting. Although the revelation of the heroine's true birth often brings a traveler into these plays, New Comedy, as Leo Salingar says, "is still curiously inward-looking ... still focused on the typical bourgeois family, embedded in familiar urban surroundings."[6] But Shakespeare gives travelers substantial and varied parts in every play, and even when he does follow the unities, as in *The Comedy of Errors* and *The Tempest*, he packs the cast with them. Moreover, travel in the comedies is from as well as into the initial society; another center is often established. Isolated from the everyday, characters are brought up against themselves and their confusions: the enforced trip to the country after which Katherina at last sees the light (4.5) anticipates other places of trouble and illumination to come. Shakespeare typically translates his characters not to another urban setting but to woodland or seascape, unknown and unknowable, rich in promise but wild and threatening and all too easy to get lost in, embodiments of what lies beyond reason and human control. For some characters all of the time, and almost all characters some of the time, the comedies are enacted in these alien settings: not only sea and forest but the alarming city of Ephesus famed for sorcerers, or a bizarre country house, or a foreign land. For Falstaff, even provincial Windsor is alien, and leads to a *catastrophe* in the forest. What might seem the most idyllic of these alternative settings are never simply places of benign escape. Belmont is throughout a place of trial, while pastoral Arden knows "winter and rough weather" (2.5.8), a harsh landlord, danger, and initial disappointment. To wander in the forest near

Athens by moonlight is to be driven frantic, "wode [mad] within this wood" (2.1.192). These secondary realms test through disorientation.

Similarly, Shakespeare's customary neglect of the unity of time means that he can present (to adopt phrases from Browning) "action in character" as well as "character in action."[7] New Comedy stresses consistency: characters are types, unchanging and undeveloping, with speech, emotions, and conduct in keeping with gender, age, and social situation. But admit the passage of time, and human identity becomes malleable and subject to change, to testing processes of growth or degradation. As Salingar has written, "Shakespeare's characters are not merely capable of being surprised by what happens to them, dismayed or delighted, like the people in Italian comedies; they can be carried out of their normal selves, 'transformed,' observe themselves passing into a new phase of experience, so strange that it seems like illusion. This is only part, indeed, of a more fundamental innovation which in its general effect distinguishes Shakespeare's plays from all previous comedies, that he gives his people the quality of an inner life" (*Traditions of Comedy*, p. 222). We can now inwardly "read" a character like Antonio the merchant, whose whole demeanor has recently changed and who professes to be at a loss with himself: "In sooth I know not why I am so sad." We can distinguish an outer and an inner self and see their relations in flux.

The central experience of most of the comedies is courtship, and, in the words of Edward Berry, "It was Shakespeare ... more than any other writer, who developed the myth of romantic marriage that has survived, though today in fragments, since the seventeenth century. And he achieved this by depicting courtship as a period of disorientation similar to a rite of transition – a nerve-racking, potentially dangerous, chaotic, but ultimately re-creative time out of which may emerge the form and meaning of marriage."[8] *Love's Labor's Lost* ends with only conditional acceptances because the women feel the men have not been through a profound confusion; their trial has not been sustained and exacting enough. "Who chooseth me, must give and hazard all he hath" (*Merchant*, 2.7.9) applies to all lovers, and not only in Belmont. Characters have to be prepared to endure risk: Petruchio and Katherina have to believe that the other will ultimately be worth trusting, Berowne has to endure apostasy and mockery, Helena to pursue and seduce the man who disdains her. The villainous Jachimo may take a gamble, but genuine lovers stake their entire happiness.

Reactions to ordeal by confusion are as various as the confusions themselves. One does not expect much disturbance in the fools and clowns who comment from the margins of events, or in the stolid individualism of Bottom, Barnadine, or Jaques, or the irredeemable self-seeking of Antonio and Sebastian in *The Tempest*, or the shallow egotism of Bianca, the shrew who will never be tamed. Little can be achieved with such blinkered self-sufficiency and self-control. But in the fundamentally benign world of most of these plays, the characters who are most loving and loveable find themselves strengthened and even transformed. Orlando survives a bewildering education in loving at the skittish hands of "Ganymed," and this confirms and reinforces his love. In the ferocious quarrels within the moonlit forest near Athens, the quartet of lovers reveal unsuspected depths of dread and emotional violence in themselves, and survive. Some of those who have trapped themselves within a confining role are made to see themselves as they really are before enduring the pain of being released. Katherina is freed from habitual shrewishness by Petruchio's unrelenting travesty of such waywardness – a robust mode of farcical comedy which is tolerable because Petruchio is clearly acting a part, because he imposes the same privations on himself as on her, and because his underlying delight in her buried self becomes clear. Beatrice and Benedick are consciously the cleverest in their social groups and indulge that cleverness as compensation for their marginal roles. They maintain their exceptional status by distancing themselves from conventional behavior, so denying the deep but commonplace attraction each feels toward the other. They are, however, magnanimous enough to endure the humiliation of admitting their ordinariness, of making themselves more ridiculous than any other intelligent and sympathetic characters in the plays.

Such characters are shaken to their depths, only to gain love, self-knowledge, and openness to experience. With others, we are less sure. It is merely one possibility at the bleaker and more open endings of *Measure for Measure* and *All's Well That Ends Well* that the passionate and yet inhibited Isabella and Angelo have in effect accepted with Benedick that "the world must be peopled" (*Much Ado*, 2.3.242), and that the stubborn and deeply disingenuous Bertram really can love the stubborn and equivocating Helena. Still other characters are too shallow for such depths of confusion. After the superficial evidence of Hero's apparent depravity in *Much Ado*, Don Pedro and Claudio dress up their hurt pride as moral outrage. For the first time in any version of this familiar story, they turn upon Hero with what Beatrice rightly terms "public accusation, uncover'd slander, unmitigated rancor" (4.1.305–06). Claudio, far from responding to the report of Hero's death with the loving regret anticipated by the Friar, maintains a self-pitying complacency to the end. Even Parolles achieves more than this: through humiliation, the cowardly braggart is learning to survive as "simply the thing I am" (4.3.333). By contrast, Jachimo in *Cymbeline* learns self-contempt and is there arrested, as Posthumus realizes in condemning him to live: "The pow'r that I have on you is to spare you; / The malice towards you, to forgive you" (5.4.418–19). Egeon and most major characters in *The Comedy of Errors* are brought into situations which heighten their sense of mortality or frailty, are in no position to work out their salvation, and escape merely by good fortune. Titania undergoes a merely arbitrary confusion. Antonio the merchant suffers more traumatically than anyone, merely to become less close to the man he loves, left on the fringes of a world where others seem at home.

Other characters are almost destroyed. Malvolio withdraws more embittered and outraged than ever. Shylock seeks the revenge of the disempowered, and is crushed. Leontes and Hermione have their lives turned upside down, without even Job's bitter-sweet compensation of new wealth and family after terrible losses. What is restored need never have been lost, while Mamillius and Antigonus remain lost beyond recall. Leontes, driven by madness into terrible wrong, endures sixteen gratuitous years at the treadmill of penance, held there by Paulina's waiting until "the gods / Will have fulfill'd their secret purposes" (5.1.35–36). The entirely sympathetic Julia of *The Two Gentlemen of Verona* is left as she began, except that Proteus is now heavily shop-soiled.

The tendency that prevails within such varied experience is that confusion in Shakespeare is primarily internal rather than external. New Comedy is situation comedy; characters are bewildered by implausibilities in the outside world – by finding the house locked up, unattended and allegedly haunted, or by a son who sometimes will and sometimes will not marry the girl his father has chosen for him. The confusions are objective in that, however mysterious they seem to some characters, the explanation is clear to the audience, and is circumstantial, not psychological. Even in adapting the *Menaechmi* – where for once chaos is not created by a deceptive slave – Shakespeare makes the major characters of *The Comedy of Errors* susceptible to the confusions in a new way because of their insecurities. As early as *Two Gentlemen* and *The Taming of the Shrew*, he anticipates his major work by locating confusion, and indeed action, primarily within the mind. There are endless mistakes of others' identity in *Errors*, but Valentine, Proteus, and Katherina have mistaken their own.

This subjective dimension gives a new depth to Shakespeare's comic endings. In New Comedy, the knot of the action is cut when social identity is sorted out, in particular when the heroine becomes eligible as a bride. What this might mean to the girl apart from her love of the young man, and the other turmoil of inner adjustments which such a discovery might have caused, is irrelevant. As in much comedy since, society at once regroups around the young couple, with injuries forgiven, wrongs repented, and almost everyone reconciled and rejoicing.

This pattern remains fundamental even within Shakespeare's richer art. The norms of expectation remain much the same: confusions will be resolved; Jack will have Jill; the group will gather in celebration. Abuses of law and power which sent shock waves through household and society at the outset are stilled. Solinus and Theseus simply brush aside the particular laws of Ephesus and Athens that formerly tied their hands; the murderous Oliver and the tyrannical Duke Frederick are converted with all convenient speed; domineering fathers withdraw their objections to would-be sons-in-law. Outsiders and newcomers who brought further imbalance into the earlier acts are now incorporated into the truer equilibrium of a society with a better disposition of power. Society becomes community, as social groupings held together by the imposition of authority relax into festivity.

Inevitably, the characters who have most engaged our sympathetic attention are at the center of this joyous escape from confusions. They have endured and now enjoy in spirit the transformation which Ariel's haunting song claims for the body of Alonso: "Those are pearls that were his eyes: / Nothing of him that doth fade, / But doth suffer a sea-change / Into something rich and strange" (*Tempest*, 1.2.399–402). In them we experience most intimately a tripartite pattern which is fundamental to comedy and to human experience at its most benign and creative: the initial, imperfect stability of the *protasis* yielding to the maze of the *epitasis* and then to the poise of the resolution. Critics have drawn valuable parallels to this pattern in, for example, seasonal festivals and in rites of passage and other ceremonies of initiation.[9]

Nevertheless, in Shakespeare's profoundly unconventional art, such norms of expectation are not always satisfied; they are submitted to interrogation even as they are being established. *The Taming of the Shrew*, for example, ends with some major characters in disarray, as the other two of the three newly wed husbands are dismissed to unhappiness by Petruchio: "We three are married, but you two are sped" (5.2.185). Comic expectations are shockingly dashed by death with Marcade's intrusion into Navarre, but even without this the lords would soon have learned that they were unready for *Love's Labor's Won*. They have to be made to work their way through their immature assurance – even though this needed lesson is made grotesque by the penance imposed on Berowne, the horror of seeking for a whole year "to move wild laughter in the throat of death" (5.2.855). Comedy is again more precarious than joyous in *Twelfth Night*, where Malvolio, Antonio, Aguecheek, and Feste end in bitter or melancholy isolation, where no joy can be taken in the prize of marriage to Sir Toby won by Maria, where at best the marriage of Olivia to Sebastian imposes conventional happiness on to a character too vivid for mere convention, and where "what's to come is still unsure" (2.3.49) in the marriage of Viola to Orsino. Instabilities and discords remain in even the most joyous of plays: in *As You Like It*, Jaques chooses to stand apart in his self-absorbed melancholy and Touchstone's "loving voyage / Is but for two months victuall'd" (5.4.191–92).

Such disturbing of comic norms extends disorientation from the characters to the audience. Watching Plautus, Terence and their successors in farce up to the present day, the audience is challenged merely to be alert and unpuritanical, to follow the intricacies of the action and enjoy what is humanly and morally preposterous just because it is preposterous. Laughter is condescending and untroubled. Some present the sister genre of comedy in similar terms: "Comedy depends for its effects upon a certain distancing. It requires a barely realized mental posture of superiority so that there can be a full deployment of that element that causes us to laugh."[10] Farce techniques which lead to such views are common in Shakespeare, and, as Bertrand Evans has shown in a classic study, much turns on the confusion generated by some characters knowing more than others of what is going on, and the audience's knowing more than all.[11]

But in practice any easy detachment is intermittent. The audience can never feel completely secure. Even at the festive ending of that most festive of comedies, *As You Like It*, we are taken aback by the unnecessary appearance, perhaps even the epiphany, of Hymen, the god of marriage. In the theatre, the effect is too often lost by having him played by a beaming Adam, Amiens, or Corin dressed up, but it should be an uncanny episode, as we wonder if this really is the god himself descended to atone heaven and earth and "bar confusion" (5.4.125). If so, it brings the rapture of the ending to both a culmination and a dispersal: in touching the joy with divine grace, it also indicates how comic endings are deeply true only of human hope.

At less elevated moments, Shakespeare makes us work in a more down-to-earth way: the opening of *The Merry Wives of Windsor* leaves us struggling to discover what all the fuss is about, and we have to pick up what we can amid all the indignation. More pervasively, Shakespeare's language makes extreme demands on us, not merely through historical change but because it is inherently and even ostentatiously difficult. Antipholus of Syracuse, for example, can find the language of his man Dromio so dazzlingly clever that he confesses: "I understand thee not" (4.3.22) – and neither do we. According to the comic theorists (influenced as usual by the elegance of Terence rather than the exuberance of Plautus), the diction of comedy "ought to be simple, easy, open, clear, familiar, and, finally, taken from common usage," a view that Ben Jonson endorsed with his stress on "deeds and language such as men do use."[12] Shakespeare, however, gives prominence to fools and other "corrupter[s] of words" (*Twelfth Night*, 3.1.36), who are bewildering in the confusion and con-fusion of their wordplay.

Love's Labor's Lost is the most flamboyant of a series of experiments played on the audience. As epitomized by Berowne's challenging line, "Light, seeking light, doth light of light beguile" (1.1.77), the language sets out to dazzle rather than illuminate. It is a Babel of characters not so much addressing one another as performing in what are virtually foreign tongues, while, exhausted but exhilarated, the audience seeks to keep up with their inventions and their confusions. The characterization is less complex, yet even here we can be shocked out of any condescension: Holofernes' rebuke of the lords' laughter – "This is not generous, not gentle, not humble" (5.2.629) – rebukes our laughter as well as that of the lords, anticipating how greater victims such as Shylock and Caliban will reduce us to respect. It is in keeping with this demanding play that it should end in such rich generic confusion: it is a comedy leading to a death, a comedy of loss, where the most sympathetic character is dismissed to a cruel penance, and where the action is rounded off first by sprightly but enigmatic songs of winter cheer and springtime fear, and then by mysterious words of farewell.

This is only the most forthright instance of a generic instability which unsettles and even perplexes us throughout the canon. Nothing is more fundamental to any literary or dramatic response than our sense of a work's genre, since this establishes the degree of seriousness and the kinds of significance likely to be present. Far from merely attaching a label, it involves niceties of tone and interpretation and the most delicate of critical tasks, and to misread genre – for example, to read a dramatic monologue as an utterance by the author himself – is to misread a work completely.[13] For this reason, Renaissance critics devoted much of their energy to defining the ideal form of genres; many were also opposed to generic mixtures. But from the first, from the threat to the life of Egeon which opens *The Comedy of Errors*, Shakespeare involves, challenges, and disconcerts us by stretching and confusing generic norms. The climactic scenes of *The Merchant of Venice* and *Much Ado* are of a tragic intensity, though bizarrely mixed with moments of comedy; *Measure for Measure* and *All's Well* are grouped with the comedies in the folio, but are pervasively bleak and bitter. What is one to make of *Cymbeline*, with its shifting levels of reality and conventionality? The density of language and volatility of dramatic effect put us on trial. In his Arden edition, J. M. Nosworthy seeks to keep his balance by treating it throughout as "romance," but this leads him to censure as indecorous or irrelevant the characters and language which are most vivid with dramatic life: Posthumus is a romance hero and therefore his terrible jealousy is "out of character" and "a deviation from the romantic norm;" in Imogen, the romantic heroine is "impaired by excessive vitality"; she is "a superb accident ... who defeated Shakespeare's intentions by coming to life"; the verse similarly contains "excellent writing but unfitted to the occasion."[14]

This is an object lesson in how to fail Shakespeare by insisting on generic decorum, yet it is a danger to which we are always vulnerable with such experimental art. Poems, according to Marianne Moore, are "imaginary gardens with real toads in them,"[15] and Shakespeare's comedies populate the imaginary gardens of romance with realities of passion and social tension. The story of *The Merchant of Venice* is driven by romance motifs: the choice among three caskets; the bond with human flesh as the penalty; the beautiful and bountiful lady in the remote palace. Yet this is also the most worldly comedy he wrote during Elizabeth's reign; his representation of the city would have been almost as recognizable to his contemporaries as Jonson's in *Volpone*. The even more disenchanted and sophisticated world of *All's Well* is similarly full of elements and motifs from folktale, with the clever wench fulfilling impossible tasks.[16] One might argue that for his own audiences Shakespeare's fantastic plots were vindicated by familiarity, since most are based on stories popular at the time, but from the outset he departs freely from his originals, so that he estranges the familiar. Or one might argue that, in the words of Stephen Orgel, such stories tell us "the terrifying truths of the inner life," their implausible surfaces releasing us from rationality into deeper patternings of experience.[17] However, this interpretation fits not only the approach to urban realism in *The Merchant*, but the other romantic and dark comedies less well than it does Orgel's subject, the simplified and rarefied world of late Shakespeare. Normally, realism and romance reflect critically and unpredictably upon one another.

Shakespeare usually starts from strong stories, but deprives us of the simple pleasures of absorption in a good tale well told. As Northrop Frye has written, "Shakespeare deliberately chooses incredible plots and emphasizes the unlikelihood of his conclusions." Moreover, "it is very seldom that a genuinely comic resolution to a play seems the 'logical' outcome of the action. There is nearly always something residually perplexing or incredible about it."[18] Shakespeare goes out of his way to stress the improbable: in the Renaissance New Comedy which is a primary source of *Twelfth Night*, *Gl'Ingannati* (The Deceived, 1538), the first meeting of the characters equivalent to Olivia and Sebastian is far-fetched but rationally explained; in Shakespeare, it is the purest chance. Shakespeare exploits the norms of comedy by a challenging extension into moods of wonder, skepticism, or tragedy. The result can be, as Frye puts it, "perplexing."

Shakespeare is quite prepared to mislead us. In *Much Ado*, for example, the Friar's authoritative prophecy – that the report of Hero's death will, if he loved her, transform Claudio's anger into remorse – is later neither borne out nor commented on. Here, as elsewhere, Shakespeare leaves his audience to make their own way through confusing situations. How, for instance, are we to interpret the judgment of Shylock? Outside the specialized world of academic criticism, this play has never managed to shake off its reputation as anti-Semitic – to be defended, if at all, on the patronizing ground that Shakespeare, as an Elizabethan, could not have known better. Certainly, the case against Shylock is made as strong as can be. His intentions are murderous from the start; Portia may lure him into a trap, but only after giving him repeated chances to show mercy, and only by subjecting him – a man who has sworn a religious oath to justify legal murder – to his own ruthless literal-mindedness. The Christian court is, by its lights, demonstrably merciful in its judgments: the Duke grants Shylock his life; on Antonio's recommendation he loses only half his goods; in the eyes of the Christian court, Shylock's enforced conversion gives him a chance of eternal bliss rather than inevitable damnation. Is it not anachronistic to find anti-Semitic prejudice among these characters? But the play is explicitly concerned with prejudice – a concept which the history of the word suggests was then rising to consciousness.[19] When Portia returns to Belmont by night after the trial, she is surprised into a new appreciation of her household musicians by hearing them afresh, out of routine: "Nothing is good, I see, without respect," she concludes (5.1.99). Respect is the consequence of paying proper attention, perceiving something without those distractions and preconceptions which can make indifferent singers of even the lark and the nightingale, and make lead seem a demeaning metal for a casket containing Portia's portrait. This prejudiced lack of respect is all too evident at the trial. The Duke grants Shylock his life explicitly to set Christian mercy above Jewish law, but once Antonio has made his proposals, the Duke retracts: "He shall do this, or else I do recant / The pardon that I late pronounced here" (4.1.391–92). The quality of mercy now becomes all too strained. Even the well-meaning Christians – not bigots like Gratiano – are blinkered by prejudice; they see Shylock "without respect," cannot do justice to his Judaism, cannot perceive how even his vindictiveness is a reaction to Christian persecution, and are blind to the destructive cruelty of their judgments. They turn away from him even as they believe they are drawing him into the fold. This, at least, is one defensible way through the maze of the judgment scene. Shakespeare puts us on trial, too, deliberately harassing us with conflicting and unresolved possibilities, confusing us with the unconscious confusion of even the more enlightened Christians' aims.

The Winter's Tale begins and ends with episodes which put us at a unique disadvantage. Nowhere else in Shakespeare is a major change in a leading character left inexplicable like Leontes' sudden plunge into insane jealousy. We share the bewilderment of the other characters. And, however well we know the play, Hermione's apparent resurrection in the last scene never fails to shock, partly because Shakespeare has misled us as never before in his insistence on her death. Paulina stage-manages the scene, and we participate in rather than merely observe the wonder and steadily increasing hopes of the onlookers; we also share their sense of all the years of loss and waste which make this as poignant a scene as any in Shakespeare. The comfortable orthodoxy of comic endings has been left far behind.

Indeed, Shakespeare's disorientation of the audience can be epitomized in how, in broad outline, his work represents two phases of progressive disenchantment with the conventional happy ending. Musical harmony depends upon difference, upon a lack of concord; rich harmonies require the assimilation of some discord – the more acute the discord, the richer the harmony. Where there is only concord, there is only blandness. Shakespeare leaves degrees of discord in all his endings (or at least, in the happiest of the comedies, leaves certain cadences of action unresolved, as with the future relations between the Antipholus twins and the sisters). The general tendency of the plays up to 1604–05 – complicated by the astonishing innovations of *Love's Labor's Lost* and the sublime gaiety within *As You Like It* – is toward ever more discordant finales. This culminates in *Measure for Measure* and *All's Well*, where the "comic" endings positively invite puzzlement, dissatisfaction, and divided responses. In the former, the last sixty lines are virtually a monologue for the Duke: the Provost responds briefly to questions and Lucio remains irrepressible, but for the rest the Duke talks on, disposing and proposing. What is one to make of a man who abruptly reveals to an intending nun that he has been tormenting and testing her by letting her believe her brother is legally murdered, and then – without anticipation or even a pause in the syntax where she might embrace and speak to her restored brother – proposes she abandon her vocation and agree to marry him? What of Isabella's silence, not only here but to his renewed proposal forty lines later? What of the reactions of the silent characters whose destinies are being disposed of? Shakespeare is either relying uncritically upon the comic convention of a happy ending after a play which in its bleakness has gone beyond comedy, or he is calling that convention into question. If the former, his artistic conscience has failed him; if the latter, he leaves us to make what we can of an entirely new and dark comic mode.

Although the four late plays are closer to the conventions of their romance origins in the joyous recognitions and reconciliations within their closing scenes, there is again a movement away from serenity. In *Cymbeline*, the sheer virtuosity of the ending seems to preclude depths of feeling;

The Winter's Tale, as I have suggested, remains as bitter as it is sweet, and *The Tempest* is little less so. Miranda may find love and a "brave new world" (5.1.183), but Prospero is for her sake reluctantly abandoning everything else he values – the arts of magic which absorb and reassure him; his affection for the responsive though untameable spirit of Ariel – and is returning to an unregenerate world, to a brother he does not trust and a dukedom he does not prize, "where / Every third thought shall be my grave" (5.1.311–12). Not only are such discords increasingly audible, but, as Anne Barton reminds us, even when these late plays are sublime in their eventual bliss they insist on their unreality: "Shakespeare does not try to conceal, he positively emphasizes the fact that his material is the archetypal stuff of legend and fairy-tale." The plays "appeal so poignantly to our sense of how we should like the world to be, and know that it is not."[20] We are left suspended between tears of joy and grief.

Shakespeare's testing and stretching of the conventions of comedy almost to destruction expresses through form how he submits traditional values and social norms to questioning. Comedy has often been seen as such a conservative genre that it is "deeply penetrated by scapegoating and victimization."[21] For Henri Bergson, laughter always aims to humiliate, and comedy is a way of insisting on conformity through fear of being mocked as eccentric.[22] For Umberto Eco, "Comedy is always racist: only the others, the Barbarians, are supposed to pay."[23] But Shakespeare transcends such reductive views. Shylock, for example, is funny only when described by Solanio and Salerio in Act 2 scene 8, never in himself. Though he is in effect treated as a scapegoat by the Christians, the play exists in order to shake and confuse prejudice such as he arouses.

Although Shakespeare rarely reexamines orthodox values explicitly, he provokes us through confusion into a reinvigorating review of them. For Bergson, comedy is intimidating and encourages complacency in those who laugh,[24] but Shakespearean comedy disturbs the audience's presuppositions. On the surface, the plays are socially conservative; Holofernes rebukes the scoffing lords for falling short of their "generous" and "gentle" birth; it is rare for a low-born character to rise high by innate worth – Helena of *All's Well* is exceptional. Nevertheless, she and Holofernes exemplify the plays' critical distinction between rank and worth, through which Orsino is made vulnerable to Feste, Don Pedro to Benedick, Duke Vincentio to Lucio, and Leontes to Paulina. Although a prince or lord has a prominent role as arbiter or spectator at the close of all but three of the sixteen comedies,[25] he is invariably brought within the ironic play of judgment. Theseus' critique of imagination and defense of "cool reason," for example, reveals little but his own confusions: he denies the reality of what we ourselves have seen, while he seeks to reduce to mere "tricks" the imaginings of the poet to which his own magnificent language has just given "a local habitation and a name" (5.1.6, 17–18).

The heroines most clearly embody Shakespeare's appraisal of social norms. The predominance of the male over the female then enshrined in religion and law is clearly affirmed in only two of the earliest and most farcical plays – by Luciana and the Abbess in *The Comedy of Errors* and eventually by Katherina herself in *The Taming of the Shrew*. The other early play, *The Two Gentlemen of Verona*, is more prophetic, locating positive values not in the well-born males but in the women and, with comical modulation, in the menservants. Dramatic vision is released from social stereotype, and from now on it is preeminently the heroines who embody the values of intelligence, sensibility, and insight. They can enjoy not only moral but social power – though often only through male disguise – and as a result, in the words of Catherine Belsey, the plays disrupt "the system of differences on which sexual stereotyping depends," opening up fissures within orthodox perceptions of gender.[26] Moreover, even though the plays end with returns to normality, the acknowledged preeminence of the heroines implies that the values embodied in them are to be carried over into the "ever after" of at least the happier plays.

In sum, Shakespeare's comedy presents states of abnormality and disarray, and the interpretative challenges they present within the humor and charm could hardly be further from Bergson's view of comedy as a reaffirmation of complacency. This sometimes confusing experience of confusion is not, however, to be confused with chaos. Hunting at dawn, Theseus invites Hippolyta up to the mountain's top to "mark the musical confusion / Of hounds and echo in conjunction" (4.1.110–11). At that point, confusion will become con-fusion and, as Hippolyta says, "one mutual cry" (117). The moment anticipates Portia on "respect"; it is a turning point of reflection that gathers up the whole play, its drawing of order out of chaos, of harmony out of a Babel of voices.

The playwright's artful shaping of disarray into expressive order is also made manifest in some charged episodes where a condition of maximum confusion is turned into dramatic order and theatrical ceremony. One of the supreme moments in Shakespearean comedy comes in *As You Like It* Act 5 scene 2 when – paralleling the music of the hunt at dawn as *A Midsummer Night's Dream* turns from vexation to bliss – Rosalind begins preparing the lovers for what will prove their marriages the next day. All are at the utmost pitch of feeling: Silvius' perennial frustration is heightened by Phebe's open love for Ganymed; Phebe is in an ardour of impatience; Orlando, now that he has seen Celia return the love of his brother, is also at a high point of love, frustration, and uncertain expectation, and has said he can no longer play the game of courtship with Ganymed; Rosalind has the excitement of knowing that her love is about to be fulfilled. Emotions are too inflamed for them to continue in the timeless, pastoral leisure of the central acts.

Here comes a passage of some fifty lines (75ff.) of echoing and antiphonal phrases ("And so am I for Phebe. / And I for Ganymed. / And I for Rosalind. / And I for no woman."), a transfiguration into new emotional complexities of those deft and piquant symmetries of confusion which Shakespeare found in Lyly, his principal forbear outside New Comic traditions.[27] It is a crescendo of devotion led by Silvius at the height of his pastoral idealism, turned by the whole quartet into a litany of rapturous adoration, though wryly qualified by Rosalind's knowing but still yearning *double entendres*. Here, if any-where in Shakespeare, we find "a more than usual state of emotion, with more than usual order" in which Coleridge sums up poetic imagination.[28] The antiphonal utterances impose order on emotional impasse – an order which we know to be justified because, like Rosalind, we know the solution. A ceremonious space is created in language for lovers who are in chaos, a ritualistic heightening and depersonalizing of emotion. It brings to full ex-plicitness other ceremonious moments and episodes which create clearings of emotional order within the confusions of characters sent astray by injustice and by passion.[29]

The episode is poignant in the pain and yearning and confusion of feel-ing, bizarre in its elevation of language, comic in Rosalind's riddling words, and joyous in that we know the play is turning toward the happiness of all who can be happy. In its ceremonious recreation of emotional muddle, it is at the heart of Shakespearean comedy, and indeed of theatrical experience. Such moments of clarification are like finding the oblique spot from which a "perspective," an enigmatic painting, is given shape and coherence. When, for example, Holbein's *The Ambassadors* is seen from an acute angle, a long grey mark emerges as a skull. As Bushy says in *Richard II*, "Perspectives, which rightly gaz'd upon / Show nothing but confusion; ey'd awry / Distin-guish form" (2.2.18–20).

NOTES

I am most grateful to Stephen Wall and Dr. Martin Wiggins for valuable comments on a draft of this chapter.

1 All quotations from Shakespeare are from G. Blakemore Evans *et al.*, *The River-side Shakespeare* (Boston and New York: Houghton Mifflin Company, 1974).
2 The exceptions prove the rule: the child "brags" inconveniently in Jaquenetta's belly, but Armado vows "to hold the plough for her sweet love three year" (*LLL*, 5.2.677, 883–84), while Lucio is compelled to marry the woman he has

wronged (*Measure*, 5.1.509ff). Angelo and Bertram are prevented from abusing Isabella and Diana.

3 Northrop Frye, *A Natural Perspective: the Development of Shakespearean Comedy and Romance* (New York: Harcourt, Brace and World, 1965), pp. 73ff., and *The Myth of Deliverance: Reflections on Shakespeare's Problem Comedies* (Brighton: Harvester Press, 1983), pp. 37–38.

4 Sir Philip Sidney, *An Apology for Poetry*, ed. Geoffrey Shepherd (London: Nelson, 1965), p. 135.

5 Stephen Orgel (ed.), *The Winter's Tale* (Oxford: Oxford University Press, 1996), pp. 25–26.

6 Leo Salingar, *Shakespeare and the Traditions of Comedy* (Cambridge: Cambridge University Press, 1974), p. 124.

7 See the original preface to *Strafford*, cited William Clyde DeVane, *A Browning Handbook* (London: John Murray, n.d.), p. 58.

8 Edward Berry, *Shakespeare's Comic Rites* (Cambridge: Cambridge University Press, 1984), pp. 31–32.

9 See especially C. L. Barber, *Shakespeare's Festive Comedy: a Study of Dramatic Form and its Relation to Social Custom* (Princeton: Princeton University Press, 1959; reprinted., 1972), and Berry, *Shakespeare's Comic Rites*.

10 Gareth Lloyd Evans, "Shakespeare's Fools: the Shadow and the Substance of Drama," in Malcolm Bradbury and David Palmer (eds.), *Shakespearean Comedy, Stratford-upon-Avon Studies* 14 (1972): 144.

11 Bertrand Evans, *Shakespeare's Comedies* (Oxford: Oxford University Press, 1960).

12 Franciscus Robortellus, *On Comedy* (1548), trans. Marvin T. Herrick, *Comic Theory in the Sixteenth Century* (Urbana: University of Illinois Press, 1964). See also pp. 214ff. Jonson: prologue to the folio version of *Every Man in his Humour*, line 21.

13 On genre, see especially Alastair Fowler, *Kinds of Literature: an Introduction to the Theory of Genres and Modes* (Oxford: Clarendon Press, 1982).

14 *Cymbeline* (London: Methuen, 1955; reprinted 1980), pp. lix-lxiii.

15 Marianne Moore, *Complete Poems* (London: Faber and Faber, 1990), p. 267.

16 For a summary, see Susan Snyder (ed.), *All's Well That Ends Well* (Oxford: Oxford University Press, 1993), pp. 1–15.

17 Orgel, *Winter's Tale*, p. 17.

18 Frye, *Natural Perspective*, p. 123; Frye, *Myth of Deliverance*, p. 6.

19 *OED* records the verb *prejudice* as bearing our modern sense of creating unfavorable bias only from 1607 and the noun from 1643. See sense 3 under both.

20 Anne Barton, *Essays, Mainly Shakespearean* (Cambridge: Cambridge University Press, 1994), pp. 180, 203.

21 T. G. A. Nelson, *Comedy: the Theory of Comedy in Literature, Drama, and Cinema* (Oxford: Oxford University Press, 1990), p. 177.

22 Henri Bergson, "Laughter," in Wylie Sypher (ed.), *Comedy* (New York: Doubleday Anchor Books, 1956), pp. 148, 72–73.

23 Umberto Eco, cited Nelson, *Comedy*, p. 178.

24 See for example the closing pages of his chapter in Sypher, *Comedy*, pp. 185–90.

25 Salingar, *Traditions of Comedy*, pp. 17, 254.

26 Catherine Belsey, "Disrupting Sexual Difference: Meaning and Gender in the Comedies," in John Drakakis (ed.), *Alternative Shakespeares* (London: Routledge, 1988), p. 190 .

27 See, for example, *Gallathea* 3.2 and the end of 3.1. For Shakespeare's absorbing of this play, see Leah Scragg, *The Metamorphosis of "Gallathea": a Study in Creative Adaptation* (Washington, DC: University Press of America, 1982).

28 James Engell and W. Jackson Bate (eds.), *Biographia Literaria*, 2 vols. (London: Routledge, 1983), II, 17.

29 Alexander Leggatt, *Shakespeare's Comedy of Love* (London: Methuen, 1974), p. 96 observes how "scenes of the most intense confusion . . . contain some of the most patterned writing."

7

CATHERINE BATES

Love and courtship

Men and women meet, match, marry, and mate. This is the eternal story which Shakespeare's comedies retell again and again:

> Jack shall have Jill;
> Nought shall go ill:
> The man shall have his mare again, and all shall be well.
> (*A Midsummer Night's Dream*, 3.2.461–3)[1]

The details may vary considerably – and all is not always well – but in every comedy this basic formula remains the same. Sometimes men chase after women. Sometimes women chase after men. Often men pursue women who pursue other men who pursue women, giving us the mad merry-go-rounds of love we find in plays like *A Midsummer Night's Dream* or *The Two Gentlemen of Verona*. Frequently women turn themselves into men for a while, like Julia, Viola, or Rosalind. Less often men get themselves turned into women, like Falstaff, or, like Bottom, into beasts. But even if their actual shape or sex remains unchanged, everyone is in some way altered by love, transmuted into something rich and strange, or "metamorphis'd" like Proteus and Valentine (*Two Gentlemen of Verona*, 1.1.66, 2.1.30). The experience of passion changes everything: one's view of the world, of the beloved, even – or above all – one's own sense of self. Characters who, out of youth, inexperience, or disinclination had hitherto remained untouched by love suddenly find themselves caught up in the maelstrom of desire where everything is thrown into moral and emotional chaos before falling into a new *Gestalt* of socialized couples which represents the final (and, with luck, stable) product of this mysterious process of human natural selection.

Thankfully, the process does not go on for ever. It may be protracted, prolonged, or excruciatingly postponed, but the period of courtship is never of infinite duration. It is always a fixed term, a brief spell during which individuals fall under the enchantment of love and bewitch each other with promises and vows. Courtship occupies a distinct period or interval, like the "midsummer madness" of *Twelfth Night* (3.4.56) or Rosalind's "holiday humor" in *As You Like It* (4.1.69). "Men are April when they woo," she pronounces, "December when they wed" (147–48). Even if it seems an eternity in the making, the whole thing is over in no time. If April's sweet showers make folk long for love, then the squally changeableness of the English spring – "Which now shows all the beauty of the sun, / And by and by a cloud takes all away" (*Two Gentlemen*, 1.3.86–87) – makes it the perfect season for blowing hot and cold and for suffering love's fervent hopes and cruel assaults. The lover has spring in his steps. As the Host cannily predicts of Fenton, the young and ultimately successful lover in *The Merry Wives of Windsor*, "he speaks holiday, he smells April and May – he will carry't, he will carry't – 'tis in his buttons – he will carry't" (3.2.68–70).

Shakespeare's comedies are about courtship if they are about anything, but they are not, in this respect, either different or new. The timeless tale of boy meets girl was as hot a topic in the New Comedy of ancient Greece, the courtly romances of the Middle Ages, or the bawdy fabliau stories of folk tradition – all of which Shakespeare drew upon for his sources – as it continues to be to this day. Moreover, out of the whole vast spectrum of human relationships – social, economic, sexual, political, and familial – it has always been this highly specific relation between prospective marriage partners which has formed the staple of romantic comedy from the earliest times. Quite why this should be is a question worth pausing a moment to consider.

Whatever form it takes, a courtship narrative always charts some kind of development or progress. It moves its protagonists from one state of being to another that is clearly differentiated. The emphasis is on process – on the characters' passage through a sequence of normally well-recognized steps toward a desired, however distant, destination. "Your brother and my sister no sooner met but they look'd," Rosalind tells Orlando, "no sooner look'd but they lov'd; no sooner lov'd but they sigh'd; no sooner sigh'd but they ask'd one another the reason; no sooner knew the reason but they sought the remedy: and in these degrees have they made a pair of stairs to marriage" (*As You Like It*, 5.2.32–38). Few courtships are as blithely contracted as this one. Indeed, the romance between Celia and Oliver is an exception, the rule in such cases being precisely those obstacles, delays, and misunderstandings which constitute the tortuous plots of most comedies of love. But, no matter how fraught or problematic a particular love affair, the courtship narrative traces a definite trajectory. Marriage may, as in a troubled play like *All's Well That Ends Well*, come near the beginning; or it may, as in *Love's Labor's Lost*, be postponed well beyond the conclusion: but in every case marriage is at least the promised end. No narrative structure is quite so teleological in its orientation, so heavily geared toward a final outcome.

Marriage – the endpoint to which courtship stories inevitably as if mag-
netically tend – is literary shorthand for the control of human sexuality
by law. In its natural state human sexuality might look something like the
world depicted in Ovid's *Metamorphoses*: a riot of rape, incest, homosexu-
ality, bestiality, sex change, hermaphroditism, species pollution, and sexual
perversion of every kind. In Ovid's text men have sex with gods, animals,
objects, each other, and themselves – as indeed do women – and more than
one character rejects the most primal taboos as artificial constraints upon
sexual expression from which the animals are blissfully exempt. Yet it is such
rules – the incest taboo, laws against consanguinity, the advisability of marriage outside the tribe, the establishment of polygamy or monogamy, and so
forth – which wrestle to control this otherwise chaotic sexuality and bring it
into some semblance of order. The laws regulating sexual conduct are second
only to language in creating order out of chaos and in distinguishing men
from the beasts. It is these laws which constitute human society – civiliza-
tion, in a word – even if, as Freud believed, that society was as a consequence
bound to be a repressive one. For these laws entail a massive reduction of all
the infinite number of possible sexual permutations down to a single kind of
allowable relation: one which specifies precisely who may have sex with
whom, for what purpose, and when.

In Shakespeare's plays this relation is marriage and with it the no-nonsense
heterosexual coupling as a result of which, as a reformed Benedick puts it,
"the world must be peopled" (*Much Ado*, 2.3.242). Such sexual relations,
licensed and endorsed by a host of social practices and solemnizations, are
what make up civil society. Since the couple is the basic building block of
the social group, matrimony celebrates not only the union of one particular happy couple but, more importantly, the absorption of that couple
into the larger group as a whole. Ultimately the individual is subordinate
to the group – something Shakespeare emphasizes in those plays which cul-
minate not with one but with two (*Two Gentlemen*, *Twelfth Night*), three
(*Midsummer Night's Dream*, *Taming of the Shrew*), or even four weddings
(*As You Like It*, eventually *Love's Labor's Lost*).

At the end of courtship's arduous journey, the chaos finally settles. Couples
submit to the laws of their society and take up their rightful positions as
mature householders and sexually responsible adults – as parents, that is. As
far as romantic comedy is concerned, this is a closed subject, as accepted and
unarguable as the long-established relationships of the parents and guardians
from which the younger generation both distance themselves and take their
cue. Once couples have (with varying degrees of serenity) arrived on the
marital shore, the curtain generally falls, for once licensed and regulated,
sexuality ceases to be interesting. Of marriage romantic comedy has little or

nothing to say, but of courtship it has to say a great deal. As William Congreve was to put it, courtship is to marriage as a very witty prologue to a very dull play.[2] For, although courtship leads like a pair of stairs to marriage, it still remains – structurally speaking – on the outside of that ordered state. And, if marriage represents sexuality regularized, then anything which precedes that state exists in an as yet unregularized state – one which calls to mind the preparatory, limbo state of the young initiate.

As just such a preliminary state – full of expectation but still awaiting final resolution – courtship is a quintessentially creative period, providing the amorphous and chaotic raw material from which order is soon to be drawn or upon which order will in due course be imposed. This is why literary courtships have traditionally opened out into a period of experiment and free play during which the rules are temporarily suspended, normal gender roles reversed, and hierarchies turned briefly upside down. It is also why the place for courtship is classically the forest, like that outside Athens in *A Midsummer Night's Dream*, or between Mantua and Milan in *Two Gentlemen of Verona*, or the Forest of Arden in *As You Like It*. For the forest is not only – as the "jolly greenwood" – an age-old locus for dalliance and fertility rituals, but more specifically (deriving from *foris*, "outside") a place that lies outside the jurisdiction of the city.[3] The forest does not necessarily specify an area of woodland but rather any wild or uncultivated place – like "the mountains and the barbarous caves, / Where manners ne'er were preached" to which Olivia threatens to banish the disorderly Sir Toby in *Twelfth Night* (4.1.48–49), or like the haunt of the outlaws in *Two Gentlemen of Verona* whose youthful crimes have thrust them "from the company of aweful men" (4.1.44). As a place which stands on the edges or outskirts of civilized society, and as refuge to all that society exiles and outcasts, the forest is a fitting place for those who have yet to take up their positions as fully fledged – that is to say, as married – citizens.

Courtship is a form of initiation rite which, in many societies, requires the parties to remove themselves to some second or "green" world from which they symbolically enact their reentry into the initiated, norm-governed group.[4] And even where specifically forest retreats do not feature as such, most of Shakespeare's comedies echo this sense of movement to and from some mysterious or sinister realm, be it Portia's Belmont in *The Merchant of Venice* or Petruchio's country house in *The Taming of the Shrew*. With marriage, the couple are finally ushered through the door of regulated sexuality and, once the gate clangs shut, this marks for them a point of no return. But before that moment they effectively stand on the threshold, rather as the rowdy singers of epithalamia made their rough music on the threshold of the bridal chamber (*thalamos*). These singers stood "at the very chamber dore ... in a large vtter roome," as George Puttenham puts it in *The Arte of English Poesie* (1588), there to play their drums and maracas (their loud and shrill music being designed, in the first instance, to drown out the screams of the virginal young bride upon "feeling the first forces of her stiffe and rigorous young man").[5] Comedies of love which center on courtship could be seen as extensions of this large outer room, and their actions could be characterized by the cacaphonous clatter there expressed.

Uniquely positioned as a transitional phase and liminal state, courtship stands just on the outside of marriage and the ordering of sexuality that it represents. Courtship thus bears a curiously ambiguous – one could say, carnivalesque – relation to the law. As a general statement, this could be said of any period or society; however, courtship was in Shakespeare's day an area of particularly intense ambiguity. From the middle of the sixteenth century, both the Church and state in England sought to clarify and pin down precisely what constituted matrimony in law. In 1597 and 1604 the Church issued a series of canons which attempted to lay down unambiguous guidelines on the conduct of wedding services, the registering of marriages, and the issue of licenses and banns.[6] Up until then, however, and even for some time afterward, there remained a good deal of variety in local practice and accepted custom. The older form of spousals in which the two parties expressed their consent to marry in words of the present tense (*per verba de praesenti*), even if made in private or without witnesses, could still, strictly speaking, constitute a binding and indissoluble union. If courtship bore an ambiguous relation to the law at the best of times, then Shakespeare reflects on the very particular ambiguities that surrounded it in his own day, when the area was greyer than usual. Courtship could be defined simply as the period of wooing and winning that we find in most of the comedies. But it could also extend to that critical period between a betrothal and its formal solemnization in marriage (as with Claudio and Julietta in *Measure for Measure*); or even, more critically still, between the latter and its physical consummation in intercourse (as with Bertram and Helena in *All's Well*). In all these cases, we can see Shakespeare opening out that strange threshold state that stands just outside the law, testing contemporary definitions of courtship and seeing just how close he could get to that chamber door without quite passing through it.

Courtship narratives thus allow writers to explore and meditate upon the chaotic nature of human sexuality and the laws that set out to govern it. In the confrontation between something fluctuating, disorderly, and ultimately yielding, and something fixed, immutable, and stern one can see how the relation of sexuality to the law might easily correspond to some fairly obvious sexual stereotypes. (Not that women are always disorderly or men inclined to the law. The impact of love is as likely to make men's fancies "more giddy and unfirm, / More longing, wavering, sooner lost and worn, / Than women's are" as Orsino discovers in *Twelfth Night*, 2.4.33–35, while it is the women who, more often than not, keep a clear head.) In the course of most courtship narratives, a match of some kind is made between sexuality and the law. But, until it is, they remain uneasy sparring partners, batting power to and fro and furiously resisting closure – for all the world like one of Shakespeare's more skeptical and sharp-tongued courting couples. It is this critical relation between love and the law that is what courtship – or literary courtship, at any rate – is really about. And indeed it is this larger theme, rather than the particular relationship between this man or that woman, which makes courtship a topic so patient of repetition and a theme capable of such infinite variation.

Courtship's habitual scene is one of revelry and misrule and Shakespeare's comedies occupy a world of moral and emotional chaos in which the rules are temporarily put on hold. But they are not chaotic plays. On the contrary, in terms of formal construction they are among the most consummately ordered in the repertoire, giving us such miracles of plotting as *The Comedy of Errors*, based on the confusion of identical twins, or *The Merry Wives of Windsor*, in which multiple plots interlock with dazzling precision to enable wives to outwit lovers and husbands, servants to outwit masters, and daughters to outwit parents all in one go. Moral chaos seems no bar to formal perfection. Indeed, it is often at moments of the greatest moral dereliction that formal patternings emerge with the greatest flourish. In Act 4 scene 3 of *Love's Labor's Lost*, the quadruple perjury of the menfolk – who, incapable of keeping their vows to abjure love, have all to a man succumbed to the charms of the French princess and her ladies – turns into a masterpiece of aesthetic design. The guilty confessions of the four men, unknowingly overheard by one another, allow Longaville to come forward and reproach Dumaine, the king to come forward and reproach the two of them in turn, and Berowne, who has been watching the whole "scene of fool'ry" from a tree (4.3.161), to come down and reproach all three, before being, in his turn, exposed by Costard, the clown. The moral high ground well and truly collapses and there are red faces all round. Yet out of the morass of hypocrisy and shame comes a scene of exquisite craftsmanship, rather as, in an opera, the very worst treachery or disagreement can be expressed in music of the most harmonious kind.

Full of patternings, symmetries, pairings, parallels, and carefully orchestrated juxtapositions, Shakespeare's comedies delight in formal contrivance. Extremely self-conscious creations, they abound with plays within plays. *Love's Labor's Lost* contains a masque of Muscovites as well as the hilarious pageant of the Nine Worthies; *A Midsummer Night's Dream* concludes with the equally hilarious "Pyramus and Thisbe"; *The Merry Wives* with "Herne the Hunter"; while the whole of *The Taming of the Shrew* is a brisk comedy laid on to entertain the drunken Christopher Sly. Prologues, epilogues, and clearly signaled shifts in register serve as framing devices to mark out these worlds inside worlds, rather as the perspective paintings of the period show glimpses of rooms within rooms or whole landscapes through the *trompe l'œil* of a casement window.

Shakespeare's characters inhabit an extraordinarily literary universe. The air positively buzzes with models, translations, analogues, clichés, and quotations. Poor Slender in *The Merry Wives* is lost without his "Book of Songs and Sonnets" (1.1.199), while Falstaff falls back on quoting Sidney's *Astrophil and Stella* (3.3.43). Like the sixteenth-century rhetorical handbooks that exhaustively list every literary trope and form, Shakespeare's comedies are crammed with orations, epistles, blasons, complaints, sermons, odes, epigrams, eclogues, and sonnets, all of which can be formally distinguished. This wealth of forms helps to drive home the power of literature to shape chaotic experience and give expression to the fluctuation of love's moods. Indeed, language itself begins to flirt and tease, turning coyly aside just when the characters thought they had finally pinned meaning down. The result is the ricocheting wordplay of a text like *Love's Labor's Lost*, where human language is shown to be totally insubstantial and lover's vows as light as air, or like *Twelfth Night*, where, as Viola remarks, "They that dally nicely with words may quickly make them wanton" (3.1.14–15). Here surface takes priority over content and, detached from meaning, language becomes a glittering display in which a brilliant turn of phrase or quick-witted repartee can take precedence over the sincere oath or sworn vow.

Formal perfection seems directly related to moral vacuum or collapse. The more morally ambiguous or contingent a situation, the more dazzling the display of wit or the more perfectly crafted the scene. It is as if an inverse relation exists between society's ordering of human behavior and the artist's ordering of his material. Where one fails, the other steps in to take its place. That artists might, in fact, be just as good at ordering matters as jurists or lawyers were was an idea seriously entertained by that shrewdest of Renaissance commentators, Michel de Montaigne. In his essay "On Experience" (translated by John Florio in 1603), Montaigne observes that social laws struggle to manage human nature at the best of times. There is a constant mismatch between the strict dictates of the law on the one hand and a human nature bent on resistance and discontinuity on the other. "There is but little relation betweene our actions, that are in perpetuall mutation, and the fixed and unmoveable lawes," he notes. Montaigne urges that laws be kept to a minimum, that they be simple, intelligible, and just.

But ultimately he despairs that any man-made juridical system will be capable of dealing with human waywardness and intractability. Ending up with his own famous incapacity to judge, to know anything, or to order his own material in any way except in "loose and disjoynted" bits and pieces, Montaigne finally (if a little disingenuously) hands the whole business over to the artist:

> I leave it to Artists, and I wot not whether in a matter so confused, so severall and so casuall, they shall come to an end, to range into sides this infinit diversity of visages; and settle our inconstancy and place it in order.[7]

Shakespeare takes up the challenge, and never more so than as a writer of comedy. For if tragedy remains, like Montaigne, generally skeptical of ordering systems, comedy delights in the one kind of order over which human beings can exert total control: the work of art. In tragedy, human ignorance, the unforeseen, and an all too messy reality intrude upon and usually destroy the most cherished schemes and best-laid plans. In comedy, by contrast, human ingenuity and its ability to invent artificial systems and worlds are upheld for celebratory admiration. This is one reason why comedy repeatedly draws attention to its own status as artifact and positively works to heighten the illusion. Comedy avoids the possibility of everything going wrong or not going according to plan by delivering us into a carefree world where actions are denuded of consequence. Comedy suspends the moral law in order to substitute another, a purely aesthetic one. Here, quite different criteria hold sway. In comedy's morally vacant space – for which, as I have shown, courtship provides the classic scenario – it is less the rules of honor or morality that count than those of symmetry and timing. Where the figures of authority are caught napping (men, fathers, magistrates, or kings) it is the others – the women, children, servants, and fools – who come forward to demonstrate their mastery of the aesthetic game. Designed to please the eye and the ear, comedy's satisfactions of pattern, repetition and cue-perfect timing are paramount, but remain as morally neutral as melody and rhythm in music, or, in painting, color and line.

Some plays, acutely self-conscious of their status as comedy, take this temporary replacement of the moral law by art as their very theme. *Love's Labor's Lost* is one such. In this play the abeyance of the law is clearly signaled from the outset. The King of Navarre and his courtiers solemnly vow to abjure the company of women and to commit themselves to a life of celibate scholarship for three long years. At this stage the law appears in all its juridico-discursive trappings – edicts, statues, schedules, signatures, and oaths – reminding us that, with all its verbal and textual paraphernalia, the law is quintessentially literary.[8] Laws are made with words, albeit words uttered, written, signed, and sealed with all the binding force of a Faustian pact. But the men's oaths are no sooner sworn than the circumstances suddenly change: the Princess of France and her ladies arrive on the scene. This turn of events, expected but overlooked, forces the men to sacrifice their word of honor to necessity – "Necessity will make us all forsworn," as Berowne dryly observes (1.1.149) – and to bend the letter of the law to suit the altered spirit of the times. With the comedy's ensuing personnel – a king, a princess, three courtiers, and three ladies – the action inevitably turns to courtship, giving us a particularly neat illustration of the way courtship takes up its position precisely when the rules governing honor and commitment are put on hold.

In this scene newly altered by love, the once iron edicts of the law dissolve into provisionality and doubt. Henceforth, the all-binding law becomes what it was always in danger of being, a mere text that is open to interpretation. In the course of the play, the men try every way they can to twist words, dodge definitions, and so wriggle out of the perjured situation into which they have put themselves. The law descends into casuistry and legalistic quibble. "A woman I forswore, but I will prove, / Thou being a goddess, I forswore not thee," Longaville demonstrates to his beloved in the best lawyerly fashion (4.3.62–63). But his equivocation is, in essence, no different from (and certainly no more honorable than) that of Costard who, although caught red-handed, tries to evade the penalty laid down by the proclamation – "a year's imprisonment to be taken with a wench" (1.1.287) – by claiming that Jaquenetta is no wench but ... a damsel ... a virgin ... a maid ...

The effectiveness of the law is fatally compromised by the men's barefaced decision no longer to mean what they say. Berowne's excuse that he but "swore in jest" (1.1.54) marks a fundamental breach of trust, for if words no longer guarantee truth then every human contract ever made must come under suspicion. Divorced from meaning, language breaks free and enjoys a new materiality all of its own. A "great feast of languages" is spread before us (5.1.37). Having "liv'd long on the alms-basket of words" (38–39), Holofernes, Nathaniel, and Armado cannibalize words horribly. But, parodic as it is, their wordplay merely echoes that of the more refined courtly characters from which it differs only in degree but not in kind. The insufferable pedant Holofernes is an obsessive cataloguer, logic-chopper, and a walking thesaurus. But his "gift" – to be "full of forms, figures, shapes, objects, ideas, apprehensions, motions, revolutions" (4.2.66–68) – is not, after all, so different in its effects from the verbal sparring matches and trials of wit played by the Princess and her ladies: "Well bandied both, a set of wit well played" (5.2.29). The love-struck Armado declares himself to be "for whole volumes in folio" (1.2.185), for making language is the oldest if most neurotic symptom of making love. But, no matter how labored, his efforts are essentially the same as those of the King and his courtiers, who are also caught in the grip of a serious logorrhea.

For all of them, the act of perjury puts their sincerity in doubt: "If love make me forsworn, how shall I swear to love?" asks Berowne (4.2.104). Shakespeare's plot thus literalizes the classic dilemma of the whole sonneteering tradition – how, if "loving in truth," to say so in feigning verse?[9] In the world of *Love's Labor's Lost*, where no one can be taken at his word, we are left only with the superficiality of empty rhetoric and external show. In the last act, the men come in disguised as Russians in order to court their women. But the latter, having donned masks and hastily swapped their lovers' tokens amongst themselves, easily trick them into wooing the wrong partners. Berowne's admission – that "we, / Following the signs, woo'd but the sign of she" (5.2.468–69) – shows only how far gone in the direction of superficiality it is possible to be.

In *Love's Labor's Lost*, the moral vacuum left by the men's perjury is, in true comic tradition, filled by art – by pyrotechnic displays of wit, by poetry, dance, songs, and shows, and by side-splitting parodies of the same. All is play, all a game. But it is brittle and insubstantial, and evidently not the way love is won. The absence of content and meaning is heavily signed here as being counterproductive. Here the mountains do not even give birth to a mouse and the lovers' Herculean labors are well and truly lost. In the pageant of the Nine Worthies in Act 5, the actors can only present Hercules as a youth. This is about as far as heroism is going to get in a play where we, like Berowne, have been sitting "To see a king transformed to a gnat! / To see great Hercules whipping a gig" (4.3.164–65). By means of such relentless deflation, Shakespeare pokes cruel fun at the claim of *amour courtois* to ennoble men through love. Instead, the lovers' efforts are finally dismissed by the Princess as the time-wasting pleasantries they are: "courtship, pleasant jest, and courtesy, / As bombast and as lining to the time" (5.2.780–81). Men who "swear in jest" (1.1.54) cannot really expect anything more.

It is entirely fitting, therefore, that the corrective restoration of meaning which is needed before the lovers can win cannot logically take place within the play whose purely ludic arena has been established from the opening scene. The women require their lovers to wait a whole year and a day after the ending, their long experience of penance and sorrow serving to resubstantiate the words that have been empty for all too long. Dumaine protests that their letters "show'd much more than jest" (5.2.785), but that is not proof enough. The women require verification. This injection of seriousness, which puts content back behind the form, goes against the more playful spirit of comedy. And this is why, as Berowne complains, *Love's Labor's Lost* "doth not end like an old play: / Jack hath not Gill" (5.2.874–75).

Ultimately, *Love's Labor's Lost* seems fairly critical of art. Wit and entertainment are all very well, and perfectly adequate for two hours' traffic upon the stage, but the direction of the play is heavily weighted toward the restoration of meaning and order at the close. The same could be said of *The Two Gentlemen of Verona*, the plot of which also revolves around an act of perjury and bad faith. Sent by his father to further himself in Milan, Proteus quickly forgets his home-grown beloved, Julia, and falls in love with Silvia, the mistress of his best friend, Valentine. Leaving Julia, loving Silvia, and betraying his friend, Proteus' "threefold perjury" (2.6.5) cuts across the otherwise neat symmetry of the two couples and provides the play with its plot. Like *Love's Labor's Lost*, *Two Gentlemen* also looks critically at the letter of love. With letters promised, exchanged, and written between lovers and absent friends, *Two Gentlemen* is one of Shakespeare's most pointedly epistolary plays. Letters literally separate speakers from their words and, with their ability to be misinterpreted or to fall into the wrong hands, they form a tried and tested plot device. At the beginning of the play, Proteus is a "little speaking" lover (1.2.29) whose courtship of Julia seems to be conducted almost entirely by post. We see the missive from him which Julia at first tears up and then rather sheepishly tries to piece back together; and we see her own reply, which Proteus (at that stage still faithful) joyfully receives: "Sweet love, sweet lines, sweet life!" (1.3.45). Once he has turned a traitor to constancy, however, Proteus' words can no longer be believed. Declarations of his new-found love are no more trusted by Silvia than by the French women in *Love's Labor's Lost*: "I know they are stuff'd with protestations, / And full of new-found oaths, which he will break / As easily as I do tear his paper" (4.4.129–31).

Unable to persuade Silvia of his good faith, Proteus begs her portrait instead: "to your shadow will I make true love" (4.2.125). Since he is denied "the substance of your perfect self" (4.2.123), he is obliged to content himself with its substitute – a work of art. His act of worship is not only empty and vain, however, but – more shockingly in post-Reformation England – idolatrous as well. Silvia gratifies his wish, but only because she recognizes that idolatry is an appropriate punishment for the faithless man, fit only "To worship shadows and adore false shapes" (4.2.130). But, as with *Love's Labor's Lost*, the whole movement of the play is directed toward putting substance back behind the empty shell, and restoring content to form. Charged with delivering the picture to Proteus, Julia (at this stage disguised as Silvia's page) makes this clear: "O thou senseless form, / Thou shalt be worshipp'd, kiss'd, lov'd and ador'd; / And were there sense in his idolatry, / My substance should be statue in thy stead" (4.4.198–201). In *Love's Labor's Lost* the restoration of word and meaning is postponed well beyond the edges of the play as sitting uneasily with that comedy's more throwaway, time-wasting world. But in *Two Gentlemen*, Shakespeare tries (less convincingly, for some) to incorporate it within the bounds of the play: Proteus' sudden and shamed change of heart in the closing scene allowing the playwright to wrap all the action up in the happy union of the two young couples – "One feast, one house, one mutual happiness" (5.4.173).

In both these plays a simple dereliction by male lovers deprives words of their meanings and threatens to leave the characters with a world where human art and language can aspire to little more than empty show. But there are other plays in which this fairly negative assessment of art is, if not altogether mitigated, at least balanced against a more positive one, and where the question of whether art might or might not order emotional and moral chaos satisfactorily is presented for the audience to judge. *Much Ado About Nothing* is a case in point. Here the action is structured around two interlocking plots in which theatrical illusion is used both to bring couples together and to drive them catastrophically apart. *Much Ado* is a tricky play. With its multitude of plots, distortions, conjectures, and hoaxes it abounds with garbled versions of different stories and shows humans operating tricks in a world of tricks. Much of the play is in prose, for this is a comedy with its feet firmly on the ground and in which human beings are made accountable for everything that happens. Shakespeare's lovers can expect no help from external sources here, like the fairies of *A Midsummer Night's Dream* or the god of marriage in *As You Like It*. In *Much Ado*, love plots are fashioned, manipulated, destroyed, and resolved by humans alone. Men and women get themselves into difficulties which only they can resolve, for, as Don Pedro puts it, "we are the only love gods" (2.2.386).

In the first of the two plots, Hero and Claudio fall victim to the evil plottings of Don John, who, as bastard brother to Don Pedro, is clearly the villain of the piece. He stages an encounter between an accomplice and one of Hero's gentlewomen at a chamber window, the aim being to compromise Hero's chastity and strike hatred in the heart of her betrothed, Claudio. As Don John's gratuitously mischievous and sinister plot transforms a happy ending into an ugly scene of accusation, public humiliation, pain, and supposed death, Shakespeare unveils the potentially evil consequences of theatrical power. The manipulative, coercive power of theatrical illusion – the ability to move, persuade, and initiate action – is demonstrated before our eyes. In the second plot, Don Pedro uses overhearing and disguise – theatrical devices which are, on the face of it, identical to those of his brother – in order to trick together Shakespeare's maverick duo, Beatrice and

Benedick: "I will in the interim undertake one of Hercules' labors, which is, to bring Signior Benedick and the Lady Beatrice into a mountain of affection th' one with th' other. I would fain have it a match, and I doubt not but to fashion it" (2.1.364–69). Generations of critics have argued that Beatrice and Benedick are secretly if unwittingly in love from the start, and that, mired in structures of thought and habits of mind that threaten to become sterile and repetitive, they have to be jolted into recognizing and loving each other. But it is equally plausible that Don Pedro makes something out of nothing, conjuring and engineering their mutual love with all the skill of the fiction writer or creative artist. Either way, his Herculean labor pays off, and the device to bring the two lovers together is presented as benevolent and good.

The story of the falsely accused woman is an ancient one, and, in all the known versions of the story, a lover is hoodwinked into thinking his beloved is unchaste – the germ of the Hero/Claudio plot. But not one of the seventeen or so contemporary versions of the story that Shakespeare may have known contains the equivalent of the Beatrice and Benedick subplot, nor the theatrical devices necessary to trick them together. Shakespeare invents Beatrice and Benedick, in other words, and inserts them into the well-known and much-rehearsed Hero story in such a way as to create a climate of comparison and debate. Competing types of theatrical trickery thus vie with each other for our approval and disapprobation – the seemingly benevolent devices of Don Pedro, and the clearly malicious, illegitimate plottings of Don John. Questions about what is good art and what bad – or, indeed, whether art should be judged by such criteria – are, in the end, left to the audience to decide. With its dualistic pairings, reversals, exchanges, and repositionings, *Much Ado* is a highly schematic play and its principle of contrast extends from the two interwoven plots to the juxtaposition of various paired themes: jest and earnest, love and war, motley and melancholy. In Dogberry's words, "comparisons are odorous" (3.5.16). In a play which hinges so often on the mistaking of words, it is as fitting that Dogberry's felicitous malapropism should sum up so much of the action as it is that his blundering constables should stumble upon the play's comic resolution: "What your wisdoms could not discover, these shallow fools have brought to light" (5.1.232–34). It is not that Dogberry and Verges possess, as innocents, a privileged access to the truth, but rather that, in a play so full of fumbling and muddle, we are left wondering if the final conclusion is in fact brought about by art at all and not, in the end, by pure accident and chance.

A play that could be said to be equally ambivalent about the power of art to order human experience is *A Midsummer Night's Dream*. For the action of this play takes place during the four days (or rather nights) before Theseus and Hippolyta solemnize their wedding, a period by the end of which

Egeus' disobedient daughter Hermia must also submit either to the husband of her father's choice or to the strict Athenian law which punishes filial willfulness with a lifetime of enforced chastity or with death. The "sealing-day" (1.1.84) which marks the final submission of human sexuality to law is thus some way off and in the time pending – a period pregnant with playful possibility – courtship takes up its typical position. Moreover, as Hermia and her chosen beloved, Lysander, promptly flee from the law into the forest – toward the sanctuary of a maiden aunt some seven leagues hence – so the arm of the law is measured and the extent of its influence shown to be strictly delimited. With four days' grace and seven leagues' distance, Shakespeare carefully plots the space–time coordinates of his carnival world within which the normal rules governing social and sexual affairs are, as one would expect, all over the place. Here marriage provides no order and instead the royal couple of the fairy kingdom, Oberon and Titania, are at jealous war, the product of their marital discord being only a "progeny of evils" (2.1.115) which disturbs the seasonal cycle and the natural order of things. The proper relation of the law to sexual expression – which in normal circumstances corresponds to the sexual stereotypes of ruling husband and yielding wife – is disrupted. As Bottom comments thoughtfully to Titania, "reason and love keep little company together now-a-days. The more pity that some honest neighbors will not make them friends" (3.1.143–45).

What we get instead is Oberon's "night-rule" (3.2.5), art's morally neutral alternative to the law-beholden rule of rational day. Oberon is the acknowledged master of this carnival world, for his pharmaceutical interventions – in the form of love potions administered here and there – represent the artist's ability to make believe. Oberon is no Don Pedro, however, for his interventions are mischievous and blatantly self-serving. He makes Titania fall head over heels in love with an ass so that, in her distraction, he can steal away her little page boy. As for his intrusion into the affairs of the Athenian lovers, he seems at first more concerned with symmetry and poetic justice than with writing happy endings. Observing Helena's fruitless chase of the once loving, now perjured Demetrius, Oberon promises that "Thou shalt fly him, and he shall seek thy love" (2.1.246). What is the point of this, however, except to transform Helena's "chang'd" Ovidian narrative – "Apollo flies, and Daphne holds the chase" (2.1.230, 231) – back into its more canonical version? On the other hand, Oberon is no Don John either, there being nothing in *A Midsummer Night's Dream* to match the sinister machinations of the bastard Spaniard in *Much Ado*. When, after their crazy forest dream is over, the four lovers awake to find everything resolved – Demetrius reconciled to Helena, Lysander to Hermia – they are asked by Theseus how such concord came from chaos. The answer is through imagination: through their collective experience of illusion, fantasy, enchantment, fiction and make-believe. As with Beatrice and Benedick, the reconciliation of the four young lovers shows the lasting and beneficial effects of being conjured to believe what's not true. At the end of the play, Demetrius still remains under the influence of Oberon's love drug, his induced passion for Helena not being neutralized by another substance, as Lysander's was. But, by returning his affection to Helena, to whom "Was I betrothed ere I saw Hermia" (4.1.172), the spell serves to neutralize his initial act of perjury – the very madness, that is, which got the whole plotful of havoc going in the first place. In this case, Demetrius' continuing delusion is marked as a return to health.

In *A Midsummer Night's Dream* the success of art in ordering human experience is held very much in the balance. As with *Much Ado*, the audience is invited to compare and contrast, to exercise judgment and come up with conclusions of its own. The power to conjure emotions is shown to have both bad and good effects. Theseus – pragmatic, worldly, wakeful, and Oberon's daytime double – is famously distrustful of the imagination: "Such tricks hath strong imagination, / That if it would but apprehend some joy, / It comprehends some bringer of that joy; / Or in the night, imagining some fear, / How easy is a bush suppos'd a bear!" (5.1.18–22). In Titania's ludicrous crush on the ass-headed Bottom and the mechanicals' terrified flight from the same we have evidence enough of the imagination's power to make fools of us all. But Hippolyta, by contrast, testifies to the imagination's more benevolent consequences. It is imagination which allows her to enter into the experience of a work of art and to engage sympathetically with it, even with Bottom's rendition of Pyramus: "Beshrew my heart, but I pity the man"(5.1.290). The power of art to move – even such bad art as *Pyramus and Thisbe* – needs no apology, no justification. And to this even the skeptical Theseus finally concedes: "No epilogue, I pray you; for your play needs no excuse" (5.1.355–56). In being allowed to dispense with their epilogue, the mechanicals are relieved of the need (much exercised elsewhere in their play) to explain the nature of theatrical illusion. That Shakespeare should provide just such an excusing epilogue to his own play, however, leaves the matter of illusion – and its good or bad effects – quizzically open to question:

> If we shadows have offended,
> Think but this and all is mended,
> That you have have slumb' red here
> While these visions did appear.
> (5.1.423–26)

The Taming of the Shrew poses the problem of art's relation to life and love's relation to art still more pointedly. In this play, Kate embodies the shrewish female who was enshrined in jest-books, ballads, sermons, folktales, and a well-populated misogynistic tradition. Petruchio steps in as the master analyst who dedicates himself to her cure. But his method is unorthodox, for he meets her supposed madness with a contrived madness of his own, one which vies to outbid her with a violence and unpredictability that is more than a match for her. Petruchio's idiosyncratic, adversarial, and bizarre behavior is quite as bad as hers, particularly during the Rabelaisian wedding scene, which is reported to us by one of the appalled guests (3.2.150–83). But the play draws an important distinction between the two. While Kate's madness is presented as emotional, subjective, and involved, Petruchio's, by contrast, is ironic, objective, and detached. If Kate is genuinely disorderly, Petruchio is disorderly by design. Petruchio's madness is crafty and methodical, and motivated all along by "meaning" (3.2.124). Petruchio's techniques are denounced by the play's patriarchal community for only as long as they believe his behavior and Kate's to be the same. No sooner are the effects of his therapy made visible – in the miraculously pliant Kate – than the community takes him back into its bosom and rewards him handsomely for his pains. Baptista doubles the dowry settled on the newly reformed bride.

Petruchio does not rest until he has transformed his future wife into the woman designed, patented, and approved of by the patriarchal society he represents, a Kate "Conformable as other household Kates" (2.1.278). There is no question, however, of Shakespeare leaving the matter there. For all the submission of this particular bride (a matter, in any case, notoriously open to question), the battle between man and woman is by no means over. When Petruchio sends his wife to fetch the other newly-weds, her sister Bianca and the Widow, Kate returns to report that they will not come to their husbands because "They sit conferring by the parlor fire" (5.2.102). A recalcitrant and unsupervised female language continues to persist even after the apparent success of Petruchio's taming methods – a secretive and vaguely insurrectionary discourse going on behind the scenes which clearly identifies Bianca and the Widow as the play's two new shrews. With its proliferation rather than elimination of disorderly women, and with Hortensio, recent recruit to the "taming-school" (4.2.54), ready to take up where Petruchio left off, Shakespeare's play announces a resigned return back to the beginning.

Shakespeare emphasizes the circularity of his plot, moreover, by running rings around the play's various audiences. There are two scenes in Act 4 (3 and 5) in which Petruchio famously forces Kate to abide by a world of his own devising – a world in which, at his whim, the morning is the afternoon, the sun the moon, or an old man a budding young virgin – for "It shall be what a' clock I say it is" (4.3.195). Kate eventually capitulates – "Then God be blest, it is the blessed sun, / But sun it is not, when you say it is not; / And the moon changes even as your mind. / What you will have it nam'd, even that it is, / And so it shall be so for Katherine" (4.5.18–22). At this point, as Hortensio observes, "the field is won" (4.5.23). The prerogative to conjure out of thin air a place, a time, a person's identity or gender is, of course, that of the playwright. It is the playwright who can, at the stroke of a pen, convert the bare boards of the stage into the vasty fields of France simply by asking his audience to "suppose" it so (*Henry V*, Prologue, 19).[10] When Petruchio invites Kate to imagine that the sun is the moon and so forth he is doing neither more nor less than the tricksy Lord who lays on "The Taming of the Shrew" in order to beguile the drunken Christopher Sly, and no more nor less, of course, than Shakespeare himself, who is all the while busy urging us to suspend our disbelief and enter into the theatrical illusion of his Padua.

With the moral laws governing human sexuality temporarily suspended during courtship, the aesthetic laws governing art and illusion neatly step in to take their place. In *The Taming of the Shrew*, Shakespeare makes the comparison between the two more pointedly than ever. A man orders his woman exactly as the artist orders his material. Here love's labors are won in the same way that an audience is won, the implication being that the success or failure of the one necessarily dictates the success or failure of the other. If Petruchio fails to win Kate by asking her to "suppose" what he asks her to, then, by the same token, the play must fail too: the audience will resist as Kate resists. If, on the other hand, *The Taming of the Shrew* succeeds in captivating its audience, or at least in making them enjoy the show, then it legitimates the most violent, coercive, not to say outrageously sexist behavior. The difficulty of resolving this notoriously contentious play is entirely of its own, quite deliberate making, for never so wittily has love been made the victim of art's success.

Aesthetic criteria and their ability to order love as well as life receive a more straightforwardly positive treatment in *As You Like It*. Deserting the tyranny and injustice caused by fraternal jealousy and internecine strife, the characters of this play flee the court for the Forest of Arden. Not only courtship's classic *locus*, the forest is also here the self-consciously specialized world of Elizabethan literary pastoral. As in Shakespeare's source text, Thomas Lodge's *Rosalynde* (1590), or that model of the genre, Sir Philip Sidney's *Arcadia* (1598), the otiose setting of the pastoral was home to the formal eclogue, colloquy, and debate. Shakespeare frequently holds up the action in order to dramatize one of those static setpiece dialogues so beloved of Renaissance pastoral: Fortune versus Nature (1.2.31ff.), or the country versus the court (3.2.11ff.). In *As You Like It* everything becomes a subject for stylized rendition. At the beginning of the play, even before the scene has shifted to Arden, the courtier Le Beau recounts the events of a recently witnessed wrestling match: "There comes an old man with his three sons" (1.2.118). As Celia comments, he begins his account for all the world like an "old tale" (1.2.119), one which might, indeed, have served as the narrative opening of *As You Like It* itself. This literarizing tendency to turn actions back into novel material is still going strong at the end of the play, when Oliver tells an apparently impersonal, third-person story of brotherly forgiveness and reconciliation that turns out to be all about himself – his recent conversion and reconciliation with Orlando.

Characters tend to see each other as stock literary types – "Signior Love," "Monsieur Melancholy," "Monsieur Traveler" (3.2.292, 293; 4.1.32) – and actions and events no sooner happen than they are turned into material for narrative or poetry. No sooner has the wrestling match between Orlando and the court champion, Charles, been concluded (in Orlando's favor) than it furnishes ample material for metaphor. Having that instant fallen in love with Rosalind, Orlando muses that "My better parts / Are all thrown down" (1.2.249–50), while the equally love-struck Rosalind comments that he has "overthrown / More than your enemies" (1.2.254–55). In the forest, nature itself becomes a glorified textbook in which the banished Duke can find "tongues in trees, books in the running brooks, / Sermons in stones, and good in every thing" (2.1.16–17). For the amorous Orlando, too, "these trees shall be my books" (3.2.5), as he proceeds to carve Rosalind's name in their trunks and to hang his verses from their branches. There is no lack of entertainment in the forest, for it provides the Duke with a "universal theatre" (2.7.137) in which the actions of men can be interpreted as carefully as works of art. The appearance of Orlando and his ancient servant Adam thus becomes a "woeful pageant" (2.7.138) upon which Jacques can moralize the seven ages of man, just as the stand-off between Silvius and Phebe can be described as a "pageant truly play'd / Between the pale complexion of true love / And the red glow of scorn and proud disdain" (3.4.52–54). There is nothing that cannot provide an occasion for literary theorizing or forensic abstraction: Jacques can moralize on the hunted deer (2.1.44) and delights to hear Touchstone "moral on the time" (2.7.29).

Art provides a running commentary upon life throughout *As You Like It*, and life provides endless material for art. The two, however, remain importantly distinct. Art does not confuse itself with life but celebrates its pretence and, in true comic fashion, reveals its artifice for all to see. "The truest poetry is," as Touchstone avers, "the most feigning" (3.3.19–20). It is within this relentlessly literary universe that, disguised for the duration as Ganymed, Rosalind woos Orlando and conjures him to woo "her" in return. The point of this play-acting is to make courtship itself into a work of art. But unlike the elegant, overly formal courtships of *Love's Labor's Lost*, this contrivance is allowed to succeed. And, if courtship occupies an ambiguous space outside the marital rule of law, then in this play – more conclusively than in others – aesthetic orders and forms are shown to provide an alternative that is more than satisfactory.

"Journeys end in lovers meeting," sings Feste (2.3.43), but *Twelfth Night* is one of the very few comedies which do not effect a journey to some second, "green" world from which to stage a reentry back into the cold light of ordinary day. In this play we are already there. The characters are either residents of the charmed and faintly unreal Illyria or are shipwrecked on to its shores in the very best romance tradition. And, if we are already within carnival's space, then we are also clearly within carnival time. Twelfth Night was the Feast of the Epiphany, the last night of the Christmas holiday and the last chance for revelry before the return to the workaday world. Shakespeare's play is not set on any one given night but extends the festival mood indefinitely, or at least for the plot's three-month duration. Whether the "twelf day of December" of which the carousing Sir Toby sings (2.3.84), Malvolio's "midsummer madness" (3.4.56), or merely "More matter for a May morning" (3.4.142), the time of *Twelfth Night* is unspecified, conjuring the open season and sensation of timelessness which operates within carnival's revelling world.

Within the holiday atmosphere of *Twelfth Night* there are no blocking parents, intransigent guardians, or strict laws of the state to thwart the young lovers. Indeed, nothing stands in anybody's way. The only problem, in fact, is Olivia's willful refusal to play by carnival's rules. The play begins with her vowing to shut herself away from male company for seven long years in order to mourn the death of her brother – a decision which, not unlike that of Navarre and his courtiers in *Love's Labor's Lost*, clearly rules against courtship. But in *Twelfth Night*, where the time for love has already arrived, the characters are called upon to enjoy the temporary freedoms of courtship and to submit to the carnival's alternative rule – the "uncivil rule" of cakes and ale (2.3.123) – which characterizes the whole mood of idleness and entertainment in Olivia's noisy household. Olivia refuses Orsino's love for no good reason, thus breaking all the laws of romantic comedy: "In your denial I would find no sense," complains Viola (disguised as Cesario, Orsino's page), "I would not understand it" (1.5.266–67). As the frustrated Orsino accuses Olivia when they finally meet face to face in Act 5, her aloofness is sheer perversity: "You uncivil lady, / To whose ingrate and inauspicious altars / My soul the faithfull"st off'rings have breath'd out / That e'er devotion tender'd. What shall I do?" (5.1.112–15). Olivia is an "uncivil lady" because, paradoxically, she has not been uncivil enough, has not entered into the spirit of misrule which comedy dictates and which governs not only her household but all of Illyria and Shakespeare's play as a whole. Not, that is, until she falls in love with Cesario. This – which happens rapidly – quickly somersaults her into the place where she should have been from the beginning, namely in a comedy. Once she has entered into the spirit of the game, Olivia sets off the bootless love chase which symptomizes the very best of Shakespearean love plots: "My master loves her dearly, / And I (poor monster) fond as much on him; / And she (mistaken) seems to dote on me," as Viola sums it up (2.2.33–35). Once it has got going, the play can run the usual course of confusions, plots, and tricks in which virtually every character is, in one way or another, abused or beguiled.

None more spectacularly, of course, than Malvolio, Olivia's po-faced steward who is gulled by means of that oldest trick in the book, a craftily mislaid love letter. In his unshakeable conviction that Olivia loves him, Malvolio is made a helpless laughing-stock and eventually locked up as being certifiably insane. When, in the final recognition scene, this, along with all the other plots and confusions, is explained and brought to light, the pranksters hope that the general forgiveness of "this present hour" (5.1.357) will extend to them and that Malvolio will, like everyone else, take it in good humor. Yet Malvolio remains coldly unforgiving, for he is the only figure in the play to resist comedy's alternative rule of disorder to the bitter end. Once Olivia has thrown away her veil and abandoned propriety at the end of Act 1, Malvolio is the only character left who is not playing the game, and the loss is manifestly his. In the discomfiting and excluding of Malvolio, moreover, Shakespeare seems to be making a stronger case than usual for the power of dramatic art. For Malvolio is drama's enemy, the embodiment of the antitheatrical prejudice, whose punctilious puritanism would, given a chance, close the whole thing down and send us all home. If anyone ends up outside the green world of Illyria then it is Malvolio, for he never really went there in the first place. But the rest of the characters (and, by implication, the audience) seem content to remain in its enchanted, laughing world where the rules of courtship and comic misrule seem to be upheld and endorsed above everything else.

NOTES

1 All references to Shakespeare are to *The Riverside Shakespeare*, 2nd edn, ed. G. Blakemore Evans et al. (Boston and New York: Houghton Mifflin Company, 1997).

2 William Congreve, *The Old Bachelor* (1693), 5.1.388, in *The Complete Plays of William Congreve*, ed. Herbert Davis (Chicago: University of Chicago Press, 1967), p. 107.

3 For some examples of amorous "greenwood" songs, see John Stevens, *Music and Poetry in the Early Tudor Court* (London: Methuen, 1961), pp. 338, 400, 408, 410.

4 For a particularly interesting discussion of this, see Harry Berger, *Second World and Green World: Studies in Renaissance Fiction-Making* (Berkeley: University of California Press, 1988).

5 George Puttenham, *The Arte of English Poesie*, ed. G. D. Willcock and Alice Walker (Cambridge: Cambridge University Press, 1936), p. 51.

6 See Martin Ingram, *Church Courts, Sex and Marriage in England, 1570–1640* (Cambridge: Cambridge University Press, 1987).

7 *Montaigne's Essayes*, trans. John Florio, ed. L. C. Harmer, 3 vols. (London: J. M. Dent, 1965), III, 323, 336.

8 On the use of the phrase "juridico-discursive," see Michel Foucault, *The History of Sexuality*, trans. Robert Hurley (Harmondsworth: Penguin, 1978), p. 82.

9 "Loving in truth, and fain in verse my love to show," the first line of the opening sonnet of Sidney's *Astrophil and Stella* (1590).

10 The Bianca subplot is drawn from George Gascoigne's play, *Supposes* (1566), itself an adaptation of Ariosto's *I Suppositi* (1509), "the verye name wherof," writes Gascoigne in his Prologue, "may peradventure drive into every of your heads a sundry Suppose, to suppose, the meaning of our supposes," cited in *Narrative and Dramatic Sources of Shakespeare*, ed. Geoffrey Bullough, 7 vols. (London: Routledge and Kegan Paul, 1957–66), I, 111.

8

EDWARD BERRY

Laughing at "others"

As a dramatic form, comedy can exist without laughter, but most of the plays that we consider comedies are engines of laughter, and one of the great pleasures of comic theatre is the feeling of exhilaration and release that laughter provides. Despite much theorizing, the causes of laughter and its significance in human life remain a mystery. The impulse to laugh, for one thing, is deeply equivocal. At times, as when we laugh "with" someone, laughter may be a mechanism by which we identify with another human being, a means of psychological and social bonding. At other times, as when we laugh "at" someone, the same physical reaction may be a form of aggressive self-assertion. The former kind of laughter, in which human and societal divisions are dissolved in communal merriment, we might call, loosely following Bakhtin, carnivalesque.[1] The latter, in which such divisions are perversely reinforced, we might call Hobbesian, after Thomas Hobbes, who defined laughter as an expression of superiority, a feeling of "sudden glory arising from some sudden conception of some eminency in ourselves, by comparison with the infirmity of others."[2] Both kinds of laughter, curiously, can strengthen certain kinds of social communion: the carnivalesque, by casting wide the net of community, implying that we are all, at some level, one; the Hobbesian, by affirming the superiority of one community in opposition to an individual or group outside it. Romantic and Saturnalian comedy tend towards carnivalesque laughter; satiric comedy, towards Hobbesian.

Theorists of laughter – Bergson, for example – often justify mockery of the Hobbesian kind as a form of social correction.[3] By experiencing the humiliation of being laughed at, so the idea goes, the victim is led to recognize his or her social deviance and rejoins the community reformed. In this way, even satirical laughter can become carnivalesque, the sense of social communion widened by the inclusion of a character or group previously estranged. Such gestures, however, occur rarely in satiric comedy; more commonly, the comic butts targeted by satiric laughter are not reformed but merely mocked, humiliated, and even ostracized. Even when such characters do perceive the error of their ways, moreover, we may feel that the laughter evoked at their expense is less rehabilitative than malicious; in such cases, we feel uncomfortable about the motives of satirists and the subversive pleasure they incite in audiences like ourselves. In general, Hobbesian satiric laughter works towards limited social communion through exclusion, forging group solidarity among privileged insiders through the mockery of outsiders, whoever they may be.

Contemporary literary theorists have grappled earnestly with this exclusionary impulse, by which members of powerful elites, with or without laughter, define their identities and achieve group solidarity by derogating less powerful outsiders, such as women, black people, foreigners, and laborers. The discourses of contemporary feminism, racial and ethnic studies, and postcolonialism, in particular, have been characterized by sustained attention to this problem. Given the nature of the dominant ideology and social ethos of Elizabethan England, one is not surprised to find in Shakespeare's comedies biases in favor of aristocratic, male, white, English, heterosexual Christians. In Elizabethan culture, such categories define a normative "self"; those who fall outside them are considered "other."

Mockery of such "others" is a common feature of Elizabethan plays. The tendency towards Hobbesian exclusionary laughter was accentuated in the period by the prestige of classical satire and by such contemporary customs as the charivari, which subjected social deviants, such as shrewish women, to raucous and festive abuse and violence. Such customs as bear-baiting and the exploitation of the mentally and physically disabled as court fools seem symptomatic of a predisposition in Elizabethan culture towards the laughter of cruelty.

If we look to Shakespeare's comedies for signs of the laughter of social exclusion, we need not search far. In *A Midsummer Night's Dream*, Bottom, a mere weaver who aspires to amaze the Duke, is transformed into an ass. In *The Taming of the Shrew*, Katherina, the shrew, is mocked, abused, and tormented into submission by Petruchio. In *The Merchant of Venice*, Shylock, the Jew, is mocked, humiliated, and eventually broken by the Christians. In *As You Like It*, Jaques, the melancholiac, serves as jester to his exiled lord. In *Twelfth Night*, Malvolio, a presumptuous steward, is tricked and humiliated by his tormentors as he lies in a dark dungeon. In *The Merry Wives of Windsor*, Falstaff, an outsider who threatens the peace of the town, is thrown into the Thames, beaten as a witch, and finally "pinched to death" by "fairies." In *The Tempest*, Caliban endures Prospero's abuse throughout the play and is finally "hunted" into submission. Although the treatment of the foregoing characters ranges widely in meaning and tonal effect – some deserve their abuse more than others, some are treated more kindly than others – they are all "outsiders" to a dominant social group and, as deviants from its norms, are all subjected to mocking laughter.

The closer one looks at the "others" in Shakespeare's comedies, however, the more questionable their "otherness" becomes. To be applied in a strict sense, the notion of "otherness" requires a rigid division of human types into diametrically opposed and stable categories. A normative "self" must be set off against a clearly defined "other": male must be opposed to female, for example, white to nonwhite, and aristocrat to laborer. The exclusionary laughter of Hobbes, the laughter of "sudden glory," depends upon such sharp divisions; we can laugh at ourselves, says Hobbes, only in retrospect, when we have become "other" to ourselves. Although Shakespeare's comedies may exploit such oppositions, setting off shrews and Jews as "others" from privileged Elizabethan norms, it does not remain bound to them. A striking feature of the Shakespearean comic experience, indeed, is the way in which the very notions of "self" and "other" become difficult to disentangle, both for characters within the plays and for audiences outside them. Exploring how this blurring of boundaries occurs may help to illuminate some of the distinctive characteristics of Shakespearean comedy.

One distinctive feature of Shakespeare's ambiguous treatment of "others" is that the exclusionary impulse behind Hobbesian laughter is never literally fulfilled. The shadow of the scapegoat hangs over many such characters – Shylock, the Falstaff of *Merry Wives*, Malvolio – but the archetypal fate of the scapegoat, expulsion from society, never occurs. Not once in Shakespeare's comedies is a comic butt driven out of society at the end of a play. The most vicious form of Hobbesian laughter, the gleeful solidarity of a mob as it glories in the expulsion of the alien, never receives expression.

Instead of being ostracized, characters who have been mocked, derided, and abused throughout a play are invariably invited to rejoin the community at the end; if they remain outcasts, they do so of their own free will. Duke Senior pleads with Jaques at the end of *As You Like It* to "stay, Jaques, stay" (5.4.194) rather than to leave society for a monastic retreat.[4] Olivia urges Malvolio to forgive and forget his humiliation at the hands of Sir Toby Belch and company, and Falstaff, having been "pinched to death" by the children of Windsor, is invited to join his mockers and "laugh this sport o'er by a country fire" (5.5.242). These gestures of incorporation at the end of Shakespeare's comedies are not sentimentalized. The characters they are directed to have usually not been reformed, and the gestures of inclusion carry with them not an idealized notion of social communion but a rueful acceptance of the inescapability of continuing social tension. Duke Senior thrives on Jaques' melancholy pessimism, Olivia's household depends on Malvolio's sobriety, and Windsor exploits Falstaff's roguery to resolve its own social tensions.

The fate of Caliban at the end of *The Tempest* might seem to be an exception to this rule. Caliban's end, however, is ambiguous. Prospero begrudgingly acknowledges his responsibility for him – "this thing of darkness I / Acknowledge mine" (5.1.275–76) – and sends him to his cell. If Caliban is imagined returning with Prospero to Milan, then he too is incorporated into society, although uncomfortably. If, as seems more likely, he is imagined left alone on the island, what seems a dreadful banishment may be a triumph. Mastery over "his" island, after all, has been his goal throughout the play, and Prospero's departure without him may represent a final acknowledgment of his right to rule alone. In either scenario, Caliban's destiny is not that of the archetypal scapegoat.

The true exception, and the one that proves the rule, is to be found in the treatment of Shylock during the trial scene in *The Merchant of Venice*. This is arguably the darkest moment in Shakespearean comedy, the point at which Hobbesian laughter is most vicious and intense. The structure of the scene is reminiscent of a bear-baiting. As judge, Portia first toys with Shylock, testing his strength of will and arousing his hopes, and then, step by "merciful" step, she strips him of his contract, his wealth, and, finally, his very identity as a Jew. He leaves the scene physically exhausted and mentally broken, never to appear again. Immediately thereafter, the festive Christians resume their romantic games, freed from the dark threat "the Jew" represents.

The trial scene proves the exception to the rule of inclusion not because Shylock is ostracized but, paradoxically, because in his case incorporation is worse than ostracism. Instead of being driven out of Venice, as might be expected, he is forcibly converted to Christianity and brought within the norms of Venetian society. He himself accepts this perverse gesture of social communion with a phrase that can only be taken ironically – "I am content" (4.1.394). Although some critics (mercifully few) argue that from an Elizabethan perspective forced conversion represents genuine mercy, the moment seems intended to shock. By losing his status as "other," Shylock loses his sense of self. The shock is accentuated because the act of forcible conversion transforms the quintessentially Shakespearean gesture of comic inclusiveness into macabre self-parody. Acceptance of the "other" seems in this case more malicious than ostracism. Despite its perversity, Shylock's incorporation into the Christian community highlights the consistency of the impulse toward inclusion of the "other," whether with benign tolerance or begrudging distaste, throughout the comedies.

For audiences, especially, but sometimes for characters on stage, the suspension of "otherness" implied in the reconciliatory gestures at the end of the comedies occurs in less predictable situations as well. With the exception of Don John in *Much Ado About Nothing*, all of the characters who play the role of "other" in the comedies are allowed at least a moment or two in which audiences, and sometimes characters on stage, are forced to see them from the inside, to acknowledge their essential humanity. At such moments, the difference between "self" and "other" dissolves. Shylock's "Hath not a Jew eyes?" (3.1.59) is the most famous of such moments because it is the least expected. Seduced at the beginning of the scene into complicity with Salerio and Solanio, whose smugly laughing contempt for Shylock breathes through their every line, we cannot help but be shocked when the victim of their callous humor is finally given voice. Sympathy, of course, does not preclude judgment – Shylock's voice turns quickly to savage vengeance – but it provokes deep ambivalence, disorienting our conception of who is "self" in this scene and who is "other." Whether the moment has any effect on Salerio and Solanio is doubtful, but the exact nature of their responses is left to the discretion of the actors or a director.

Similar shifts in perspective occur in our experience of Caliban, at moments when we are temporarily freed from our theatrical dependence on Prospero's view of him. In the midst of plotting to kill Prospero with Stephano and Trinculo, for example, Caliban attempts to give courage to his drunken companions by informing them of the "sounds, and sweet airs" of the isle, "that give delight and hurt not." He tells them of the dreams provoked in him by such sounds: "The clouds methought would open, and show riches / Ready to drop upon me, that when I wak'd / I cried to dream again" (3.2.136–43). His vision has no discernible effect on Stephano and Trinculo but tends to disorient audiences, who suddenly sense a responsiveness to beauty within a character whom Prospero compulsively rejects as no more than a depraved "other." Some critics argue that Caliban's sensitivity is no more than that open to savage beasts, who are proverbially soothed by music; even if we interpret Caliban as bestial, however, the poetic power of the moment dissolves the boundaries between human "self" and bestial "other," creating affinity rather than distance. A similar sympathy for Caliban is evoked wordlessly later in the play when he is hunted as an animal by Prospero, whose "dogs" are named, appropriately, Fury and Tyrant (4.1.254–62).

The hunting of Caliban is at the extreme end of persecution of the "other" in the comedies, but the symbolism of predator and prey recurs in many situations. Falstaff is comically "hunted" in *Merry Wives*, brought to the ground as a stag, encircled, and "pinched to death" by "fairies" whose appearance

is announced by hunting horns and the sounds of dogs. Although not literally hunted, Malvolio is cruelly baited by his tormentors, who imprison
him in a dark dungeon and try to brainwash him into a state of insanity.
Although audiences tend to wince as this jest threatens to go beyond the
bounds, the tormentors themselves seem little touched by Malvolio's plight,
and it is left to Olivia at the end of the play to express sympathy: "Alas,
poor fool, how have they baffled thee!" (5.1.369). Although Olivia maintains her distance as mistress of the household, her use of the word *fool*
as a term of endearment and her use of *thee* rather than *you* suggest that
her insight into her own folly has prompted a feeling of empathy with the
plight of the "other." Throughout the comedies, then, unexpected shifts in
perspective disorient both audiences and some onstage characters, collapsing
if only momentarily the differences between insider and outsider, "self" and
"other."

Not only is the boundary between inside and outside disturbed in
Shakespeare's representations of the "other," but the categories that define
these characters are themselves unclear and unstable. To think about the
"other" customarily means adopting fixed social categories unalterably opposed to each other: men vs. women, for example, native vs. foreigner, or
white vs. nonwhite. In Shylock's case, the categorization is simple enough:
he is a Jew, his opponents are Christian. In most other cases, however, categorization is much more difficult. In what sense, exactly, is Malvolio mocked
as "other"? He is a steward, a social category that hardly seems important
or general enough to deserve satire in its own right. "Sometimes he is a kind
of puritan" (2.3.140), says Maria, but her equivocal phrasing prevents strict
identification with a religious group, and his tormentors make nothing of his
religious identity. Maria's conclusion is that Malvolio is, above all, an "affection'd ass" (2.3.148), and even Olivia accuses him of being "sick of self-love"
(1.5.90). But these attributes are not contained by social categories at all.
Malvolio's tormentors, moreover, represent diverse social identities themselves: Feste is a court jester, Fabian is a servant, Sir Andrew and Sir Toby are
both knights, and Maria is Olivia's gentlewoman. Malvolio is thus "other" to
each of them in a different way. Each of these characters, moreover, bears him
a somewhat different grudge. A similar complexity is apparent in the Falstaff
of *Merry Wives*. In his case the complexity arises because of the multiplicity
of social types he contains. He is a threat to Windsor, presumably, because
he is a potential seducer of other men's wives. But he is also a poacher, a
drinker and feaster, a thief, a disgrace to knighthood, a foreigner to Windsor,
an old man, a fat man – and one could go on. His "otherness" is not a single,
fixed point but shifts from relationship to relationship throughout the play.

To many recent critics, Caliban's "otherness" fits within the familiar category of the native person, the victim of colonial oppression. Prospero the colonialist, from this perspective, invades the island and enslaves the aboriginal inhabitant. The problem with such readings is not that they are wrong – they speak to something in the play as well as in the history of its reception – but that they deny the role of Caliban its sense of mystery. Who, exactly, is Caliban? The very nature of his being is uncertain. The language that other characters use to describe him blurs the boundaries between humans and beasts, and, in the case of Prospero, between humans and devils. Shakespeare's fondness for metamorphosis often collapses distinctions between the human and the animal realms, and often, surprisingly, in ways that invite sympathy for animal "otherness." In *A Midsummer Night's Dream,* Bottom the weaver, translated into an ass, reveals asinine qualities, including a desire to scratch and eat hay, but they are endearing qualities, arousing affection and understanding rather than contempt. In *Merry Wives,* Falstaff's most sympathetic moments occur when, in disguise as Herne the hunter, he fantasizes about himself as a Windsor stag.

Perhaps the most complicated mixing of categories in Shakespeare's treatment of the "other" occurs in the roles of the disguised heroines, such as Julia in *Two Gentlemen of Verona,* Portia in *Merchant of Venice,* Rosalind in *As You Like It,* and Viola in *Twelfth Night.* Although it may seem odd to think of such dominant characters as "other" in plays that seem to celebrate them, the dominant patriarchal ethos of Elizabethan England makes them so, and signs of their equivocal status occur throughout the plays. The most significant token of their "otherness" lies in the plays' remorseless drive toward patriarchal marriage, which converts them all, finally, into wives to husbands whose social power outreaches their depth of character. To categorize the disguised heroines as merely "female," however, and therefore as categorically "other," is to distort the paradoxical nature of their theatrical roles. Each of these characters is a shape-shifter, capable of calling into question the very nature of identity itself. In the most complicated case, that of Rosalind in her game of courtship with Orlando in *As You Like It,* we witness a boy-actor (Shakespeare keeps us conscious of the actor behind the role) playing a young woman, Rosalind, playing a young man, Ganymed (who, in mythology, was Jove's cupbearer and male lover), playing a young woman, Rosalind. In such a case as this, the very notions of gender, and, more broadly, of "self" and "other" become confused.

Consider, for example, a single moment in the story of Julia, the betrayed heroine of *Two Gentlemen of Verona.* In disguise as a man, Sebastian, she is forced to woo Silvia on behalf of her own unfaithful lover. Moved by

Silvia's unexpected sympathy upon discovering Julia's betrayal, "Sebastian" tells how "he" once wore Julia's clothes to play the part of Ariadne:

> Madame, 'twas Ariadne passioning,
> For Theseus' perjury and unjust flight;
> Which I so lively acted with my tears
> That my poor mistress, moved therewithal,
> Wept bitterly; and would I might be dead
> If I in thought felt not her very sorrow.
>
> (4.4.167–72)

Here we have a boy-actor playing a young woman, Julia, who plays a young man, Sebastian, who as a boy-actor once wore Silvia's clothes to play the role of a fictitious young woman, Ariadne. The moment in which "Sebastian" finds "himself," moreover, reenacts the play of Ariadne, for Julia is at this moment conveying the pathos of her situation, her lover's "perjury and unjust flight," to Silvia as a sympathetic audience. Such moments seem designed to call into question the very stability of social and psychological identity that the notions of "self" and "other" imply.

Not only are the categories of "otherness" mixed in Shakespeare's comedies; they are also viewed from multiple perspectives. The result is that laughter at the "other" is always framed within a context that unsettles its tendency to evoke feelings of "sudden glory." Holofernes, for example, is mocked throughout *Love's Labor's Lost* as a pedantic schoolmaster, infatuated with the Latin language. When he plays the role of the great leader of the Jews, Judas Maccabeus, both the incongruity of the part and his own ineptitude provoke his aristocratic audience to great witticisms at his expense. Although his exasperated protest "this is not generous, not gentle, not humble" (5.2.629) prompts the Princess to sympathize with his plight, his tormentors, the young men, seem ironically unmoved. Yet the scene is framed to suggest that, although they are immune to the irony, the young men too are inept role-players, puffed up with their narcissistic desire to immortalize themselves by creating an heroic academe. Who, then, is "other" to an audience, the simple pedant Holofernes or his sophisticated mockers? A similar effect occurs in the same scene when Don Adriano de Armado, mocked throughout the play as a braggart Spanish soldier, unexpectedly achieves a kind of dignity, expressing his intention to "right" himself "like a soldier" (5.2.724–25) and marry the pregnant Jaquenetta. None of the young aristocrats shows a comparable ability to reform. Although by social role and national identity both Holofernes and Armado seem safely categorized as "other," to be mocked at will, the play's framing irony extends the mockery to the mockers themselves.

This kind of irony, in which laughter recoils against the laugher, is intensified by Shakespeare's tendency to unify his multiple plots by thematic mirroring. In *A Midsummer Night's Dream,* for example, the young aristocratic men also delight in mocking the inept performances of their social inferiors. The play that is performed by Bottom and his "hempen homespuns," however, "Pyramus and Thisbe," parodies the young lovers' own misadventures, and their obliviousness to the fact calls attention to their own lack of self-knowledge. Like Bottom and Flute, they too have played the roles of irrational young lovers, and badly. In a more serious vein, the theme of Christian charity provides an ironical framework for the "otherness" of Shylock in *The Merchant of Venice.* Shylock's vengefulness marks him as a Jew, an "other" to the Christians, who espouse the doctrine of mercy that Portia enunciates in the trial scene. Yet as the scene unfolds, Shylock's vengefulness comes to seem almost indistinguishable from a Christian charity that outwits and breaks him. An ironic hint of this dislocation of the categories of "self" and "other" occurs at the beginning of the trial scene when Portia, presumably unaware of the irony and intent on establishing herself as an impartial judge, asks, "which is the merchant here? and which the Jew?" (4.1.174).

The metadramatic tendencies of the comedies widen the scope of this ironical framing of "otherness." Much of the mockery of "others" occurs in situations that show the characters as actors or role-players. Falstaff receives his comeuppance in *Merry Wives* as he parades his lustiness disguised as Herne the hunter. Malvolio enacts the fantasies of greatness inspired by Maria's forged letter before an unobserved audience of his tormentors. Jaques not only plays the role of melancholy traveler but performs the most famous setpiece in Shakespeare – "all the world's a stage, / And all the men and women merely players" (2.7.139–40). Both the pageant of the Nine Worthies in *Love's Labor's Lost* and the performance of "Pyramus and Thisbe" in *A Midsummer Night's Dream,* as I have shown, feature common men mocked by their social superiors as they attempt to play roles unsuited to them. By calling attention to the theatricality of "otherness," Shakespeare makes of it not an essential quality of being but a social role. Since the theatrical metaphor is never limited to "otherness," moreover, the entire world of the plays tends to become a stage and all the other characters merely players as well. In *Twelfth Night,* Malvolio plays the role of lord of the household, while Olivia plays the role of mourner, Orsino of lover, and Viola of her brother, Sebastian. The shifting perspectives induced by these constant reminders of the theatricality of life tend to blur the boundaries between "self" and "other," making all characters "players," and in that sense "other" even to themselves.

Perhaps the subtlest instance of Shakespearean metadrama undermining the mockery of the "other" occurs in *The Taming of the Shrew*. In this play, it seems, Shakespeare lets the crudest of patriarchal fantasies have its day: the stereotypical shrew, the kind of woman subjected to charivaris or the wearing of scold's bridles in Elizabethan England, is here "tamed" into the role of the model wife. Yet the play in which Katherina is tamed is a play within a play, performed at the request of a hunting lord, who uses it to show the beggar, Christopher Sly, how grand it is to live his kind of life. The roles of the hunting lord and Christopher Sly in the Induction run parallel to those of Petruchio and Katherina in the play within the play: in each case, a member of the lower orders is persuaded to accept a new and "better" identity. The parallel between the hunting lord and Petruchio is accentuated by the fact that both are hunters: the one has just returned from a stag hunt, the other applies to the "taming" of his wife the methods used to tame falcons: "My falcon now is sharp and passing empty, / And till she stoop, she must not be full-gorg'd" (4.1.190–91). Since Katherina's taming occurs in a play put on to please a hunting lord, who desires to celebrate his kind of life before a mere beggar, is it not possible that the focal point of this play, Petruchio's mastery over Katherina, represents a wish-fulfillment fantasy for hunting lords and an ironic critique of their swaggering sense of masculine prowess? If such an irony were allowed to emerge in a production of the play, then the "otherness" of Katherina might be displaced on to Petruchio and the social type he represents. Such a reversal of roles might seem far-fetched – debate on this controversial play is unlikely to end soon – but its mere possibility highlights the way in which Shakespearean metadrama complicates the representation of "otherness."

Complexity of another kind arises if we consider the settings of the comedies. One conventional way of categorizing "otherness" is through national or even local identity. "Foreigners" are often the butts of comic laughter, and for Elizabethan Londoners the category included not only Europeans but Welsh, Scots, Irish, northerners, and townsfolk from anywhere else in England. In *Merry Wives*, Windsor's inhabitants include two such types: the Welsh priest, Evans, and the French physician, Caius. Their linguistic ineptitude makes them easy targets for laughter, both among the English in Windsor and, presumably, among the English at the Globe theatre. The laughter of the Windsorites, however, is also expressive of a more local patriotism: although English enough, Falstaff and Fenton are both mocked by the Windsorites for being "foreigners," interlopers in Windsor from the world of the court, a mockery that includes both civic identity and social rank. Such mockery would presumably play well before audiences of Windsorites – many critics feel that the values of the Windsor citizens inform the play – but not before audiences at court or at the Globe, where the ethos of Windsor might itself seem alienating and "other." When Falstaff mocks Evans for making "fritters" of the English language (5.5.143), then, who is "other" – Evans for being Welsh, Falstaff for being a non-Windsorite, or the Windsorites who mock both of them but whose small-town complacency may itself seem "other" to a courtly or urbane audience?

Merry Wives is Shakespeare's only English comedy. The question of an "otherness" dependent upon national or local identity becomes even more difficult in all the other comedies, in which the settings are either foreign or fanciful or some mixture of the two. Theseus, for example, the Duke of Athens in *A Midsummer Night's Dream,* is about as stable a representation of a "self" as we find in the comedies; many critics take him as the moral center of the play. From his condescending but amused and tolerant vantage point, Bottom the weaver and his "hempen homespuns" are irredeemably "other," as they might seem to Elizabethan aristocrats at the Globe. What happens to this stable "self," however, if we remind ourselves that the play is set not in contemporary England but in an ancient Athens inhabited by English fairies and that, even more importantly, Theseus is a character from Greek mythology who distrusts poetry? Not only Theseus but the imagined world in which he lives is "other" to an audience, Elizabethan or modern.

A similar confusion characterizes *The Taming of the Shrew*. This play is set mainly in Padua, although its characters come from other Italian cities as well: Katherina and her family are Paduans, Lucentio is a Florentine, Vincentio is a Pisan, and Petruchio is a Veronese. The induction to the play, however, is set in Warwickshire. If Katherina is "other" as a shrew, then perhaps everyone else in her plot, including Petruchio, is also "other" as an Italian, all of them exotic and distant creatures in the eyes of a hunting lord and beggar from somewhere near Stratford. To London audiences, moreover, even the Stratfordian perspective might well have seemed comically alien.

The question of national identity is potentially even more unsettling in *The Merchant of Venice*, for here it merges with questions of ethnicity and religion. As a Jew, Shylock is easy prey to Elizabethan Christians. If Shylock seems a negative stereotype of a Jew, however, then how is an Elizabethan audience to deal with the fact that he is a Jew in Venice, not Elizabethan London? Negative stereotypes of Italians also abound on the Elizabethan stage – stereotypes involving, among other things, Machiavellian intrigue, lust, revenge, foppishness, frivolity, and, above all, nasty Catholicism. "An Englishman Italianate is the devil incarnate," concludes Queen Elizabeth's tutor, Roger Ascham, as he bemoans the influence of Italy upon young English gentlemen.[5] The "otherness" of Roman Catholicism, in particular, recurs obsessively throughout Elizabethan literature, including such major works as Spenser's *Faerie Queene*. In such a context, is it possible that Elizabethan audiences might have been unsettled by the clash of two "othernesses" in *The Merchant of Venice*: Shylock's "Judaism" and a Venetian Catholicism, the latter as tainted in its own way by legalism as the former? Perhaps the "mercy" that Shylock receives in forced conversion is a Catholic, not a Christian mercy. If such were the case, perhaps the appropriate response to the trial scene would be the one that Mercutio makes to the feuding Montagues and Capulets in *Romeo and Juliet:* "a plague a' both your houses" (3.1.106).

Thus far I have examined the "other" as someone to be mocked, and have considered ways in which that mockery is deflected or unsettled through moments of empathy, the mixing of categories, the employment of multiple perspectives, including that of metadrama, and exotic settings. In each of these cases, I have argued, Shakespeare blurs the boundaries between "self" and "other," undermining the tendency toward pure Hobbesian laughter. Yet there is another, more paradoxical way in which Shakespeare achieves this effect. If, as I have shown, shifts in theatrical perspective may incite in us a sympathetic identification with the "other," they may also incite in us a more mysterious feeling of appreciative wonder at the mystery of "otherness" itself. There is something in Shakespeare's representation of "otherness" that engenders not mockery but awe.

Characters set off as "other," curiously, tend to have pregnant imaginations. They dream, and their dreams evoke wonder, both in them and us. Caliban, as I have shown, gives an account of his dreams, and, although it apparently has no effect on Stephano and Trinculo, it awakens in us the knowledge that the character transcends Prospero's reductive image of him. In *Twelfth Night,* Malvolio's outrageous fantasy of awakening from a nap with Olivia and then playing with "some rich jewel" while Toby approaches and curtsies to him captures the overweening hypocrisy of a man who lectures others on knowing their place, but it also speaks for a fertility of invention in its own way astonishing. Up to this point in the play, he has seemed a man with no inner life at all. Falstaff too indulges in wonderful fantasies, one of which enables him to revel in thoughts of sexual prowess for which there is no other evidence in the play: "For me, I am here a Windsor stag, and the fattest, I think, i' th' forest. Send me a cool rut-time, Jove, or who can blame me to piss my tallow?" (5.5.12–15). His ensuing image of his immense body being divided like that of a stolen buck, each of his lustful and admiring women receiving one of his haunches, transforms the laughter of mockery into that of delighted admiration. At such moments, characters whom we are invited to mock as "other" reveal a creative energy and resiliency that makes their very "otherness" a source of transcendent power.

The epitome of this kind of transformation, and one of the touchstones of Shakespearean comedy, occurs in *A Midsummer Night's Dream* when Bottom the weaver is courted by Titania, the queen of Fairies. Bottom is a simple man, a "hard-handed" man, and his name suggests his position in both the bodily and social hierarchies. He is therefore an easy object of laughter for an audience whose prevailing social norms celebrated heads and aristocrats. And Shakespeare indulges us in such amusement. When Bottom is transformed into an ass, the joke prompts laughter because it literalizes a condition we have already perceived in his narcissistic certainty that he can perform any theatrical role to perfection. The ass head appears by magic as an emblem of his asininity.

This Hobbesian framework for the scene of Bottom's transformation, however, is undermined by what actually transpires. With his ass head on his shoulders, his tendency to scratch, and his yearning for hay, Bottom is of course a laughably bestialized figure. Titania's worship of him, moreover, is a mere fantasy, the result of Oberon's potion. The situation as a whole seems likely to evoke the laughter of "sudden glory": we are invited to mock a fool from the perspective of the King of the Fairies. But the scene is built on a reversal of expectations. Instead of being mocked, Bottom's asininity is celebrated – or, more accurately and paradoxically, is both mocked and celebrated. His conviction that he can play any role is marvelously proved true: he masters his fear with a song, he responds to Titania's overtures with courtly wit, and he responds to the attentions of his courtiers – Peaseblossom, Cobweb, Moth, and Mustardseed – with unaffected nobility and grace. In reversing our expectations in such a way, Shakespeare plays upon the paradoxical symbolism inherent in the figure of the ass itself, for the animal is not only a simple and foolish beast but the one chosen to witness the Nativity and to bear Mary and Christ on their travels. In the image of Bottom at Titania's court, what seems to be simple mockery of a "hard-handed" man becomes a paradoxical epiphany of "otherness" to which the appropriate but unexpected response is a laughter of wonder. As Bottom himself observes upon awakening, his dream "hath no bottom" (4.1.216).

Laughing at the "other" in Shakespearean comedy, then, is more complicated than it might seem to be. The signs of "otherness," certainly, are present. Characters are mocked, sometimes savagely, for, among other things, their social rank, their ethnic status, their gender, and their national identity. And audiences become complicit in that laughter. The closer we examine such mockery, however, the more difficult it becomes to view it from a stable perspective. The victims of comic abuse are not driven out of society, as we might expect, but invited back in. At moments when they are most vulnerable, moreover, such fools and villains are depicted from the inside out, evoking in audiences a sudden jolt of empathy. Categories of "otherness" multiply and mix together. An apparently all-pervasive irony makes of "otherness" a fun house of mirrors, in which all the world may become a stage of fools. Our vantage point on "others" within a play may be dislocated by settings that make the entire world of the play "other" – either recognizably "foreign" or bizarrely exotic. Finally, in a move that more than any other deflects Hobbesian laughter, the very "otherness" of the "other" may evoke wonder rather than contempt.

To explore the reasons for this inability to pin down the category of "otherness" in Shakespeare's comedies would take us beyond the scope of this chapter. We might look for them, however, in a variety of places: in the equivocal nature of Shakespeare's own subject position in Elizabethan society, as actor, businessman, Stratford boy, Londoner; in the variety of social perspectives brought to bear by audiences of his plays, which could include apprentices, merchants, courtiers, men, women, merchants, crypto-Catholics, Londoners, country people, and aliens; and in the volatility of conceptions of identity in the period, which created ambiguity and tension around such notions as gender, social rank, and religious, civic, and national identity. Although hardly a comic utterance, King Lear's anguished cry "who is it who can tell me who I am?" (1.4.230) voices a question that spans the Elizabethan and Jacobean periods.

Whatever the ultimate reasons behind the instability of the notion of "otherness" in the comedies, it helps us to understand some ways in which Shakespearean comic form is distinctive. Let me highlight four such ways. First, Shakespearean comedy is not essentially a comedy of abuse; although abuse occurs, the satiric impulse behind it is generally relatively mild and deflected in the wide variety of ways we have already explored. Secondly, Shakespearean comedy is not essentially a comedy of stereotypes, or of stereotypical categories; although stereotyping occurs, by mixing categories and shifting perspectives Shakespeare achieves an illusion of psychological complexity that prevents stereotyped responses. Thirdly, although critics sometimes try to locate in individual characters, such as Theseus in *A Midsummer Night's Dream* or Rosalind in *As You Like It,* a normative point of view, Shakespearean comedy is not a comedy of a fixed perspective; irony, whether harsh or tolerant and benign, eventually undermines every position that we may desire to anchor ourselves upon. Fourthly, Shakespearean comedy is not a comedy that implies in human beings a stable psychological or social identity; in this respect, Jaques' "all the world's a stage" speaks for the comedies as a whole. To summarize these negative attributes more positively, we might conclude that Shakespearean comedy disorients, breaks down psychological and social boundaries, finds laughter in the very fluidity and mystery of human experience, and perpetually calls into question who is "self" and who is "other." Such laughter never allows us to rest for long in the Hobbesian feeling of "sudden glory" or to celebrate our "self" by excluding an "other." A more likely response to "otherness" in Shakespearean comedy is that of the long-gone American cartoon character, Pogo: "We have met the enemy, and he is us."

The quest for "otherness" in Shakespeare's comedies has thus brought us full circle, back to the initial distinction between carnivalesque laughter, which widens the net of social communion, and Hobbesian laughter, which narrows it. Such broad distinctions inevitably oversimplify, of course, and we have uncovered enough cruelty in Shakespearean laughter to call this one into question. As a whole, however, Shakespearean comedy includes many different kinds of laughter, and our focus on a narrow range of comic characters, those at the periphery of social norms, has accentuated the importance of the Hobbesian. If, as I have shown, the "otherness" even of such characters is itself unstable and insecure, then we may safely conclude that a pure laughter of social derision plays a limited role in Shakespearean comedy. In its widest sense, the word *carnivalesque* is not a bad one to describe a more inclusive and distinctively Shakespearean kind of laughter – a kind that temporarily breaks down social and psychological boundaries between privileged "selves" and excluded "others."

One reason for calling such laughter carnivalesque is that it erupts, like carnival merriment, as a disturbance in the normal routine of life; the term prevents sentimentality, therefore, by reminding us that less liberating kinds of laughter also exist. Most of the laughter in the comedies occurs during the period in the middle of the plays when normality is disrupted by the confusions of mistaken identity, amorous intrigue, and misadventures of various kinds. With the sense of reconciliation and renewal that usually marks the end of the comedies, comes as well a return to normal life. With this return, the plays look forward to the reconstruction of social norms and categories suspended or violated in the course of the action. Malvolio is invited into the charmed circle at the end of *Twelfth Night* not to become Olivia's husband but to resume his role as steward. Rosalind, in *As You Like It*, gives herself to her father and to Orlando so that she may dwindle into the role of a wife. Bottom the weaver, having achieved a triumphant death as Pyramus, will return to his loom. The carnival thus comes to an end, and, despite comic gestures toward social renewal, the resumption of the conventional social order puts people once more in their places. Social divisions and hierarchies are restored and, along with them, the prospects for Hobbesian laughter. Yet in audiences, and perhaps also among some characters on stage, the memory of carnival lingers, and with it a skepticism about the categorizing of social experience that divides "selves" from "others" in ways that are neither stable nor secure.

NOTES

1 See Mikhail Bakhtin, *Rabelais and his World*, trans. Hélène Iswolsky (Cambridge, Mass.: MIT Press, 1968).

2 Thomas Hobbes, "Tripos," in *English Works*, ed. William Molesworth (1840; reprinted. Aalen: Scientia, 1962), IV, 46.

3 Henri Bergson, *Laughter*, trans. Cloudesley Brereton and Fred Rothwell (London: Macmillan, 1911).

4 Citations to the plays refer to G. Blakemore Evans *et al.* (eds.), *The Riverside Shakespeare*, 2nd edn (Boston and New York: Houghton Mifflin Company, 1997).

5 Roger Ascham, *English Works*, ed. William Aldis Wright (Cambridge: Cambridge University Press, 1904), p. 229.

9

ALEXANDER LEGGATT

Comedy and sex

In the opening scene of *The Two Gentlemen of Verona* the title characters have an abstract, literary debate about love, introducing their ideas with the formula "writers say" (1.1.43, 46).[1] The principal lovers at the beginning of the play are Proteus and Julia, who communicate by letter and whom we never see together until Act 2 scene 2, when they are forced to part. Love seems a matter of words, disembodied and unfulfilled, all theory and no practice. In Act 2 scene 5, however, Launce, the play's principal clown, gives a different view of it. When his colleague Speed asks about Proteus and Julia, "how stands the matter with them?" Launce replies, "Marry, thus: when it stands well with him, it stands well with her" (19–21). In our era, sex has been as relentlessly theorized as any human activity. For Shakespeare's clowns it is a simple, practical matter. There is nothing to debate, though there may be something to illustrate: elsewhere in the scene Launce uses his staff as a comic prop; he could use it here.

Launce's name, a variant spelling of "lance," makes this sort of comedy appropriate to him. Moreover, he is accompanied in his major scenes by his dog Crab. It is not just that sex brings out the animal in humanity, though Shakespeare uses that idea elsewhere: Falstaff appears for his final encounter with the wives of Windsor as a stag at rutting-time, and in *Cymbeline* Posthumus imagines that Jachimo in bed with Imogen "Like a full-acorned boar ... / Cried 'O!' and mounted" (2.5.16–17). It is rather that Launce's dog, not a figurative animal but the real thing, on stage, is invariably the most unpredictable, distracting, and engaging of performers. Whatever is bothering the human characters, he has his own agenda. He will yawn, scratch, lie down, look up – and the actor playing Launce has to work with whatever he does, accepting the fact that no matter how skilled he is the dog can always upstage him. Launce's dog embodies the reductiveness of comedy, its tendency to deflate our pretensions by bringing us down to the low physical realities that demand our attention when we would rather be declaring love or expounding philosophy: the need to scratch, the need to urinate, the need for food and sex.

This reductiveness operates throughout the comedies. Exhorting his colleagues to love, Berowne in *Love's Labor's Lost* goes from the romanticism of "when Love speaks, the voice of all the gods / Make heaven drowsy with the harmony" to the Launce-like practicality of "Advance your standards, and upon them, lords; / Pell-mell, down with them!" (4.3.318–19, 341–42). Given the secondary meaning of "nothing" as "vagina,"[2] there is a similar reductiveness in the title of *Much Ado About Nothing*: for all the passion it unleashes, that is what the slandering of Hero is finally about. It is for a similar reason that the clown Lavatch in *All's Well That Ends Well* wants to get married: he asks the Countess's goodwill "In Isbel's case and mine own" (1.3.23), where "case" has the same secondary meaning as "nothing." Comedy's self-questioning uneasiness about its own procedures operates here:[3] Lavatch's joke is part of his persistent cynicism about sex, and far from taking his routines with a good grace the Countess finds them out of place and offensive, calling him "a foulmouthed and calumnious knave" (1.3.56–57). In *Measure for Measure* sex is for Claudio quite literally a matter of life and death; but for Pompey and Lucio it is groping for trouts in a peculiar river, putting a ducat in a beggar's dish, filling a bottle with a funnel (1.2.89; 3.2.123, 166). On the one hand this alerts us to the absurdity of Vienna's antifornication law: as Lucio complains, "Why, what a ruthless thing is this . . . for the rebellion of a codpiece to take away the life of a man!" (3.2.111–12). But this trivializing and impersonal view of sex takes a less amiable turn in Lucio's treatment of Kate Keepdown. Having got her pregnant he abandons her: if it was just the rebellion of a codpiece, why should he think about the consequences? The reductive jokes that simply amuse in the early plays acquire a darker edge in later ones, as part of a general development to which this chapter will return.

The leveling quality of sexual joking has a more positive function in *The Taming of the Shrew*. In the first meeting of Katherina and Petruchio, it is a game they both can play. He can taunt her, "Women are made to bear, and so are you," and she can taunt him right back: "No cock of mine. You crow too like a craven" (2.1.200, 227). Whatever actors may do, in the text he never hits her; but she hits him, when on "What, with my tongue in your tail?" (2.1.218) his joking goes too far. The jokes suggest a sexual chemistry between them; in this arena they meet on equal terms, and she can sometimes set the rules. One way in which Petruchio asserts his dominance is to preach "a sermon of continency" (4.1.171) on their wedding night, and it is not clear that within the action of the play their marriage is ever consummated. The way he deprives Katherina of food may suggest symbolically that it is not. We might have feared he would assert his mastery by forcing sex on her, and we may wonder if not having sex with Petruchio is really a deprivation.

But if sex is the great leveler, then arguably Petruchio sees in it a dangerous potential for equality, even an area in which Katherina could master him; and so he deprives her of it at least until her taming is complete.

Like the distracting presence of Launce's dog, sex is a comic threat to characters like Petruchio, who are playing for control. In *Love's Labor's Lost* the ladies of France mock and dominate their lovers, and finally put them off for a year. The men want consummation, the women can wait, and this puts the women in charge. But when the Princess glimpses the King on horseback and comments, " 'a showed a mounting mind" (4.1.4), she may be revealing not just the King's desires but her own; at least she is prepared to think about it. Beatrice in *Much Ado About Nothing* claims to despise Benedick, but when she calls him "Signor Mountanto" (1.1.29) the reference is to an upward blow in fencing, and the more they protest their indifference to each other the more these antilovers seem to be dwelling on the act they claim not to want: Benedick will not "hang [his] bugle in an invisible baldrick," Beatrice does not want Benedick putting her down (1.1.231, 2.1.269–71). In *A Midsummer Night's Dream* Quince and his acting company are concerned that their play should be as decorous and inoffensive as possible, and when Quince calls Bottom "a very paramour for a sweet voice" Flute is quick to correct him: "You must say 'paragon.' A paramour is, God bless us, a thing of naught" (4.2.11–14). Keeping their language clean, however, is a losing battle: Pyramus and Thisbe demand to see the wall's chink, they speak of kissing its hole and its stones, and Pyramus complains the lion has deflowered Thisbe (5.1.176, 189–90, 200, 288). Like the dog yawning and scratching when some necessary question of the play is to be considered, the actors' inadvertently sexual language keeps breaking the decorum they are at such pains to establish.

Here we touch on one of the paradoxes of Shakespearean comedy. The physical reality that betrays the pretensions of language is itself a matter of language: sex is embodied in words. In *Love's Labor's Lost* Costard and Maria describe a passage of sexual banter as though fitting speeches together were itself a kind of copulation: "By my troth, most pleasant. How both did fit it!" "A mark marvellous well shot, for they both did hit it!" (4.1.129–30). Or, as Stephen Greenblatt puts it, "Dallying with words is the principal Shakespearean representation of erotic heat."[4] Some of the bawdry comes in scenes that are quite self-consciously about language. William's Latin quiz in *The Merry Wives of Windsor* is typical: thanks to Sir Hugh Evans' Welsh accent and Mistress Quickly's alert mishearings, the textbook dryness of the lesson is enlivened by the spoken equivalent of graffiti in the margins: "focative case," "*Genitivo – horum, harum, horum*" (4.1.46–63). Part of the fun is that the more Quickly objects to the lesson's impropriety, the more improper she makes it. Learning a language is no more an innocent activity here than it is in *Henry V*, where the French princess anticipates the English conquest by learning English words for the parts of her own body, ending with puns on "foutre" and "con" that (like Quickly) she finds shocking and cannot resist repeating (3.4).

Writing, printing, and reading all have erotic overtones. In *The Merchant of Venice*, when Nerissa threatens to sleep with the lawyer's clerk, Gratiano declares he will "mar the young clerk's pen" (5.1.237). Receiving duplicate love letters from Falstaff, the Windsor wives object to being put in the press (*Merry Wives*, 2.1.73–75). Beatrice is chagrined, Leonato reports, at finding in her own writing " 'Benedick' and 'Beatrice' between the sheet" (*Much Ado*, 2.3.141–42). Malvolio's examination of what he thinks is Olivia's handwriting gets quite intimate: "These be her very c's, her u's, and her t's; and thus makes she her great P's." Sir Andrew's innocent question, "Her c's, her u's, and her t's. Why that?" (*Twelfth Night*, 2.5.85–88), helps the audience spell out the pun (Williams, *Glossary*, pp. 87–88).

The spoken no less than the written word has its own erotic power. In *All's Well That Ends Well* it is an encounter with Parolles, whose very name means "words," that snaps Helena out of her initial mood of reticence and despair and into a determination to win Bertram against all odds. Parolles changes her mood by talking wittily against virginity. As she banters with him Helena goes from "Man is enemy to virginity; how may we barricado it against him?" to "How might one do, sir, to lose it to her own liking?" (1.1.114–15, 151–52). The erotic power of language takes a darker turn in *Measure for Measure*, where the eloquence of Isabella's rhetoric breeds Angelo's desire for her, and he catches the process in a pun: "She speaks, and 'tis such sense / That my sense breeds with it" (2.2.147–48). In William's Latin lesson the sex is all harmless talk; but we hear that in the background story of *The Tempest* Miranda taught Caliban language, and he tried to rape her. What Prospero sees as an assault on her honor Caliban attributes to his breeding instinct (1.2.350–54); but could this also be an instance of the dangerous erotic power of words?

Given this link between language and sex, there is more than just a word game in Feste's wish that his sister had no name. Agreeing with Viola that it is easy to dally with words and make them wanton, he adds, "her name's a word, and to dally with that word might make my sister wanton" (3.1.19–20). In *Much Ado About Nothing* it is in words, and words alone, that Hero is made wanton. Don Pedro and Claudio seem disposed to believe Don John's accusation even before they see anything; and the speeches of Claudio and his fellow men are for a while enough to break Leonato's faith in his daughter. Kenneth Branagh's 1993 film lets the characters and the audience see Margaret and Borachio copulating at a window. In the play the audience sees nothing; the trick is done with words. Even in the reported encounter, what Margaret and Borachio are doing at the window is not making the beast with two backs but talking (4.1.83–91). Throughout the play Margaret jokes about sex: with Hero and Beatrice on Hero's wedding morning (3.4.23–35, 60), with Benedick as the finale approaches (5.2.6–22). Don John's plot casts her, in a kind of bed trick, as a sexually active version of Hero; but we never see her in that role, and Borachio insists on her innocence (5.1.296–98). If there is a true parallel between her and Hero it is because she is sexually active in words alone (her own words in this instance) and when Benedick offers to write her a sonnet "In so high a style ... that no man shall come over it" there is a touch of frustration in her punning retort, "To have no man come over me! Why, shall I always keep below stairs?" (5.2.6–10).

Jaquenetta in *Love's Labor's Lost* seems to be the converse of Margaret. She says very little, but at the end of the play she is pregnant. She embodies the leveling power of sex: as Costard says of her, "This maid will serve my turn, sir" (1.1.290), so Berowne calls Rosaline "one that will do the deed / Though Argus were her eunuch and her guard" (3.1.196–97). What one man hopes for the other complains of; but the women, different in every other respect, are by this account sisters under the skin. As Margaret is the unwitting instrument in the slandering of Hero, Jaquenetta is involved in the exposure of Berowne. In another link between the women, Costard mistakenly gives Rosaline the letter Armado wrote to Jaquenetta; and Jaquenetta gets Berowne's letter to Rosaline, which she hands over to the King. This accidental misdirection may be the inspiration for the Princess' trick of deliberately changing tokens so that the men woo the wrong women. It is an ironic demonstration of the impersonality of sex, of the principle that in the dark all cats are grey.

As Prospero's sudden thought of Caliban breaks up his wedding show for the lovers, the news of Jaquenetta's pregnancy shatters not only Armado's impersonation of Hector but the whole show of the Nine Worthies. It is hard to stand on one's classical, heroic dignity when faced with a paternity suit involving a dairymaid. Jaquenetta seems to embody by her mere presence the leveling, impersonal, and disruptive power of sex. But again we need to notice the importance of words. Berowne is exposed not when he is caught in a compromising position but when Jaquenetta shows the King his letter. Moreover, it is Costard who says Jaquenetta will serve his turn; it is Costard who claims she is pregnant by Armado. Our evidence, such as it is (she is not even on stage at this point) is not her belly but his talk. If Margaret talks persistently about sex, Jaquenetta inspires sex talk in others; but it is still talk.

Two of the most striking female presences in the early comedies are in fact not present at all: it is talk that creates the kitchen wench in *The Comedy of Errors* and the milkmaid Launce thinks of marrying in *The Two Gentlemen of Verona*. In both cases the talk is bawdy: Dromio, turning the wench into an image of the world itself, declares, "I could find out countries in her," though when asked about The Netherlands he replies, "I did not look so low" (3.2.5–6, 138). All fire and fat, she embodies the male fear of female sexuality that the Courtesan also inspires: "light wenches will burn" (4.3.54–55). This fear returns, with the safety check of comedy removed, in Lear's disgust at the centaur-woman with the sulphurous pit beneath her waist. There is gentler, more rueful comedy in Launce's account of his milkmaid. Her physicality is more domestic and comforting: she milks, brews, washes, and spins. But while Launce claims she will not be liberal of her tongue or her purse, "of another thing she may, and that cannot I help" (3.1.344–45). He seems prepared to accept her misdemeanors even more philosophically than he accepts Crab's. *The Comedy of Errors* hinges on comic fear, *The Two Gentlemen of Verona* on the comedy of forgiveness, the tolerance of offense. In each case an offstage wench, created by the sexually alert language of the man who describes her, captures the spirit of the play.

Yet Shakespeare's theatre was not a theatre of words alone. In the stage action there is sometimes a displaced sexuality. When in *The Comedy of Errors* Antipholus and Dromio of Ephesus try unsuccessfully to break into their own house, are they just breaking into a house? Dromio's line, "Shall I set in my staff?" (3.1.51) suggests not. There the words help the *double entendre*, as they do when Malvolio breaks open Olivia's letter and notes that it is sealed with the figure of Lucrece.[5] But we may not need words when Portia's suitors insert keys into caskets in order to open them, or when Portia and Nerissa slide rings on to their husbands' fingers. The joke about Benedick and Beatrice between the sheets is acted out on stage by Julia in *The Two Gentlemen of Verona*: reassembling the fragments of a torn letter, she finds her name and that of Proteus and folds them together: "Now kiss, embrace, contend, do what you will" (1.2.130). Watching Orlando throw down Charles the Wrestler gives Rosalind ideas: "Sir, you have wrestled well and overthrown / More than your enemies" (1.2.244–45). This invites us to think back on the wrestling match, one man pinning another to the gound, and rewrite it in imagination as a same-sex encounter anticipating the same-sex love scenes in Arden. There is in all such cases a kind of visual *double entendre*, often but not always helped by the *double entendre* of language.

As Hero suffers from the power of words, Imogen in *Cymbeline* suffers from the materializing of sex in visual language. Jachimo equates taking her

honor with taking Posthumus' ring; either theft would be easy (1.4.91–94).
Entering her room while she sleeps, he takes a bracelet from her arm, and
his language as he does so is erotically charged: "As slippery as the Gordian
knot was hard!" (2.2.34). At the sight of the bracelet, which Jachimo, teasing
Posthumus, suddenly displays and just as suddenly hides again (2.4.97–98),
Posthumus' faith crumbles. Jachimo has in fact done nothing: but his entry
into Imogen's room, emerging from a trunk like a rising serpent, and his
prowling about the bed noting the marks on her body, have a disconcerting
erotic power that can make the audience almost as ready as Posthumus to
credit his lies. He has done nothing, but in the *double entendre* of the stage
action it feels as though he has entered her body by entering her space,
possessing her as he possesses her bracelet.

Double meanings are the stock in trade of comedy when it deals with sex.
Is the needle in *Gammer Gurton's Needle* really just a needle? Is the china
scene in *The Country Wife* really about china? And what are we to think of
the oral fixation on muffins and cucumber sandwiches in *The Importance
of Being Earnest*? Alerted by the double meanings of language and stage
pictures, we are prepared to see in a more general way the sexual dimension
of activities that are not overtly sexual. In *Love's Labor's Lost* Sir Nathaniel
innocently compliments Holofernes on his role as a teacher: "their sons are
well tutored by you, and their daughters profit very greatly under you," to
which Holofernes replies, "if their daughters be capable, I will put it to them"
(4.2.73–78). This is the erotic dimension of the teacher–pupil relationship,
which has led to scandal after scandal in the real world. In *All's Well That
Ends Well* the doctor–patient relationship is eroticized (another scandal in
reality) when Lafew leaves Helena with the King: "I am Cressid's uncle, /
That dare leave two together" (2.1.99–100). Is there a touch of Angelo's pun
on "sense" when Helena argues the King into letting her attempt the cure,
and he replies, "what impossibility would slay / In common sense, sense
saves another way" (2.1.179–80)?

Arrested for his role in the sex trade, Pompey in *Measure for Measure*
complains, "'Twas never merry world since, of two usuries, the merriest was
put down" (3.2.6–7). Money is bred illegitimately in the counting-house as
children are bred illegitimately in the brothel. In comedies by Shakespeare's
Jacobean contemporaries, the link is made by a recurring plot device in which
a usurer is tricked into marrying a prostitute. Moneylending is eroticized in
The Merchant of Venice: Shylock, having equated his breeding of money
with the breeding of sheep (1.3.76–94), names as the penalty in his bond
with Antonio, "an equal pound / Of your fair flesh" (1.3.148–49). He goes
on to deny that Antonio's flesh has any commercial value, and insists the bond
is just a joke: but the unnecessary, disconcerting adjective "fair" makes the

claim sound erotic, and when he is robbed of his jewels and the Venetians mock him for losing his "stones" (2.8.20–24), it sounds as though they are verbally disabling him as a sexual threat.

In *Measure for Measure* sex is bound up with the workings of the law. When the executioner Abhorson objects to having Pompey as his assistant, the Provost retorts, "Go to, sir, you weigh equally; a feather will turn the scale" (4.2.30–31). Pompey, who feels quite at home in prison, settles into his new job with puns on "turn" that apply equally to sex and hanging (4.2.56–59). As Lear imagines the beadle lusting for the whore he whips, *Measure for Measure* sees a perverse sexuality in the law that regulates sex. Angelo's attempt to blackmail Isabella is the most obvious example, but even the well-meaning Escalus, setting out to question Isabella, declares "You shall see how I'll handle her," giving Lucio an opportunity he cannot resist: "Marry, I think, if you handled her privately, she would sooner confess; perchance publicly she'll be ashamed" (5.1.280–86). Male authority and female subjection in public life are reflected in the power relations of sex. While Claudio and Juliet made love "Mutually" (2.3.28), Angelo demands that Isabella "lay down the treasures of your body" and "Fit thy consent to my sharp appetite" (2.4.96, 162). Arguably, the Duke frustrates Angelo's design only to enact a similar design of his own. In his disguise as a friar, he seems needlessly defensive about being left alone with Isabella: "My mind promises with my habit no loss shall touch her by my company" (3.1.179–80). When he proposes marriage his offer, however surprising, is legal and proper; but in the same way that Angelo has said, I'll save your brother if you go to bed with me, the Duke says, in effect, I saved your brother, now go to bed with me.

As there is a doubling between sex and other activities like teaching, moneylending, and law enforcement; so there is a doubling within sexual activity itself. In the bed tricks that occur throughout comedy one kind of sexual relationship pretends to be another: thus, in Colley Cibber's late Restoration comedy *Love's Last Shift* the heroine wins back her wayward husband by pretending to be an attractive courtesan and tricking him into committing adultery with her. In Ben Jonson's *The New Inn* the tailor Snuffe and his wife pretend to be a countess and a footman running off for a weekend together. There is a hint of married adultery at the end of *The Merry Wives of Windsor* when Ford tells Falstaff, "To Master Brook you yet shall keep your word, / For he tonight shall lie with Mistress Ford" (5.5.238–39). He will make love to his wife, not as her husband but as the adulterous lover he pretended to be. Behind the joke may be a hint that this game of make-believe will revive their relationship, as it does in *Love's Last Shift*.

In *All's Well That Ends Well* Bertram sleeps with his wife Helena, thinking she is the Florentine maid Diana. He unwittingly consummates the marriage he has refused to consummate, and the effect is more complicated than
Ford's throwaway joke. Parolles, to whom Bertram gives the unpleasant task
of telling Helena her wedding night has been postponed, claims the delay
will merely "make the coming hour o'erflow with joy / And pleasure drown
the brim" (2.4.46–47). Given Bertram's real coldness to Helena, the words
ring particularly hollow. Helena describes the actual consummation more
ambiguously as "wicked meaning in a lawful deed, / And lawful meaning
in a wicked act" (3.7.45–46). It is not just that the whiff of adultery makes
the act seem socially disreputable, as Diana's mother the Widow suspects
(3.7.4–7). We hear enough of the crassness of Bertram's sexual feeling, cutting across the fancy language of seduction, to sense that Helena will encounter not a great lover but a randy young man who is merely satisfying an
urge: "give thyself unto my sick desires, / Who then recovers" (4.2.35–36).
He later describes the encounter as just one of "sixteen businesses" (4.3.84)
he has despatched in a busy night.

Helena's feelings are more complicated: "But O, strange men! / That can
such sweet use make of what they hate" (4.4.21–22). The hate may be the
hate he has expressed for her personally; or she may have detected the misog-
yny that lies behind his attitude to Diana as someone to take and forget;
or both. That was the contemptuous kind of "love" he made; yet she can
still describe his use of her as "sweet," and she later tells him, "when I
was like this maid, / I found you wondrous kind" (5.3.310–11). There was
something for her, something she values, even in an act to which he himself was ultimately indifferent. At the most practical level, she is now pregnant, and according to the medical theory of the time this means she must
have had an orgasm.[6] Perhaps the sheer impersonality of sex means that
as there can be less in it than one hopes for, there can also be more. It escapes the control and the intentions of the people who indulge in it, and
Helena has taken more pleasure from it than Bertram had any thought of
giving.

Yet Diana, his intended target, is so put off by Bertram that she vows to
stay single and have nothing to do with men (4.2.73–74). Her own view of
married sex is that her mother "did but duty" (4.2.12). In *Measure for Measure* Mariana takes the equivalent of Helena's role, substituting for Isabella
in Angelo's bed. Nothing is said of her sexual feelings or her possible pregnancy: the encounter simply leaves her as "nothing . . . neither maid, widow,
nor wife" (Lucio helpfully suggests she may be a punk) (5.1.183–86) until
she is rescued from this limbo by marriage. While there may be something
positive in Helena's ambiguous encounter with Bertram, it leaves Diana with

bleak feelings about sex, and Mariana's similar encounter leaves her, for a while at least, with a blank identity.

The substitutions that give a double meaning to sexuality take a darker turn in *Cymbeline*. Against her own intentions, Imogen rouses men's desires by putting them off. That is the effect she has on Cloten and Jachimo. Even her husband Posthumus recalls that she restrained his "lawful pleasure" with "A pudency so rosy the sweet view on't / Might well have warmed old Saturn" (2.5.9–12). While Helena finds unexpected pleasure in Bertram's callow lovemaking, Imogen sees in Posthumus, the man she loves and has married, something she needs to resist; and the two other men who attempt her, Jachimo and Cloten, are in different ways images of Posthumus.

When Jachimo enters her bedchamber it was Posthumus, by accepting the wager, who sent him there; Jachimo is trying Imogen's chastity on her husband's behalf. His entry into her chamber is like a bad dream entering her sleeping imagination: she has been reading the story of Tereus' rape of Philomel, the tale that haunts *Titus Andronicus*, and as she reaches the point "Where Philomel gave up" (2.2.46) she falls asleep and Jachimo emerges from the trunk. Prowling the room, he compares himself to Tarquin (2.2.12–14). It is as though sleep has released a sexual fear made all the stronger by her waking restraint. Something like this happens in *A Midsummer Night's Dream*. All through the play sexuality is restrained: Theseus waits impatiently for his wedding night, but he waits; Helena brushes aside Demetrius' threats of rape by appealing to his virtue; and Hermia insists that Lysander lie a proper distance away from her. When Hermia has a nightmare of a serpent crawling on her breast and eating out her heart, is she paying the price for all this restraint? While this is a literal dream, Jachimo's invasion of Imogen's bedchamber is a symbolic one; but is it too the product of restraint? And if so, does it rebuke that restraint or justify it? Jachimo by one possible reading represents the violence of male desire which Imogen has been fighting off, rightly, even in her husband.

While Jachimo is lyrically sinister, Cloten is crude: "I am advised to give her music o'mornings; they say it will penetrate." He tells the musicians, "If you can penetrate her with your fingering, so; we'll try with tongue too" (2.3.11–15). Jachimo studies her body, voyeuristically, keeping a few inches away from it; Cloten imagines handling and probing it. Jachimo's role as a Posthumus substitute is oblique. Cloten's is alarmingly direct: he plans to rape Imogen while wearing her husband's clothes. Guiderius kills and beheads him before he gets anywhere near carrying out his plan. Yet he lies with Imogen after all: in what may be Shakespeare's most grotesque bed trick, she awakes from a drugged stupor into a nightmare, lying beside a headless man who is wearing her husband's clothes, and whom she takes to be Posthumus himself. She surveys his body and finds it to be her husband's body – his hand, his foot, his thigh, his muscles (4.2.312–14). Only the head is missing. Going not just by the clothes but by the body, she cannot tell her husband from the hateful buffoon who wanted to rape her, any more than Bertram can tell the wife he hated from the girl he wanted to seduce. This time the doubleness created by the plotting conveys a darker view of married sex than we get in Helena's ambiguous encounter with Bertram, and a much darker view than Ford's casual joke. And this time the bed tricks are not offstage, to be created for us by words; we see Imogen in bed, with Jachimo hovering over her, and we see her lying with Cloten.

In *Cymbeline* the ordeal of experiencing through plot equivocation the dark side of sex is the heroine's; in *Pericles* it is the hero's. At the start of the play Pericles comes to Antioch, as Bassanio comes to Belmont, to win a bride by solving a riddle. His desire "To taste the fruit of yon celestial tree / Or die in the adventure" (1.1.22–23) suggests he is coming to Antiochus' daughter as to the fruit of Eden; this will be his initiation into knowledge. Or into death: the beautiful princess appears surrounded by the severed heads of previous suitors who have failed the test, and her father calls her "golden fruit, but dangerous to be touched" (1.1.29). The riddle he has to solve is a sinister *double entendre*: "I am no viper, yet I feed / On mother's flesh which did me breed" (1.1.65–66). The bride he hopes to win is committing incest with her father. Realizing the truth, Pericles recoils in words that make the scene an ironic rewriting of Bassanio's winning of Portia: "Fair glass of light, I loved you, and could still, / Were not this glorious casket stored with ill" (1.1.77–78).

The archetypal quality of the scene suggests a rejection not just of this one woman, but through her (and with a pun on "gate" as "vagina") of sexual experience itself: "For he's no man on whom perfections wait / That, knowing sin within, will touch the gate" (1.1.80–81). Even back home in Tyre, Pericles finds "Here pleasures court mine eyes, and mine eyes shun them" (1.2.6) and he flees compulsively across the Mediterranean as though afraid that Antiochus and what he represents could pursue him any-where. At Pentapolis he finds his true bride in Thaisa, whose cheerfully frank desire for him purifies the cannibalistic language of the Antioch rid-dle: "All viands that I eat do seem unsavoury, / Wishing him my meat" (2.3.33–34). Yet though he loves Thaisa in return he is still afraid, partic-ularly of her father Simonides, and he refuses to admit his feelings until father and daughter force them out of him. The father–daughter configu-ration, and the fact that other knights have come to woo Thaisa, make Pentapolis at once a purified version of Antioch and a place touched by its shadow.

This fear, dispelled by Pericles' marriage to Thaisa, returns when she apparently dies in childbirth in a storm at sea, and he yields too quickly to the sailors' demands that her body be tossed overboard to rid the ship of impurity and calm the storm. According to Cerimon, who finds Thaisa and restores her to life, "They were too rough / That threw her in the sea" (3.2.81–82). The family is sundered, it seems, by the arbitrary plotting of romance; but the plotting carries the suggestion that they are somehow afraid of each other. Thaisa assumes she will never see her husband again, and retreats to Diana's temple as a vestal (3.4.7–10). Far from cherishing the newborn Marina as a memory of her mother, Pericles leaves her to be raised at Tarsus and vows never to cut his hair or shave his beard until her wedding day. It is as though, with Antioch still in his memory, he is afraid of his relationship with her, keeps away from her, and puts himself through a symbolic ordeal until she is married and out of his reach.

Even when, not knowing his identity, Marina comes to rescue Pericles from the catatonic state of mourning into which he has retreated on the false news of her death, his first reaction to her is to cry "Hum, ha!" and push her away. Her response, "if you did know my parentage, / You would not do me violence" (5.1.86, 102–03), suggests that once again he has been too rough. When the truth comes out in what may be the most stunning of Shakespeare's reunion scenes, he calls her "Thou that begett'st him that did thee beget" (5.1.200), and the riddling language seems at once to recall and to purify the riddle of Antioch. The reunion is complete when Pericles and Marina find Thaisa in Diana's temple at Ephesus. Thaisa, so frank about her feelings when she first saw Pericles, is initially wary: "If he be none of mine, my sanctity / Will to my sense bend no licentious ear" (5.3.30–31). But he is hers, and the inhibitions fall away. This time Pericles has found Thaisa not in her father's court but in Diana's temple, and the shadow of Antioch is finally lifted.

Marina, on the other hand, finds her husband in a brothel, where she has come having been kidnapped by pirates, and where he has come to do business. Her employers expect great things of her, and advertise her accordingly: "Bolt, take you the marks of her, the colour of her hair, complexion, height, her age, with warrant of her virginity, and cry, 'He that will give most shall have her first.' Such a maidenhead were no cheap thing, if men were as they have been" (4.2.55–59). In this market virginity raises a girl's value, as it does in the other market of marriage. Marina preserves that virginity, preaching virtue to the customers, sending them off to hear the vestals sing, and reducing her employers to comic frustration. She particularly impresses the governor Lysimachus, who comes in a wonderfully ineffective disguise – "Here comes the lord Lysimachus disguised" (4.6.15–16) – and with a breezy entrance line: "How now? How a dozen of virginities?" (4.6.19). After some talk with Marina, however, he pays for her virginity in a way her employers never intended, giving her gold for *not* having sex with him, and leaves protesting not that he is now disgusted with the brothel and cured of his corruption, but that he was never corrupt and the place has always revolted him (4.6.105–12). Then why did he come at all? The contradiction, like the disguise that implies shame and fools no one but himself, suggests his own contradictory feelings about sex, feelings he resolves only when he meets Marina.

This is the man she marries. As Imogen's husband doubles with a would-be seducer and a would-be rapist and Bertram is both a husband consummating his marriage and a careless adulterer, so behind the Pericles family story lies the fear of incest, and Marina, her virginity on display, wins a husband who comes to her as to a prostitute, the sex trade shadowing the marriage market as Antioch shadows Pentapolis. There may be a similar doubling in *The Tempest* in Miranda's marriage to Ferdinand. Prospero is at once delighted with his future son-in-law and deeply suspicious of him. When it becomes clear that Ferdinand is smitten with Miranda, Prospero casts a spell that makes him symbolically unable to use his sword, then imprisons him. Even after the young man has passed the test, Prospero lectures him obsessively about not anticipating the wedding night. Behind all this lies Prospero's memory of Caliban's attempt to rape Miranda. Giving Ferdinand Caliban's old job of piling logs, Prospero seems to be testing the Caliban in him. The result is characteristically double: the lover and the would-be rapist seem as opposite as they could be, yet we begin to think of them together and to see behind the one the shadow of the other. The show Prospero creates for the lovers to celebrate their betrothal imagines fertility without sex, in a wedding to which Venus and Cupid are conspicuously not invited. And it is the thought of Caliban that breaks up the show: on the surface, Prospero is reacting to Caliban's political rebellion; but beneath this may be the memory of Caliban's attack on Miranda, a memory as hard to dispel as Pericles' memory of Antioch.

This doubling of one character with a darker one, one act with a darker one, links back to the comic *double entendres*, verbal and visual, of earlier and less troubled plays. If we joke about sex, it is because we joke about things that make us uneasy. Some of the threats are everyday: the brothel scenes of *Measure for Measure* and *Pericles* are full of pox jokes that function like the government health warning on a packet of cigarettes: "The poor Transylvanian is dead that lay with the little baggage ... Ay, she quickly pooped him. She made him roast meat for worms" (*Pericles* 4.2.22–25). Sex is fatal in other ways. The sex–death connection, captured in the pun on death as orgasm, can be romantic, as it is for Antipholus of Syracuse when he calls Luciana a siren luring him to his fate – "He gains by death that hath such means to die" (3.2.51) – or for Claudio when he declares, "I will encounter darkness as a bride / And hug it in mine arms" (3.1.84–85). But *Measure for Measure* equates sex and death in a grimmer way in the law that applies the death penalty to fornication, and in his first scene Claudio describes sex as eating rat poison (1.2.128–30). In *All's Well That Ends Well* sex is equated with death for both Bertram and Helena. Lavatch says of the danger Bertram faces in war: "The danger is in standing to't; that's the loss of men, though it be the getting of children" (3.2.41–42); and in the plotting Helena's encounter with Bertram in bed is juxtaposed with the false news of her death. They do, as Lavatch predicts, get a child; but only after going together into a symbolic death. After death, the judgment: as Lear sees the sulphurous pit in the female body, Mistress Ford thinks of sex with Falstaff as going "to hell for an eternal moment or so" (2.1.46–47). The wives plan to tease his desire "till the wicked fire of lust have melted him in his own grease" (2.1.64–65). It is a return to the comic–apocalyptic fear of the female body in *The Comedy of Errors*, with the sexes reversed. More seriously, in *Measure for Measure* the body that disgusts Angelo is not Isabella's but his own: he imagines himself lying by her like "carrion" by "the violet in the sun" (2.2.172–173), an image that will be dramatized when Imogen wakes beside the dead Cloten.

It may sound as though the cheerfulness about sex embodied in Launce's "stand well" joke turned, as Shakespeare explored the subject more deeply in his middle and later plays, into unease, even horror, as the mask of comedy came off and the fear that lies behind laughter emerged. Critics of a biographical turn used to speculate that something happened to Shakespeare in mid-career that darkened his view of sex. Anthony Burgess' novel *Nothing Like the Sun* (1964) imagines him catching syphilis. But in fact the doubleness – this time the doubleness in the plays' attitude to sex, the light as well as the dark – persists. In *The Tempest* the threat of Caliban is countered not just by Ferdinand's vows of premarital chastity but by the frank delight he and Miranda take in each other. However admirable Marina's chastity may be, there is something ludicrous in the instant reformations she produces. And in *The Winter's Tale* the darkness is exorcised. The opening scenes are unpromising: Polixenes declares that the childhood innocence of his early life with Leontes ended when they met their future wives, and Hermione warns him, "Of this make no conclusion, lest you say / Your queen and I are devils" (1.2.82). To enter puberty is not to mature into fulfillment but to fall into sin. Leontes' sudden jealousy triggers a queasiness about sex, including a pornographic close-up of the act itself: "It will let in and out the enemy / With bag and baggage" (1.2.205–06). His fantasies color everything: Camillo's innocent use of the word *satisfy* sends him into a fury (1.1.231–33). It is all summed up in the words with which his jealousy first strikes, words which echo Dromio on the kitchen wench and the Windsor wives on Falstaff: "Too hot, too hot!" (1.2.108).

When the old shepherd finds the infant Perdita abandoned in Bohemia, his suspicions are the same as those of Leontes, but his attitude turns the play around: "There has been some stair-work, some trunk-work, some behind-door-work. They were warmer that got this than the poor thing is here. I'll take it up for pity" (3.3.72–74). Disgust and anger are succeeded by comic tolerance, and he takes up the child Leontes abandoned to death. Sex means not death but new life, and life is worth preserving. The sexual body is no longer too hot, merely warm. Autolycus sings merrily of spring, summer, and tumbling in the hay (4.3.1–12), and one of his ballads warns of the fate of a woman who "was turned into a cold fish for she would not exchange flesh with one that loved her" (4.4.278–80). Leontes sees guilt in innocence; the shepherd's servant misreads Autolycus' ballads in the opposite direction, calling them "so without bawdry, which is strange, with such delicate burdens of dildos and fadings, 'Jump her and thump her'" (4.4.193–95). The sexual comedy of the ballads is linked with the frank sexuality of Perdita's feelings for Florizel. She imagines him covered in flowers,

> like a bank for Love to lie and play on,
> Not like a corpse; or if, not to be buried,
> But quick and in mine arms.
>
> (4.4.130–32)

Thomas Bowdler's *Family Shakespeare*, expurgating the play for decent nineteenth-century readers, paid tribute to this passage by cutting it.[7] Sex for Perdita is not death but life, not enemy action with bag and baggage but play. The Bohemia scenes not only turn the story around; they dispel its uneasiness about sex, so that Leontes can greet the restored Hermione with words that rescind the "too hot, too hot!" of his early jealousy: "O, she's warm" (5.3.109).

Yet the final scene of *The Winter's Tale* is not just a simple celebration of the body. Hermione begins the scene as a statue, a work of art. Autolycus the ballad singer is a master of disguise, and Ferdinand and Perdita are dressed up respectively as a shepherd and the queen of the feast. As in the early plays sex is talk, in *The Winter's Tale* it goes from the dark illusions of Leontes' fantasy through the dressing-up of comic disguise and festivity to the benevolent illusions of art. It is still make-believe. And this reminds us of a pervasive *double entendre* in the theatrical occasion itself. The Antonio of

The Merchant of Venice loves Bassanio, and the Antonio of *Twelfth Night* loves Sebastian. Disguise gives a homoerotic dimension to the love scenes played by Orlando and Ganymed, Olivia and Cesario. But for the most part the sexual relationships of Shakespeare's comedies are heterosexual; and there are no women on stage. When the heroines go into disguise the dialogue is full of jokes that remind us of the boy beneath the woman: Viola's "A little thing would make me tell them how much I lack of a man" (3.4.302–3), Portia's "They shall think we are accomplishèd / With that we lack" (3.4.61–62). There are no sexual acts on stage, only words and pictures; and it is words and pictures that turn boys into women (and sometimes back again), calling on the audience's willingness to accept a theatrical *double entendre* and take a boy for a girl. Sex in the theatre is talk, play, illusion. Christopher Sly, transformed to a lord, is offered anything he wants; but when he demands to go to bed with his boy-wife, he finds there is something he cannot have.

In *Love's Labor's Lost* Boyet and Rosaline talk themselves through a sex game, full of lines like "she herself is hit lower. Have I hit her now?" (4.1.118). To the last question Rosaline replies, in effect, no: "Thou canst not hit it, hit it, hit it, / Thou canst not hit it, my good man" (4.1.125–26). It is all talk, and can never be anything but talk. But the moralizing opponents of theatre in Shakespeare's time did not leave it at that. They noted the prostitutes in the auditorium, the brothels in the neighborhood; they speculated darkly about what went on between the men and boys in the tiring-house; they told stories of women tempted into sex by what they saw in the playhouse.[8] To Rosaline's rebuff Boyet replies, "An I cannot, cannot, cannot, / An I cannot, another can" (4.1.127–28).

In *As You Like It*, through disguise and talk Rosalind plays a sex game with Orlando in the Forest of Arden, which functions like the stage itself as a place where sexual relations can be dramatized in the form of play without the commitment (or the danger) of reality. But Orlando tires of the game and Rosalind promises, "I will weary you then no longer with idle talking" (5.2.50–51). They remain characters in a play, their relationship in that sense forever unconsummated like that of the lovers on Keats' Grecian urn. Rosalind in the Epilogue promises she would kiss the men in the audience *if* she were a woman – which she is not. Whatever the actors do when the play is over is their business; but Rosalind, punning and mischievous to the last, gives the audience, who have spent an afternoon with comic illusions and comic talk that dance around the reality of sex, an agenda for the evening: "I charge you, O men, for the love you bear to women – as I perceive by your simpering, none of you hates them – that between you and the women the play may please" (Epilogue, 13–16; on "play" see Williams,

Glossary, p. 238). Feste ends *Twelfth Night* by declaring "our play is done" (5.1.407); in the *double entendre* of Rosalind's challenge to the audience, it is about to begin.

NOTES

1 All references to Shakespeare are to David Bevington (ed.), *The Complete Works of Shakespeare* (New York: HarperCollins, 1992).
2 Gordon Williams, *A Glossary of Shakespeare's Sexual Language* (London and Atlantic Highlands, N.J.: Athlone Press, 1997), p. 219.
3 On comedy's tendency to question itself, see Alexander Leggatt, *English Stage Comedy 1490–1990: Five Centuries of a Genre* (London: Routledge, 1998), pp. 136–57.
4 Stephen Greenblatt, *Shakespearean Negotiations: the Circulation of Social Energy in Renaissance England* (Berkeley and Los Angeles: University of California Press, 1988), p. 90.
5 David Willbern, "Pushing the Envelope: Supersonic Criticism," in Russ McDonald (ed.), *Shakespeare Reread: the Texts in New Contexts* (Ithaca and London: Cornell University Press, 1994), p. 185.
6 See Kate Aughterson (ed.), *Renaissance Woman: Constructions of Femininity in England* (London and New York: Routledge, 1995), pp. 57–58.
7 Donald Hedrick, "Flower Power: Shakespearean Deep Bawdy and the Botanical Perverse," in Richard Burt (ed.), *The Administration of Aesthetics* (Minneapolis and London: University of Minnesota Press, 1994), p. 96.
8 Ibid., p. 88; and Andrew Gurr, *Playgoing in Shakespeare's London* (Cambridge: Cambridge University Press, 1987), pp. 206–07.

10

Language and comedy

Both the linguistic detail and the cultural ramifications of Shakespeare's comic language are extremely complex. In order to elucidate them, what I propose to do is focus on four interrelated themes, illustrating each one by reference to one or two particular plays: rhetoric and society in *Love's Labor's Lost*; logic and laughter in *As You Like It*; gender and language in *Measure for Measure* and *As You Like It*; and context and quotation in *Twelfth Night*.[1]

Rhetoric and society

A chief resource for the language of Shakespeare's comedies and a source of the ideas about language debated in them is the art of rhetoric. Elizabethan rhetoric has often been associated almost exclusively with stylistic ornamentation and obscure names for figures of speech, but for the Elizabethans much more was at stake in their adaptation of this ancient art of persuasion to social and literary uses of the English tongue. An ideal of eloquence and its constitutive power for social organization was key. As Thomas Wilson, in his *Art of Rhetoric*, recasts Cicero's celebration of the orator's godlike powers for his English Protestant readers, "the gift [from God] of utterance" repairs the fall of man, with eloquence the chief instrument for bringing men "to live together in fellowship of life, to maintain cities, to deal truly, and willingly to obey one another." Wilson also gives what seems a very idealistic notion about the power of eloquence to fashion social harmony a fascinating turn when he observes how persuasion into community is also persuasion to subjection: "For what man, I pray you ... would not rather look to rule like a lord than to live like an underling," he asks, "if wit had not so won men that they thought nothing more needful in this world ... than here to live in their duty?"[2] This darker thought links the eloquent rhetorical underpinnings of the social order to the mechanisms of what we would today call ideology, succinctly defined by Terry Eagleton as ways people are made "to invest in their own unhappiness."[3] What I want to suggest here is that Shakespearean comedy also raises questions about the relation between rhetorical eloquence and social organization. As if in answer to Wilson and Cicero, however, the excellences of language do not necessarily tend toward peace-making and social harmony.

In the 1550s, when Wilson wrote his celebration of eloquence, its potential application to the English tongue that was to be Shakespeare's instrument was in grave doubt, for the vernacular in comparison to Latin or Greek was deemed by many to be "indigent and barbarous,"[4] no fit instrument out of which to fashion literary masterpieces or social order, too impoverished to advance learning or debate theology . But by the 1590s, when Shakespeare began to produce his stylish comedies, perceptions of English had changed, due partly to the successful translation of religious texts and partly to the cultivation by English poets of rhetoric. When Shakespeare made eloquence his chief object of attention in *Love's Labor's Lost*, he was not merely indulging a seemingly unstoppable showmanship in words that was fostered by his interest in rhetoric. He was also at once celebrating and critiquing – even if he did set this play of eloquence in France – what contemporaries saw as the triumphant coming of age of English. Indeed, in making his vernacular play an exhibit in rhetoric, showing that English could do as much with words as Latin, he was helping to make it happen.

The story of how the "[s]weet smoke of rhetoric" (3.1.60) is both the central subject and the chief linguistic resource of the "great feast of languages" (5.1.35–36) that is *Love's Labor's Lost* has been told often, perhaps best by William C. Carroll and Keir Elam.[5] But the basic outlines are worth retelling, particularly because many of the rhetorical figures used in great profusion here continue to heighten, structure, and enliven Shakespeare's comic dialogue throughout his career. We ignore the building blocks of his verbal art if we ignore the rhetorical figures. The frequent allusions within this play and others to rhetorical terminology make it clear, nonetheless, that Shakespeare, far from identifying rhetoric merely with style, was familiar with the holistic five-part Ciceronian structure, which included invention (the finding of matter and arguments), disposition (the arrangement of material), style (the expression of ideas in pleasing language), memory (strategies for retaining ideas and speeches), and delivery (use of voice and gesture). Self-reflective commentary about the language is very common in Shakespeare's comedies, and rhetorical terminology crops up especially often in *Love's Labor's Lost* because almost all the characters behave as observers and critics of other people's language practices. Thus, the pedantical Holofernes denounces Berowne's "invention" while praising that of the Roman poet Ovid (4.2.155–57, 123–25). The courtiers, however excessive their own rhetoric, exhibit their refined taste by critiquing Armado's overblown "style" (1.1.196). Boyet takes delight in imagining how the ladies' scorn will disable their speech-making lovers' rhetorical strategies for "memory," and he reports an overheard lesson in delivery where the lords instructed their boy-emissary in "[a]ction and accent" (5.2.149–50, 99). But, as Holofernes' persistent question – "What is the figure, What is the figure?" (5.1.59) – registers, the main obsession of the play's characters *is* with the refinement of style and the copious variation of expression. Indeed, an analysis of *Love's Labor's Lost* can readily turn into an encyclopedia of rhetorical figures, so prolific and various is their display, and what follows will give only a small sampling.

Rhetorical figures have usefully, though with imprecise boundaries, been divided into *schemes* (such as alliteration), which manipulate word and sentence patterns, and *tropes* (such as metaphor), which effect changes from the usual signification of words. The preferred embellishments in *Love's Labor's Lost* are the schemes, including, for example, many variations on patterned repetition. Some focus on stylized beginnings, like Holofernes' performance in *alliteration*, the scheme which repeats opening consonant sounds – "The preyful Princess pierced and pricked a pretty pleasing pricket" (4.2.56); others on stylized endings, like his *homoioteleuton*, which repeats similar word endings – "Most barbarous intimation! Yet a kind of insinuation, as it were, *in via*, in way, of explication" (4.2.13–14). *Ploce* repeats words at frequent intervals, as in Berowne's "Light seeking light doth light of light beguile" (1.1.77), whereas *isocolon* and *parison* repeat phrases of equal length and corresponding structure, as in Nathaniel's "pleasant without scurrility, witty without affection" (5.1.3–4). Then there are the more complicated patterns, virtuoso schemes like *antimetabole*, which repeat words in converse order: "They have pitched a toil; I am toiling in a pitch" (4.3.2–3), says Berowne, setting his outward and inward experience into a heightened relation.

The habit of word repetition and inversion slides seamlessly into the pervasive comic strategy of wordplay. Drawing on an early modern English vocabulary rich in homonyms and words with multiple meanings, *Love's Labor's Lost* and all the comedies revel in repetition-based verbal ambiguities and shifting significations. For various devices we would today all group together as "puns" (a word Shakespeare would never have heard), Elizabethan rhetoricians drew more discriminating terminology from their classical sources. For example, the term *antanaclasis* was used to refer to a word repeated in shifting senses, as where Berowne shifts between "light" meaning "truth" and "light" meaning "physical illumination" in the word repetition illustrated above; whereas the term *paronomasia* referred to shifting between words similar in sound, like "suitor" and "shooter," when Boyet asks "Who is the shooter? Who is the shooter?" and Rosaline answers "Why, she that bears the bow" (4.1.107–09). *Syllepsis* draws out two meanings with one use of a word, as where Berowne activates both the rhetorical term "style" and the like-sounding climbing "stile" in his mocking dig at Armado's high language: "Well, sir, be it as the style shall give us cause to climb in the merriness" (1.1.196–97). Probably the most versatile pun for the dramatist, since it facilitates the dialogic interplay among the characters, is *asteismus*, where the play on words is between speakers, with the answerer returning an unlooked-for second meaning: "All hail, sweet madam, and fair time of day," the King of Navarre greets the Princess of France, who answers him back as if he had made a weather report, " 'Fair' in 'all hail' is foul, as I conceive" (5.2.339–40).

While all of Shakespeare's comedies exploit schemes of repetition and wordplay, to flesh out its eloquence *Love's Labor's Lost* exploits more than others the verbal devices conducive to copious speech, or elegant variation. Two principal devices are *synonymia*, the heaping up of words of like meaning, and *periphrasis*, or circumlocution, used especially in the speech of characters whose verbal excesses are explicitly satirized, like Armado and Holofernes. Speaking of Costard talking and "consorting" with a woman, Armado draws thus "out the thread of his verbosity" (5.1.16): *"I did encounter that obscene and most preposterous event that draweth from my snow-white pen the ebon-coloured ink, which here thou viewest, beholdest, surveyest or seest"* (1.1.234–37). Brian Vickers has rightly argued for the "functional nature" of rhetorical figures in Shakespeare's plays, establishing also a development from "stiffness" to "flexibility" in their use from early to late in his career ("Use of Rhetoric," pp. 90–91). *Love's Labor's Lost* is, however, the play in which the figures are exhibited quite explicitly for their sheer virtuosity as embellishments of language. This is not to say that the use of embellished language is unmotivated within the play, though it more often marks social dysfunction than decorum (the fit of language to speaker, situation, and addressee) or communicative competence. Armado's linguistic overreaching, for example, is linked to his social delusions, imagined by him as an effective means to cement a familiar and profitable relation with the King.

Comedy is perhaps the literary genre most explicitly concerned with people's behavior within social formations, and Shakespeare's excellence as a comic dramatist – no matter what he brings from the learned arts of rhetoric and logic, the dramatic conventions of Italy, Greece, and Rome, and the literary artifices of Lyly and Ovid – depends on his keen observation of how language works in actual social contexts. No one would hold up *Love's Labor's*

Lost, with its unusually heightened artifice of styles, as naturalistic in its language, but it nonetheless sets up a model for a comic commonwealth to be repeated and expertly varied in later plays.[6] Mikhail Bakhtin has identified as fundamental to the social dimension of language use what he calls "dialogized heteroglossia," that is, a plurality of languages in interplay reflecting all manner of social variation – the languages of different generations, regions, classes, occupations, educational backgrounds, and the languages of different situations, social occasions, business negotiations, power relations, and the like.[7]

Shakespeare's comedies multiply linguistic differences, or what sociolinguists call "varieties,"[8] to emulate or create multilanguaged and stratified social worlds. Thus, in *Love's Labor's Lost*, Shakespeare "quotes" or invents languages for different occupations (curate vs. schoolmaster), different generations (the "tender juvenal" Moth vs. the "tough señor" Armado [1.2.11–12]), and different social classes or "sorts" (the upper sort in the lords and ladies, the middling sort in the schoolmaster and curate, and the lower sort in the clown, dairymaid, and constable). Of course, Shakespeare's multilanguaged comic world differs from Bakhtin's multilanguaged real world in "quoting" or appropriating styles from literary as well as from life contexts. For example, Moth's smartalecky quips borrow from the chop-logic of his comic predecessor John Lyly's pages, while the love talk of enamoured males – in virtually every comedy – draws on Petrarchan conventions. Shakespeare's comic heteroglossia also differs in the patterning and coordination of its dialogic interplay, for in multiplying varieties he is not simply aiming at truth to life or rhetorical decorum. He is also multiplying opportunities for the stylistic counterpointing, collisions, cross-talk and mistakings his comedy thrives upon. Armado's copious circumlocution, "*That unlettered small-knowing soul*," set against Costard's laconic "Me?" (1.1.242–43) can be read as a paradigm for this key tool of Shakespearean comedy: the encounter of styles.

Acts of differentiation are rarely separable from acts of evaluation, and, in its cross-class stylistic encounters, *Love's Labor's Lost* illustrates a pattern whereby lower-class language behaviors are distinguished partly by incompetence that is intended to trigger laughter. Jaquenetta cannot read the letter that comes her way, Constable Dull stumbles into malapropisms ("reprehend[ing]" the "Duke's own person" [1.1.179–81]), and Costard is ignorant of word meanings like "remuneration" and "guerdon" (though clever, however incorrect, at guessing at meanings through context). Hence, there is a political dimension to the formal stylistic encounters of the comic dialogue. Richard Helgerson has argued that Shakespeare and his theatre company align themselves by means of the history plays with aristocratic and monarchic concerns. In promoting the eloquence of English, in the nationalist project of having "as else the Greeks... the kingdom of our own language," Shakespeare is said in the histories to work against the popular, to purge "signs of... barbarism."[9] But *Love's Labor's Lost* incorporates strategies into the dynamics of its cross-talk that pull against any such exclusionary alignment. Comic barbarities of language of one kind or another are displayed by virtually every social group, and the lower-class styles are well suited within the artfully contrived stylistic encounters to expose the overblown excesses of aristocrats like Berowne and of their imitators, the middle-ranking overreachers like Armado and Holofernes. Shakespeare's capacity to manage this double-edged linguistic critique across classes is helped by the rhetorical tradition's association of superfluous eloquence with abuse or barbarism, so that the over-cultivation of the play's foremost linguistic virtue is continually being turned over to vice. The rhetorical tradition, with its careful attention to audience psychology, would also have helped equip Shakespeare to imagine and play to composite audiences, pleasing all by aiming the comic mockery in all directions. Indeed, it is the failure to have assimilated rhetoric's lessons about audience address, about suiting the word to its hearer, that makes the lords and the play's other linguistic overreachers most vulnerable to critique and mockery. Rosaline pins down the sense in which the verbal behavior of the lords, however well framed their styles, nonetheless falls short of genuine civility: "A jest's prosperity lies in the ear / Of him that hears it, never in the tongue / Of him that makes it" (5.2.849–51). Civility and the pursuit of eloquence imagined as copious and embellished language, this critique of Berowne would seem to suggest, do not always go as fully together as Thomas Wilson's idealistic proposition would have it.

If, flouting prescriptions for drama like Sir Philip Sidney's that repudiate the mingling of kings and clowns,[10] Shakespeare's comic art of language thrives on the social differentiation and mixture of styles, *Love's Labor's Lost* nonetheless also critiques and exposes the politics of linguistic differentiation. One might imagine that the maturing of the English language, the expanding of its resources in the early modern period, could spread the gift of enriched possibilities for expression among those without a privileged education in Latin and Greek, so that a newly eloquent English could have, in effect, a democratizing and socially cohesive potential. The Latin lesson in *The Merry Wives of Windsor* (4.1), with a boy and his tutor's Latin learning set against an uneducated woman's bawdy Englishing of terms, certainly makes it clear that Shakespeare saw the practice of bilingualism in England as a social divider. But *Love's Labor's Lost* draws attention to how the elaboration of English and the cultivation of its eloquence can also multiply possibilities for social discrimination. It presents a dynamic whereby characters themselves elaborate and exaggerate linguistic differences within English usage to index and enhance their own social capital. Armado, Holofernes, and Nathaniel, for example, are always working to establish their own worth by differentiating their language practices from the "rude multitude": "We will be singuled from the barbarous" (5.1.82, 74–75). Their strategies for distinguishing high and low, civility and rudeness, often backfire, as when Armado's Latinate diction yields the rude image of Navarre dallying "with my excrement" (5.1.96). Linguistic stratification in the play, then, does not merely construct characters as socially positioned and provide the fun of comic verbal collisions. It is also made the occasion to reflect on how social agents – playing out their own struggle for superiority and distinction – are themselves, in Pierre Bourdieu's words, "producers" of "acts of classification,"[11] makers of social division. In *Love's Labor's Lost* the quest for eloquence, far from simply summoning social subjects into harmonious subjection, actively engages them in competition.

Logic and laughter

Logic for convincing argument and rhetoric for eloquent persuasion were inseparable partners in Elizabethan thinking. These two basic arts would have been known to Shakespeare as school subjects, but the proliferation of English manuals which recommended themselves to the ambitious as tools for self-advancement and even to zealous Protestants as logical self-defense against the devil suggests that they were also popular subjects. A key to understanding Shakespeare's inventiveness in comic language is to see how seamlessly he assimilated what he learned from logic and rhetoric with what he learned from observation of everyday conversation and of how people around him negotiated social relations in language. What is important about Shakespeare's language is almost always explicitly reflected upon in his plays, and his own comic practice seems to reflect Tranio's subversive advice for his master's education in *The Taming of the Shrew*, to "Balk logic with acquaintance that you have / And practise rhetoric in your common talk" (1.1.34–35). Shakespeare's contemporaries debated in the verse tributes of the folios whether "art" or "nature" made for his unmatchable fluency with language, but it might be more accurate to focus on his ability to see the unheralded artistry informing "natural" conversation and to find in the learned arts not only the means to heighten language but also insights into the mechanisms and interest of the ordinary, the seemingly trifling, the everyday. This section focuses on what Shakespeare's comic language does with logic.

As You Like It, one of Shakespeare's mature comedies, sounds much more like conversation in the easy cast of its dialogic exchanges than the relatively early *Love's Labor's Lost*, but its language both in prose and verse, when attended to in detail, is quite remarkable for its accent on logic and disputation. Indeed, Jonas Barish identified "logicality" as the distinguishing feature of Shakespeare's comic prose, what most clearly marks it off from Ben Jonson's. His emphasis is not on formal patterns of logic like the syllogism, but on a pervasive habit of treating discourse as if it were argument and, above all, a characteristically disjunctive habit of syntax.[12] It is really the skeletal structure underlying the sentences that Barish is concerned with – Shakespeare's practice of splitting ideas into balanced and symmetrical elements and sharpening the divisions between them into oppositions or antitheses, often with the help of rhetorical schemes of repetition, such as *isocolon* and *parison*:

> ROSALIND   Unless you could *teach me to forget a banished father*, you must not *learn me how to remember any extraordinary pleasure*.
>
> (1.2.3–6; emphasis added)

> ORLANDO   Besides *this nothing that he so plentifully gives me, the something that nature gave me* his countenance seems to take from me.
>
> (1.1.16–18; emphasis added)

These strongly marked disjunctive elements are often sorted and linked within sentences by a characteristic subset of conjunctions, those that stand out as "logical hinges": the cause-and-effect renderers, "for," "therefore," "so...that"; the makers of conjectural alternatives, "if...if not"; the form of qualification, "though...yet"; and many other logical dividers such as "the one...the other," "either X or Y," "not X but Y," "rather X than Y," or more simply "but," "or," and "yet" (Barish, *Ben Jonson*, pp. 24–36):

> ROSALIND   [Nature] hath sent this natural for our whetstone; *for* always the dullness of the fool is the whetstone of the wits.
>
> (1.2.51–53; emphasis added)

> ORLANDO   ... *if* I bring thee *not* something to eat, I will give thee leave to die; *but if* thou diest before I come, thou art a mocker of my labour.
>
> (2.6.11–13; emphasis added)

> PHEBE   Think not I love him, *though* I ask for him.
> 'Tis but a peevish boy – *yet* he talks well –
> *But* what care I for words? *Yet* words do well ...
>
> (3.5.109–11; emphasis added)

ROSALIND   [Time ambles] With a priest that lacks Latin, and a rich man that hath not the gout, *for the one* sleeps easily because he cannot study, and *the other* lives merrily because he feels no pain.

(3.2.313–16; emphasis added)

Given the rambling amorphousness of less cultivated sixteenth-century prose, the logicality of Shakespeare's comic syntax – a development from the more rigid patterning of John Lyly's euphuistic style – plays a critical role in giving structure to the sentence, intensifying its capacity to highlight key or comic elements, and making it a flexible instrument suited to a wide range of uses.

Beyond this general cast of the syntax, in *As You Like It* as in other comedies Shakespeare finds more surprising functions for logical language. Language has many uses in Shakespeare's comedies, but important among them is the least utilitarian – to surprise with pleasure, to trigger laughter. The witty fools of Shakespeare's mature comedies, like Touchstone and Feste, are the purest comedians in words. Their language is sheer performance, with the measure of its success coming in the immediate responses, or failures of response, from an audience. But how does it work? Does Touchstone draw on established structures in any predictable way to prime the pumps of his wit, or is his performance without script, spontaneous, just sparking off the remarks of whoever comes his way? Part of the answer is that the fool is a logician. Among his most basic tools is the syllogism, a form which sets out a dispute or argument in terms of three propositions: a disputable claim (the hoped-for conclusion), backed up by two interrelated reasons, or premises, from which the hoped-for conclusion should self-evidently follow. Touchstone and Feste, however, do not function as formal logicians, who – like mathematicians – use the forms of syllogism set out in the art of logic to demonstrate, based on infallible premises, truths that must hold no matter what audience may be addressed. Their working methods are closer to those of practical disputants trained up in the overlapping field of rhetoric, who begin with premises grounded in opinions, shared beliefs, or trusted maxims and aim through their arguments to secure the adherence of particular audiences to the disputable claims they advance. For the Elizabethans, this persuasion to adherence, sometimes symbolized as the open hand of rhetoric as opposed to the closed fist of logic, was the reasoning valued for real-life situations.[13]

This is the predictable pattern, then, in the comic patter orchestrated by the fool into the give and take of conversation between himself and other onstage characters. A disputable claim is advanced – in the comic transformation of the fool's wit, generally a claim that looks preposterous or absurd:

TOUCHSTONE   Wast ever in court, shepherd?
CORIN   No truly.
TOUCHSTONE   Then thou art damned.

(3.2.31–34)

Then reasons are asked for and proffered, with the fool drawing for material here on precepts acceptable to his audience, knowledge they will grant that they share with him; and, finally, the fool draws out of the syllogism – producing a shock of pleasure – the discovery of his preposterous conclusion:

CORIN   For not being at court? Your reason.
TOUCHSTONE   Why, if thou never wast at court, thou never saw'st good manners; if thou never saw'st good manners, then thy manners must be wicked, and wickedness is sin, and sin is damnation. Thou art in a parlous state, shepherd.   (38–43)

But what could make such a learned procedure of argumentation funny? It is partly the preposterous matter the clown proves, and partly the false moves he makes to produce his proof, for the fool always depends on fallacious arguments. An important trigger of the laughter is the incongruity between the predictable forms and their ludicrous outcomes: chaos is less funny than rule-governed predictability that is startlingly violated. A related trigger is the incongruity between the high-prestige forms of learning that provide the mechanism for the fool's sophistical wit and the low subjects he very often touches upon, some trifling and some bawdy.

Not only is the fool a logician, of course, but in Feste's description of his own methods, he is also a "corrupter of words" (*Twelfth Night* 3.1.34–35), who exploits the ambiguities and double meanings of words. Punning repartee, as we have seen, is in itself a mainstay of Shakespearean comedy, with the words of one speaker always being bandied back in different senses, whether playfully or incompetently, but it is interesting to see how logic and ambiguity are partnered in a special way in the language of the fools. Logic handbooks such as Thomas Wilson's *The Rule of Reason* encouraged their readers to train in the explicit identification of the fallacies or "colored reasons" making for deceitful arguments – with verbal subtleties and ambiguities the chief fallacies.[14] Thus, Touchstone uses a homonymic pun to distort his proof to Celia that "I should bear no *cross* if I did bear you, for I think you have no money in your purse" (2.4.10–11; emphasis added). Or, carrying to an extreme Wilson's category of the fallacy "parting ... words that should be joined" (161), Touchstone thus analyses the "shepherd's life": "Truly, shepherd, in respect of *itself*, it is a good life; but in respect that it is a *shepherd's life*, it is naught. In respect that it is *solitary*, I like it very well; but in respect that it is *private*, it is a very vile life... As it is a *spare* life, look you, it fits my humour well; but as there is *no more plenty* in it, it goes much against my stomach.' (3.2.11, 13–21; emphasis added).

Though I have been drawing on the designated "fools" for examples of how comic wit works through the contamination of logical forms by verbal ambiguity, these strategies spill over into the wit displays of characters like Rosalind. She puts Touchstone down when he derides Orlando's tree-decorating verses as "bad fruit," with a complex display of reasoning that turns on a pun between medlar (the fruit) and meddler: "I'll graff it with you, and then I shall graff it with a medlar. Then it will be the earliest fruit i' th' country; for you'll be rotten ere you be half ripe, and that's the right virtue of a medlar" (3.2.114–18). And even the country wench Audrey, who seems the least suited audience for Touchstone's conversation, participates in the logic games. When he joins together the words "foul slut" to justify his choice of Audrey as a partner who will satisfy his desire, she exposes the fallacy of "joining...words that should be parted" (Wilson, *Rule of Reason*, p. 161): "I am not a slut, though I thank the gods I am foul" (3.3.31–33).

Not every audience member will relate to the pleasures of analyzing the fool's or other character's wit for the more exotic fallacies of word use. It is futile, finally, to pin down *the* pleasure effect of the fool's language, since much of its virtuosity is in how the language is geared to the variable pleasures of multiple or composite audiences. The pleasure of Touchstone's wit seems to take as moody a man as Jaques by surprise when he finds his "lungs" begin "to crow like chanticleer, / That fools should be so deep-contemplative" (2.7.30–31). A kind of bifurcation or complexity in the pleasure Jaques derives from Touchstone's humor is suggested by his double-edged effort at analysis: "And in his brain, / Which is as dry as the remainder biscuit / After a voyage, he hath strange places cramm'd / With observation, the which he vents / In mangled forms" (2.7.38–42). On the one hand, Jaques' words align him with a listener whose pleasure is in analysis, for he uses a terminology that identifies quite precisely the basis of Touchstone's humor in the art of logic: "places" are the "topics" of logical "invention," which are meant to help generate "observation," which in turn serves as material for his mangling of logical "forms." On the other hand, Jaques' imagery associates Touchstone's humor with "low" bodily processes, specifically an uncomfortable process of digestion and evacuation. He catches up the high and low aspects of the fool's humor in this characterization, and with it another aspect of Shakespeare's attentiveness to the mixed constituencies of his audience. Indeed, in the framing of its humor, the play *As You Like It* quite explicitly engages in practices of audience analysis and segmentation of a kind familiar in Shakespeare's day from rhetoric and still commonplace today in advertising: most of Touchstone's comic routines, for example, begin with an exploratory survey of audience assumptions ("Hast any philosophy in thee, shepherd?" [3.2.21–22]), while the boy–lady epilogue, Rosalind, separates the audience into "men" and "women," playing provocatively on what he/she has to offer each segment.

Beyond laughter, logical forms of disputation permeate *As You Like It* for serious uses which effectively illustrate Shakespeare's characteristic blending of the social and artistic. "Welcome," says the feasting Duke Senior three times to a hungry Orlando and his weakened servant Adam, replicating one of the most common utterances of everyday social conversation, and then, at quite surprising length, articulating by means of a developed argument the logic of his welcome:

> If that you were the good Sir Rowland's son,
> As you have whisper'd faithfully you were,
> And as mine eye doth his effigies witness
> Most truly limn'd and living in your face,
> Be truly welcome hither. I am the duke
> That lov'd your father.
>
> (2.7.194–9)

Here, the question of the validity or rightfulness of the Duke's action in welcoming Orlando is thematized and treated as if it were open to dispute, with a reason being offered to justify it – that Orlando may be Sir Rowland's son. The Duke goes on to spell out the elided premise (for I, the Duke, loved Sir Rowland) that must join in to tie down the conclusion (then I, the Duke, should love Sir Rowland's son). But first, he offers reasons why the initial premise, which was stated hypothetically ("If that you were ... Sir Rowland's son"), should be granted – first, Orlando's own testimony and, second, their physical likeness.

However extraordinary it may seem to find someone building up a complex argument for the trifling social speech act of welcoming someone, the reasoning out of practical actions may underlie more everyday speech than we imagine. H. Paul Grice has, for example, established that conversation is built on inference-making,[15] even if the premises are characteristically elided and logical hinges unmarked. Shakespeare's heightened articulation of practical logic in utterances like the Duke's is an important ingredient in his art of constructing dramatic character out of language. G. R. Hibbard has aptly commented on the contribution of argumentation to lifelike characterization: "The reality [characters] assume in our minds owes far more, perhaps, than most critics have recognized to their ability – which is, of course, their author's ability – to give ... admirably argued and compelling reasons and explanations for their doing the things they want to do and intend to do."[16] *As You Like It* is full of such explicitly articulated reasons for actions and practical decisions, like Adam's articulation of why, though he is old, Orlando can be comfortable taking him on as a servant (2.3.46–55). As if in imitation of the reasoning Shakespeare works out to position a dramatic role in its social matrix, the disguised Rosalind actually reasons out how, as a man rather than a woman in distressed circumstances, her role is to "comfort the weaker vessel," so that her resulting gendered speech action is announced with the force of a logical conclusion: "therefore courage, good Aliena" (2.4.4–5, 6–7).

Beyond a tactic for character realization, the logic of the Duke's "welcome" also exemplifies the pastoral comedy's implicit experiment with "the rule of reason" as a principle for social harmony. Behind the logical discourse in Arden is a conjecture about the plausibility of rational disputation as a basis for social community.[17] The openness of the Duke's forest community to logical disputation is part of what sets it in explicit opposition to the court of Duke Ferdinand and the estate of Orlando's brother Oliver. The preceding plot action had in a sense already motivated the calling of "welcome" into dispute when Duke Frederick, without permitting disputation, refused to welcome Orlando as the victor at the wrestling match. Indeed, the validity of Duke Senior's "welcome" as an argumentative conclusion had already been indirectly examined and critiqued in Rosalind and Celia's exchange after Frederick's expulsion of Orlando:

ROSALIND   The Duke my father loved his father dearly.

CELIA   Doth it therefore ensue that you should love his son dearly? By this kind of chase [argument], I should hate him, for my father hated his father dearly; yet I hate not Orlando.   (1.3.27–31)

But the point is not so much whether Duke Senior's reasoning is valid as what his reasoning contributes to the repair and maintenance of his community. Sudden eruptions of aggression or violence characterize the hierarchical world outside the pastoral Forest of Arden in this play, presided over by patriarchal rulers or superiors who put a stop to the self-assertions of inferiors by "stern commandment" (2.7.109) or outright force. Just as Thomas Wilson proposes (and *Love's Labor's Lost* tests out) "eloquence" as a mechanism of social cohesion, the forest world tests out disputation. It may be Touchstone who makes the most persuasive case for the potential effectiveness of argumentation as a corrective to violence, in his disquisition on the "virtue in If" as "the only peacemaker" (5.4.102). In his anatomy of degrees in giving the lie, the delaying action of logical division and back-and-forth disputation postpones or mitigates aggression, while the "if" formulation characteristic of hypothetical syllogisms, positing alternatives, opens up a space amidst difference for potential agreement. The hypothetical syllogism is highlighted in Rosalind's peacemaking, which wraps up the comedy: "if," she secures advance assent from Phebe, "you do refuse to marry me, / You'll give yourself to this most faithful shepherd?" (5.4.13–14), repeating a similar formulation with the various candidates for marriage matches. Nonetheless, Rosalind's full participation in the disputation community of the forest partly serves to mask an ideological blindness inherent in the ideal of a rational community in which mutual understanding can be achieved through disputation without force. An ideal of rational community based on dialogic persuasion and intersubjective assent tends to assume a democracy of access to the conversation in all circumstances, whereas gender and class inequalities in any realistically imagined world dictate, through circumstances as simple and invisible as the access to turn-taking or topic-initiation, a hierarchy of access. Only a Rosalind turned Ganymed, a woman with the conversational access of a man, in a fantasy world like Arden, as Shakespeare knows well, could even begin to enter into the conditions for free disputation. Once again, Shakespearean comedy touches on the cultural politics of its own discourse practices.

Gender and language

Where Shakespeare's tragedies are almost barren of women's speech scripts that one would want to identify with or emulate, the comedies are remarkable for their frequent representations or fantasies of women's language as competent, eloquent, fluent, witty, or powerful. Rosalind, Portia, Viola, and Beatrice among others are all permitted, within the comic universes of discourse in which they have being, not only to speak copiously and well, but also to be listened to and responded to, not only to be appreciated and given credit for their words, but also to do things with words – to change minds, transform situations, harm others, and help them. It seems something to celebrate, given the constant dreary prescriptions in Elizabethan writings and culturally authoritative texts that women should be silent, chaste, and obedient, that silence is the best eloquence for women, that the "woman should learn in silence with all subjection," that she should not be suffered "to teach, nor to usurp authority over the man, but to be in silence" (1 Timothy 2:11–12), so that women will not be following their inclinations to "wax wanton" or "to be idle, wandering about from house to house; and not only idle, but tattlers also and busybodies, speaking things which they ought not" (1 Timothy 2:11, 13). Even if the comedies do repeat some of the stereotypes – for example, when Rosalind generalizes of women "You shall never take her without her answer unless you take her without her tongue" (4.1.162–64) – they seem to give voice in the voices and reception of their heroines to some different and attractive viewpoints. Easy as it may be, however, to admire Shakespeare's comic heroines, feminist and other political criticisms have brought out good reasons for proceeding with caution, lest the positive representations do the gentler work of ideology and imprison the admirer in an unwitting subjection – whether to stale family values or conventional sexual roles. This question is too broad to investigate fully in this chapter, which will instead gesture through two examples drawn from *As You Like It* and *Measure for Measure* at the complexity with which the comedies treat questions about women's language.

Feminist criticism in the past decades has raised the vexed question of whether or not women's language differs from men's. It is interesting to find this issue given explicit attention in Rosalind's assertion that Phebe could not have written the letter that Silvius delivers to her: "I say she never did invent this letter. / This is a man's invention, and his hand" (4.3.28–29). What Rosalind means is not immediately transparent, and one needs to unpack her reasons one by one, for they pull in many interesting directions. With regard to Phebe's handwriting, one might wonder if Rosalind is associating a particular script with femininity – perhaps "the sweet roman hand" attributed to Olivia in *Twelfth Night* (3.4.26) – and discerning the letter to be in a less graceful English or secretary hand, perhaps, such as the hand in which Shakespeare himself wrote. It would seem not, however, for her reasons the letter cannot be in Phebe's handwriting are that "She has a leathern hand, / A freestone-colour'd hand. I verily did think / That her old gloves were on, but 'twas her hands. / She has a hussif's hand" (4.3.24–27). This reasoning immediately complicates the issue of gender difference in language by intermixing the variable of sex with the variable of class: Phebe could not have written the letter because she does not belong to the leisured or educated class that writes, or writes with any fluency or refinement. This immediately breaks down any simple one-to-one correspondence between sex and language, as, indeed, recent researchers into this question have generally found it necessary to do.[18]

Yet the characterization of the style as "a man's invention" seems to pull in a different direction. From one angle it seems to bring into play a simple and unreliable stereotype of feminine versus masculine styles: "Why, 'tis a boisterous and a cruel style, / A style for challengers. Why, she defies me, / Like Turk to Christian. Women's gentle brain / Could not drop forth such giant-rude invention, / Such Ethiop words, blacker in their effect / Than in their countenance" (31–36). But Rosalind is being disingenuous in her description of the letter, teasing and leading on Silvius, who believes the letter expresses anger in a naturalistic way, about the "cruelty" or tyranny to which it gives voice. The cruel voice of Phebe is "man's invention" in the quite different sense that the whole Petrarchan interplay that the Silvius–Phebe subplot draws upon between a besotted and poeticizing male lover and a cruel, tyrannous, and usually silent female beloved is "man's invention" – the product of a virtually uninterrupted masculine tradition in love poetry. If the letter gives voice to the "cruel fair" of Petrarchan convention on whose pattern Phebe is drawn, then Rosalind is uncovering a fuller sense in which "she" "never did invent this letter." Still, the episode is complicated by yet one further dissonance between the letter Rosalind eventually reads and her prefatory descriptions of it. The letter is a poetic response by the normally silent and objectified Petrarchan beloved to her situation, the opening up in verse of the "woman's heart" (45) and mind. But where we might expect the verse to be completely circumscribed within the already scripted postures of the Petrarchan convention, all "man's invention" of woman's voice as Rosalind has hinted, there is something more to this verse that might give us pause. Compared to the Petrarchan shards hung on trees by Orlando and quoted and parodied around the forest, Phebe's verses are competent, even eloquent. The couplets are not jingling send-ups, and they say something new about Phebe's confused attraction to Ganymed. The unconventionality of the emotion expressed seems to gesture – to the extent any verbal expression can – at authenticity, as if a woman was indeed finding and speaking her mind, even if her "voice" has only "man's invention" to work with and transform. Of course, this hint at the possibilities for inventing a female literary voice can only remain the merest hint – positioned as it is in a male-authored play presented in a theatre without female actors. Nonetheless, the insight that women's literary meanings may have to be made out of men's language is one that has been prevalent in recent feminist criticism opening up early modern women's writing. Cruelly, Rosalind, whose own linguistic inventiveness and pleasure are opened up by her verbal cross-dressing, turns a deaf ear to the interest of Phebe's language, so that if it manages briefly to voice something we might call "female" longing in an alternative same-sex, cross-class tune, it nonetheless gets no serious hearing before the comedy moves on to honor Hymen and celebrate conventional heterosexual unions.

If Phebe's verses raise some complexities attending the production of women's language, Isabella's situation in the darker comedy *Measure for Measure* treats the complexities of reception. If Shakespeare had had a talented sister Judith, feminist scholars have frequently asked since Virginia

Woolf first set forth this question,[19] what conditions within Elizabethan culture might have either enabled or restricted her ability to accomplish something of importance with her words? The answers have most often focused on restrictions that prevented women from developing the verbal fluency of their male counterparts, especially restricted access to education and the inhibiting prescriptions linking silence with virtue. Yet Shakespeare's comedies often depict female characters with verbal facility, or "linguistic capital,"[20] equal to or greater than that of the male characters. Giving Isabella and Angelo matching language and logic in *Measure for Measure*, Shakespeare explores how sex differentiation in language can arise in reception rather than composition. Angelo's words, when Isabella suggests she will appeal against his wrong-doing beyond him to a wider audience, bring out clearly how real-world disputations do not occur on a level playing field, how power relations and access affect speech reception: "Who will believe thee, Isabel? ... my place i' th' state, / Will so your accusation overweigh / That you shall stifle in your own report" (2.4.155–59). As startling to Isabella, who expects her speech to be rated according to the force of her arguments, is the masculine assumption that her speech "power" derives as much or more from something extraneous to her linguistic ability: "in her youth / There is a prone and speechless dialect / Such as move men," her brother Claudio explains, relegating to secondary status his recognition that "beside, she hath prosperous art / When she will play with reason and discourse" (1.2.163–66).

Among the most puzzling aspects of this play is why the voluble Isabella, so forceful a disputant in the first half, so quietly diminishes into being "ruled" (4.6.4) in her speech by the Friar/Duke in the second half. In his sociolinguistic analysis, Pierre Bourdieu has argued that speakers learn over time within their habitual speech contexts to self-censor. *Anticipated* speech reception, based on a history of reception that yields a "practical expectation ... of receiving a high or low price for one's discourse" ("Economics," p. 655), comes to affect speech production. Shakespeare seems to be suggesting something similar, that Isabella's experiences of reception in the first half condition her speech inhibition in the second half: she is, in a sense, unlearning her educated fluency in real-world speech contexts. Ironically, the speech restrictions imposed on Isabella in the convent of the Saint Clare order at the outset of the play will likely sound unliveably severe to most audience members, however much Isabella herself longs for stricter "restraint": "When you have vowed, you must not speak with men / But in the presence of the prioress; / Then if you speak you must not show your face, / Or if you show your face you must not speak" (1.4.4, 10–13). Shakespeare recognizes and draws to our attention, in the linguistic trajectory of Isabella outside the convent, how the tacit regulation of women's speech through the subtleties of its reception in everyday contexts can be just as restrictive.

Context and quotation

Among the most obvious uses for language in comedy is to serve the plot – both to narrate action not represented on stage and to carry forward and clarify onstage events. More interesting, however, are the comic episodes where plot and language become unglued, as often occurs in plays developing situational comedy, such as *Twelfth Night*. The comic plotting engineers a whole series of well-timed and fantastic deceptions and mix-ups which generate discrepancies in awareness among the characters. As Fabian aptly suggests when Malvolio acts on his mistaken knowledge that his mistress Olivia loves him, "If this were played upon a stage now, I could condemn it as an improbable fiction" (3.4.122–23). Situations where twins are repeatedly mistaken for one another or where a disguised woman stirs the sexual desire of another woman can be funny enough in themselves, but Shakespeare also makes them occasions for linguistic performances. The plot situations defamiliarize and reaccent the characters' expressions, turning the most commonplace talk into "strange speech" (5.1.61). Thus, when Viola disguised as Cesario tells Olivia, "I am not what I am" (3.1.139), the literal sounds figurative, like riddling or metaphysical speculation. Or the comic effect can be broader, with the comic contexts prompting characters to make exquisitely self-revealing misinterpretations. "Wilt thou go to bed, Malvolio?," Olivia suggests, concerned with the mental health of her steward, and prompts the misled Malvolio's answer, as if to a sexual proposition: "'To bed? Ay, sweetheart, and I'll come to thee'" (3.4.27–29). Or characters bump up against the different social accents of each others' words as if they are talking different languages:

> SEBASTIAN I prithee vent thy folly somewhere else,
> Thou know'st not me.
> FESTE Vent my folly! He has heard that word of some great man, and now applies it to a fool. Vent my folly! ... I prithee now ungird thy strangeness, and tell me what I shall "vent" to my lady. Shall I "vent" to her that thou art coming?   (4.1.9–16)

Here and in many other examples, one character quizzically repeats another character's words. Part of the effect is to focus audience attention on situated language practices and social inflections that would normally escape notice – here the differences in speech one addresses to a stranger (as Sebastian reads the situation) and speech to a familiar acquaintance (as Feste, mistaking Sebastian for Cesario, reads it).

The script of *Twelfth Night* is a tissue of quotation, with characters continually reiterating the words and phrases of others. This may seem to mark off its language as artificial, an advanced formal experiment involving dialogic play with rhetorical schemes of repetition. Taken together with the baroque *"mise en abyme"* effects[21] of the defamiliarizing plot contexts, these language practices may come across as artistic games cut off from the social life of discourse. But Bakhtin's probing analysis of the qualities of everyday social discourse can help us to see how the literary and the social are in fact working together here. For Bakhtin, a person's speech is not helpfully described as a matter of individual expression, with the speaker drawing personal language selectively from a unitary language system, finding his or her "own words." Instead, he emphasizes how speech is shaped and developed in interaction, with speakers always "quoting," assimilating, reworking, and reaccentuating the words of others: "in the everyday speech of any person living in society, no less than half," he claims, "of all the words uttered by him will be someone else's words" (*Dialogic Imagination*, p. 339). Someone else's words do not just enter into one's speech as lexical items one could have found equally well in a dictionary or thesaurus: they come with attitude, an evaluative accent – what Feste clearly hears and responds to in Sebastian's "vent." When Sir Andrew Aguecheek appropriates Cesario's "'Odours,' 'pregnant,' and 'vouchsafed'" (3.1.88–89), or when Feste repeats Malvolio's slur about laughing "at such a barren rascal" (5.1.365–66), Shakespeare, like Bakhtin, makes us hear how people's words come out of "other people's mouths," "other people's contexts" and are "populated – overpopulated – with the intentions of others" (*Dialogic Imagination*, p. 294). Nor are the citation practices that interest Bakhtin in social discourse limited to direct quotation of particular people, though he insists its importance has been overlooked. Routinized "speech genres," the recycled behavioral scripts for bargaining, greeting, promising, or love-making constitute another important form of "citation" in social discourse.[22] Since romantic comedy deals precisely with the most often reproduced forms of social behavior, especially those pertaining to courtship and love-making, areas where not even such individualists as Beatrice or Benedick in *Much Ado About Nothing* can escape repeating the usual "truth tired with iteration"[23] like "I love thee" (4.1.280), it makes sense that Shakespeare should focus on these forms of social citation in his comedies.

Thus, the comedies highlight the status of social discourse as citation and response, and not only where improbable plots throw reaccented quotations into relief. The plays draw upon a wide variety of framing strategies in order to hold up stretches of language for observation and self-reflective comment.[24] Frames frequently employed to estrange and elicit heightened attention to verbal styles include the use of a concealed onstage audience and the onstage recitation of a character's letter. For example, when Malvolio quotes himself in a way that also "quotes" what he takes to be the language of a higher social rank, the reaction of the concealed onstage audience of Fabian, Sir Andrew, and Sir Toby sets his pretentious words and the evaluative social attitudes they carry into high relief:

MALVOLIO I extend my hand to him thus, quenching my familiar smile with an austere regard of control –
SIR TOBY And does not Toby take you a blow o' the lips, then?
MALVOLIO Saying "Cousin Toby, my fortunes, having cast me on your niece, give me this prerogative of speech" –
SIR TOBY What, what!   (2.5.62–68)

Similarly, the accents of Malvolio's angry indignation at his imprisonment are framed, type-cast by citation, and mocked when Feste offers to read his letter in a loud voice – "'By the Lord, madam'" – insisting, when Olivia objects to this mocking reaccentuation, that in reading madness one "must allow *vox*" (5.1.285, 288).

The estranging frames of Shakespeare's comic art provide perspective on many different kinds of language activity – from Petrarchan love sonnets through displays of rhetorical figures to everyday social speech acts and conversational rules – and they achieve a wide range of effects, from bemused wonderment through metalinguistic attention and deconstructive critique to explicit parody and hilarious send-up. Keir Elam's excellent study of comic discourse particularly accents the metalinguistic play and the thematization of language achieved by Shakespeare's positioning of language games within frames: "It is ... the game-frame dialectic, exploiting language as activity and as object, that lends Shakespearean comedy much of its discursive momentum and depth" (*Universe of Discourse*, p. 21). These are important insights, though they may focus attention too exclusively on formal experimentation in language. In this chapter I have tried to add another dimension by reading Shakespeare's formal artistry in comic language together with some of its cultural ramifications. I have argued that the learned arts and the social life of language equally inform Shakespeare's comic discourse and that the plays themselves explore the cultural politics of their own discourse practices.

NOTES

1 In this chapter, Shakespeare's plays are quoted from the following editions: *As You Like It*, ed. Agnes Latham, Arden Shakespeare (London: Methuen, 1975); *Love's Labour's Lost*, ed. H. R. Woudhuysen, Arden Shakespeare (Walton-on-Thames, Surrey: Thomas Nelson, 1998); *Measure for Measure*, ed. Brian Gibbons (Cambridge: Cambridge University Press, 1991); *Much Ado About Nothing*, ed. Sheldon P. Zitner (Oxford: Oxford University Press, 1993); *The Taming of the Shrew*, ed. Ann Thompson (Cambridge: Cambridge University Press, 1984); *Troilus and Cressida*, ed. Kenneth Muir (Oxford: Clarendon Press, 1982); *Twelfth Night*, ed. Roger Warren and Stanley Wells (Oxford: Oxford University Press, 1994). I am indebted to Paul Stevens, who commented on a draft and made some very helpful suggestions, which I have incorporated.
2 Thomas Wilson, *The Art of Rhetoric* (1560), ed. Peter E. Medine (University Park: Pennsylvania University Press, 1994), pp. 41–42. For Marcus Tullius Cicero on the orator's eloquence in relation to social organization, see *De Oratore* (On the Making of an Orator) trans. E. W. Sutton and H. Rackham, 2 vols. (Cambridge, Mass.: Harvard University Press, 1959), I, 22–27.
3 Terry Eagleton, *Ideology: an Introduction* (London: Verso, 1991), p. 13.
4 Letter of Richard Eden to Sir William Cecil, 1562, quoted from Richard Foster Jones, *The Triumph of the English Language* (Stanford: Stanford University Press, 1953), p. 18.
5 William C. Carroll, *The Great Feast of Language in "Love's Labour's Lost"* (Princeton: Princeton University Press, 1976); Keir Elam, *Shakespeare's Universe of Discourse: Language-Games in the Comedies* (Cambridge: Cambridge University Press, 1984). Particularly useful general treatments of rhetoric in Shakespeare include Sister Miriam Joseph, *Shakespeare's Use of the Arts of Language* (New York and London: Hafner, 1947), and Brian Vickers, "Shakespeare's Use of Rhetoric," in *A New Companion to Shakespeare Studies*, ed. Kenneth Muir and S. Schoenbaum (Cambridge: Cambridge University Press, 1971), pp. 83–98.
6 For a detailed and useful study which treats Shakespeare's comic language in relation to social formations, see Camille Wells Slights, *Shakespeare's Comic Commonwealths* (Toronto, Buffalo, and London: University of Toronto Press, 1993).
7 Mikhail Bakhtin, *The Dialogic Imagination: Four Essays*, ed. Michael Holquist, trans. Caryl Emerson and Michael Holquist (Austin: University of Texas Press, 1981), pp. 272 and 262–63. On the relevance of Bakhtin's ideas of social discourse to Shakespeare's language, see Lynne Magnusson, *Shakespeare and Social Dialogue: Dramatic Language and Elizabethan Letters* (Cambridge: Cambridge University Press, 1999), especially pp. 8–11.
8 For a discussion of varieties of early modern English with some examples from Shakespeare, see Charles Barber, *Early Modern English* (1976; Edinburgh: Edinburgh University Press, 1997), pp. 1–41.

9 Richard Helgerson, *Forms of Nationhood: the Elizabethan Writing of England* (Chicago and London: University of Chicago Press, 1992), pp. 1 (letter of Edmund Spenser to Gabriel Harvey, 1580, as quoted by Helgerson) and 245.

10 Sir Philip Sidney, *A Defence of Poetry*, ed. J. A. Van Dorsten (Oxford: Oxford University Press, 1966), p. 67.

11 Pierre Bourdieu, *Distinction: a Social Critique of the Judgement of Taste*, trans. Richard Nice (Cambridge, Mass.: Harvard University Press, 1984), p. 467.

12 Jonas A. Barish, *Ben Jonson and the Language of Prose Comedy* (1960; New York: W. W. Norton, 1970), p. 23. For other useful discussions of logic in Shakespeare and Elizabethan drama, see Joseph, *Shakespeare's Use of the Arts of Language*, especially pp. 174–241 and 354–85; Allan H. Gilbert, "Logic in the Elizabethan Drama," *Studies in Philology* 32 (1935): 527–45; and Hardin Craig, "Shakespeare and Formal Logic," in *Studies in English Philology: a Miscellany in Honor of Frederick Klaeber*, ed. Kemp Malone and Martin B. Ruud (Minneapolis: University of Minnesota Press, 1929), pp. 380–96.

13 Ch. Perelman and L. Olbrechts-Tyteca, in *The New Rhetoric: a Treatise on Argumentation*, trans. John Wilkinson and Purcell Weaver (Notre Dame and London: University of Notre Dame Press, 1969) have tried to renew this tradition of practical reasoning in the twentieth century and provide an excellent account of its history and concepts.

14 Thomas Wilson, *The Rule of Reason Conteinying the Arte of Logique* (1553), ed. Richard S. Sprague (Northridge, Calif.: San Fernando Valley State College, 1972), especially pp. 156–76. I have modernized the spelling of quotations from this text. The phrase "colored reasons" is from Dudley Fenner, *The Artes of Logike and Rethorike* (1584), reprinted in *Four Tudor Books on Education*, intro. Robert D. Pepper (Gainesville: Scholars' Facsimiles and Reprints, 1966), sig. E1v, p. 176.

15 H. Paul Grice, "Logic and Conversation," in *Speech Acts*, ed. Peter Cole and Jerry L. Morgan, vol. III of *Syntax and Semantics* (New York: Academic Press, 1975), pp. 41–58.

16 G. R. Hibbard, *The Making of Shakespeare's Dramatic Poetry* (Toronto, Buffalo, and London: University of Toronto Press, 1981), p. 53. Karen Newman also examines how realistic characterization deploys rhetoric and, to a lesser extent, logic in *Shakespeare's Rhetoric of Comic Character: Dramatic Convention in Classical and Renaissance Comedy* (New York and London: Methuen, 1985).

17 Jürgen Habermas, *Reason and the Rationalization of Society*, vol. 1 of *The Theory of Communicative Action*, trans. Thomas McCarthy (London: Heinemann, 1984) suggests a continued interest in imagining ideal social structures based on rational communication.

18 On the complex factors governing gender identity, see Vimala Herman, *Dramatic Discourse: Dialogue as Interaction in Plays* (London and New York: Routledge, 1995), p. 254.

19 See, for example, the collection of essays on "Teaching Judith Shakespeare," ed. Elizabeth H. Hageman and Sara Jayne Steen, which make up a special issue of *Shakespeare Quarterly* 47.4 (winter 1996).

20 For Pierre Bourdieu's economic metaphor for linguistic exchange, which employs this terminology, see "The Economics of Linguistic Exchanges," trans. Richard

Nice, *Social Science Information* 16 (1977): 645–68 and *Language and Symbolic Power*, ed. John B. Thompson, trans. Gino Raymond and Matthew Adamson (Cambridge, Mass.: Harvard University Press, 1991).

21 Elam's characterization of the element of "formal self-reflection" in Shakespeare's comic language in *Universe of Discourse*, p. 23.

22 See Mikhail Bakhtin, *Speech Genres and Other Late Essays*, ed. Caryl Emerson and Michael Holquist, trans. Vern W. McGee (Austin: University of Texas Press, 1986), especially pp. 60–63.

23 *Troilus and Cressida*, 3.2.166.

24 On the framing of language games in Shakespearean comedy, see Elam, *Universe of Discourse*, pp. 18–23.

11

BARBARA HODGDON

Sexual disguise and the theatre of gender

> Stage love will never be true love while the law of the land has our heroines
> played by pipsqueak boys in petticoats!
> Viola de Lesseps in *Shakespeare in Love* (1998)[1]

Desiring to equate "stage love" with "true love," Viola, the heroine of *Shakespeare in Love*, alludes to the corporeal conundrum that weaves through Shakespeare's "transvestite" comedies – *Two Gentlemen of Verona*, *The Merchant of Venice*, *Twelfth Night*, and *As You Like It* – where boy actors playing women cross-dress as men in dazzling doubles acts that offer up a spectrum of flexible sex-gender identities, confounding the body's "truth." Viola herself performs an equally provocative doubles act: fulfilling her wish to be "Valentine and Silvia too," she breaks and remakes the gender conventions of the all-male Elizabethan stage, and does it twice. Disguised as "Thomas Kent," she auditions for Shakespeare's company by reading *Two Gentleman of Verona's* Valentine (3.1.174–81),[2] wins the part of Romeo and becomes Will Shakespeare's "true love" as well as his authorial muse; for their "real-life" story, in which Viola's romance with Will and the theatre momentarily postpones an arranged marriage with Lord Wessex, grounds *Romeo and Juliet's* fictional one. The film articulates the connection between the two by cross-cutting between bedroom and stage and, as pillow-talk transforms into theatrical poetry, by linguistic "cross-dressing": Will's lines are revoiced by the "real" boy actor playing Juliet, Viola's by "Thomas Kent" as Romeo. When Will, in bed, slyly asks, "Will thou leave me so unsatisfied?" and Viola responds, "That's my line," prompting Will's "It's my line, too," textual mischief heightens their sexual pleasure, foreshadowing another transformation. For when the real boy actor's voice changes, Viola plays Juliet to Will's Romeo – a performative transgression protected by none other than a fairy-godmother-like Queen Elizabeth, who affirms Shakespeare as the poet of true love, enabling his commercial success. Finally, both stories of lost love again are transformed through the film's fantasy ending, which rhymes two images: Will, in his study, writing Viola's name and her first line in *Twelfth Night* ("What country, friends, is this?") on a blank parchment page; and Viola herself, walking on an expansive sandy shore.

Turning early modern theatrical practice into a highly marketable post-modern product, *Shakespeare in Love* plays with two theatres of gender: the one embodied by the cross-dressed boy player; the other, as in most present-day stagings of Shakespeare's comedies since the Restoration, by a woman. A hybrid, the film claims Elizabethan authenticity by staging an array of cross-dressed male performances – the boy actor's Juliet, Juliet's Nurse, and Will's drag-parodic "Miss Wilhelmina," Viola's chaperone. Yet the film's own conventions of cinematic realism also exploit Gwyneth Paltrow's beautiful body and luminous face to joke away the boy player's history, replacing one body with another to occlude the *performance* of gender. Significantly, Viola gets cast not because she is a better actor than the boys and young men but because they speak Marlowe's lines and she speaks Shakespeare's. After all, affirming that an actor becomes "real" when speaking *Shakespeare*'s words is part of the film's project, which also commits to Viola's hopelessly romantic desire to see life as theatre (forgetting that conventions govern both) and to elevating a theatre of the "really real" that privileges the woman actor over the boy player. But precisely because it makes double claims on how sexual disguise does performance work – what it invites actors *to do* and spectators *to imagine* – *Shakespeare in Love* opens up the problematics of gender performances, those appearing on urban London stages during the sixteenth century's last decade as well as in subsequent stagings and corporeal styles.

"Girl-boys" and discursive bodies

The cross-dressed boy actor offers a starting point, for his figure calls into question the relationships between actor, female character, and male disguise within theatrical representation. Did spectators accept the convention, ignore the boy actor's gender, read him as her? In their eyewitness accounts of Elizabethan and Jacobean performances, John Manningham, Henry Jackson, and Simon Forman write about the fictional women characters they saw as if those characters were female persons.[3] Distinguishing between "beguiling the eyes of the world in confounding the shapes of either sex" and theatrical representation, Thomas Heywood affirms that spectators, recognizing "youths attired in the habit of a woman by their names," knew that they were "but to represent such a Lady at such a time appoynted."[4] But Elizabethan moralists could not imagine the boy player "just" as a convention, for he stood at the center of a virulent attack on the theatre as a deceptive practice that contaminated "natural" or God-given identity with counterfeits of "true" originals, enticed spectators with devilish shape-changings and unsettled the very fabric of a culture based on stable hierarchies of social class and sex-gender, the latter reinforced by biblical prohibitions against cross-dressing.

Attempting to recuperate early modern cultural conditions, new historicist and materialist feminist critics have revitalized this antitheatrical prejudice. Speaking of the theatre as a site of social struggle and of the sexually ambivalent boy player as one sign of a sex-gender system in crisis, these critics imagine London's playhouses as dangerously sexualized sites where English culture's "intense anxieties" could be staged and their "transgressive erotic impulses" released.[5] Yet their rehearsal of Puritan polemics not only tends to confuse theatrical representation with real-life behaviors (much like Viola de Lesseps) but to consider the boy player as a site of sexualized discourse rather than as a body in performance. Appearing on stage, how do bodies – that of the cross-dressed boy actor and that of the woman who plays the cross-dressed part – carry meanings, especially those of sex and gender? What work do they perform? And how do spectators read them? A look first at how Shakespeare's texts stage the comedies' cross-dressed parts and then at how particular players inhabit those roles can help to discover the pleasures and dangers of gender play on Shakespeare's stage as well as in subsequent performances.

Reading bodies: sights and sounds

What instructions do Shakespeare's comedies offer for disciplining the boy actor's body as female and for managing sexual disguise? In Shakespeare's theatre of gender, the most obvious signs were voice and costume. Troubled by how to match their bodies to roles, *A Midsummer Night's Dream's* amateur actors settle for mimicking the boy player's unbroken voice. Even Flute the bellows mender's "coming" beard will not prevent him from playing "the lady that Pyramus must love": "You may play it in a mask and you may speak as small as you will" (1.2.45–46). The workmen's play, of course, mocks a theatrical vocabulary inherited from an earlier emblematic drama that was being superseded by more realistic performance modes; in the later comedies, voice becomes an increasingly playful register of gender. When Portia, contemplating her "device," vows to "speak between the change of man and boy / With a reed voice," the line invites vocal flexibility, marks her disguise as a performance (*The Merchant of Venice*, 3.4.66–67). In the later *Twelfth Night*, sound collapses distinctions between sexed bodies and social roles, enhancing comic confusion: Cesario/Viola's "small pipe" identifies her as both "boy" and "woman"; neither Olivia nor Antonio hears any difference between her and her brother Sebastian.[6] And just as voice twins Cesario/Viola with Sebastian, so does costume, permitting brother to transform into sister, sister into brother.[7] On the early modern stage, clothes made the man – and woman. In the culture, regulatory sumptuary laws prescribed dress codes for both, as well as for all classes and professions within the social hierarchy: the detailed lists in Philip Henslowe's inventory reveal the care and expense involved in providing appropriate garments for each identity that walked the Rose Theatre's stage.[8] Drawing on the attributes of the boy player and on familiar social codes, Shakespeare's theatre held Hamlet's famous mirror up to its body-conscious culture as much as to "nature," "minding true things by what their mock'ries be" (*Henry V*, 4.0.53).

Fashioning femininity also depended on more complex signs. To trick Christopher Sly into thinking he is a lord, *Taming of the Shrew*'s "real" Lord devises a charade in which his page Bartholomew counterfeits Sly's wife. The Lord's servants are to "see him dressed in all suits like a lady," but their attitudes toward him – calling him "madam" and "do[ing] him obeisance" – also shape the artifice. Moreover, the page must ape the body manners of "noble ladies / Unto their lords," speak his part "with soft low tongue" and use "kind embracements" to enhance his performance (Induction, 1.102–14). "*Act* like a lady": the familiar expression, characterizing femininity as susceptible to mimesis, speaks more than it knows about how gender performances depend on repeating behaviors which reenact or re-experience a socially established set of meanings.[9] That these particular attributes, associated with a fantasized ideal of feminine submissiveness, are those which, under Petruchio's tutelage, Katherina (willingly or unwillingly) reperforms, lends Bartholomew's "drag" impersonation retrospective meanings that reverberate, through a slippage between class and gender, marking "boy-servant" and "woman" as interchangeable *social* categories, each dependent on a "lordly" master's will.

Malvolio's description of Cesario/Viola – "in standing water between boy and man" (1.5.142) – suggests the indeterminant status of the adolescent male who was neither one nor the other – in Valerie Traub's phrase, "a middle term."[10] When boy players shared the stage with adult males, their femininity was partially defined by physical difference; but scenes where one or several women characters appear together relinquish that difference, relying on dialogue and/or "pure" performance.[11] Consistently, the moment where a comic heroine cross-dresses prompts a discussion that calls attention to the gap between fictional and material bodies. When *Two Gentlemen of Verona*'s Julia contemplates disguising herself as "some well-reputed page" to follow her true love Proteus, her maid Lucetta maps the latest male fashions onto the female character:

LUCETTA   What fashion, madam, shall I make your breeches?
JULIA   That fits as well as 'Tell me, good my lord,
                What compass will you wear your farthingale'.
                Why even that fashion thou best likes, Lucetta.
LUCETTA   You must needs have them with a codpiece, madam.
JULIA   Out, out, Lucetta, that will be ill-favour'd.
LUCETTA   A round hose, madam, now's not worth a pin
                Unless you have a codpiece to stick pins in.
                                                        (2.7.50–56)

On one level, this conversation depends on knowing that Julia and Lucetta are "really" boy players who have what the fictional Julia lacks to fill her codpiece and on the inappropriateness of women dressing as men. But since their dialogue reveals a kind of "double-voicing" in which both female character *and* boy player speak, sometimes from 'inside' the role, sometimes from "outside" it, the exchange works to validate fictional femininity by insisting that masculinity itself is merely a "passing matter," a function of fashion. Later, when Julia fears Proteus has betrayed her, she recalls how she had "lively acted" the part of Ariadne, a mythical figure who hanged herself when abandoned by Theseus (4.4.159–64), refashioning her femininity through another performance that "suits" her imagined situation.

Whether clothed by costume, fictional role, or both, Shakespeare's heroines repeatedly send up male body parts as well as masculine dress and behaviors as they step into male disguise. As she prepares to lose her fictional self in the equally fictional Balthazar, Portia says she will assume "a manly stride," tell "puny lies" about romantic encounters and practice "a thousand tricks of these bragging jacks" (*Merchant*, 3.4.64–78). Playing straight man, Nerissa's "Why, shall we turn to men?" expands the erotic options of the body joke: their counterfeit may turn fictional women into "real" men, may make the women turn to (other?) men, may (will?) turn boy players to men, may make boy players seek out male companions. But in the later trial scene, cross-dressing takes on a different bodily charge, equating masculine *sexual* power with social power.

Repeatedly, Shakespeare's comedies play on insides and outsides, insisting that sexual disguise conceals a female body beneath a male façade. Claiming that she has no doublet and hose in her disposition, *As You Like It*'s Rosalind sends up gender stereotypes in a barrage of questions about Orlando, proving herself a woman with excessive speech (3.2.179–80; 3.2.200-204ff.). When she is forced to duel with Sir Andrew Aguecheek against her will, picking up the sword confirms Viola/Cesario's manhood, but her inability to use it "proves" her feminine. Acknowledging the play between fictional and "real" bodies and between female character and male disguise, "A little thing would make me tell them how much I lack of a man" (3.4.268–69) – usually spoken as an aside – calls attention to both Viola and Cesario as *performances*. Even moments when a character loses control of her masculine performance sustain the theatrical fiction of a feminine psychological interiority. Thinking she has lost Proteus, Julia faints, quickly recovering her "disguise of love" and then as quickly revealing herself – a strategy Shakespeare complicates in *As You Like It* when, hearing of Orlando's wound and seeing the bloody napkin, Rosalind faints, "outing" her female character – and her "hidden" desire (4.3.156–74).

Tailoring sexual disguise

The Two Gentlemen of Verona prefigures the workings of sexual disguise that later plays borrow selectively and expand upon. Julia's name as a page, Sebastian, transfers to Viola's twin in *Twelfth Night*, her servant's disguise also connects her with Viola, and the ring exchange that resolves the plot reappears, differently figured, in *The Merchant of Venice*. With Speed, Julia assumes a clown-like persona, as does Viola with Feste and Rosalind with Touchstone. Whereas disguise of any kind permits its wearer to escape the confinements of a single position or voice and to perform as *another*, romantic heroines use *sexual* disguise to occupy other-gendered space, both imaginary and "real," and to explore the emotional or psychic territory of that "other."[12] For Julia as for Portia, Viola, and Rosalind disguise enables them to "be" men: to act as messengers, delivering love messages or objects (and, in Rosalind's case, an epilogue); to become male confidants and tutors; to escape domestic space where, clothed by a role, they voice opinions, assume masculine modes of authority, and intervene in public affairs.

Momentarily forgetting the boy player for their own politics of reading, the first wave of feminist and psychoanalytic critics saw Shakespeare's cross-dressed heroines as early modern precursors of "liberated" postmodern women. Reading both boy player and woman actor as *performers*, however, invites reconsidering such liberation less as the result of adopting masculine guises and traits than as a theatrical strategy that, by putting gendered expectations and responses into play, enables the critique of stereotypical ideologies. If, as some critics conjecture, such play unsettled early modern categories of gender and class in a culture officially hostile to same-sex desire and cross-class marriage, present-day thinking about sex and gender, which associates cross-dressing with marginal sexualities lying outside heterosexual norms and wraps boyish androgyny, effeminacy, and transvestism into one package labeled gender transgression,[13] can appear no less anxious, delimiting the flexibly gendered bodies that Shakespeare's comedies put into play.

Each play tailors sexual disguise to its own sociocultural milieu and gender politics. Julia's disguise highlights her fidelity (later echoed in *Cymbeline*'s Imogen), enabling her to observe Proteus wooing Sylvia as well as to forgive his sexual betrayal in a somewhat unsatisfactory resolution that traffics in women's bodies in order to celebrate male friendship. *The Merchant of Venice*, however, straddles two forms of disguise and gender performance. Shylock's daughter Jessica dons boy's clothes in order to escape her father's oppressive household and to choose her own husband; like her father's servant Launcelot Gobbo, she changes livery to change service, moves from Shylock to Lorenzo, from one master to another. Like Perdita in *The Winter's Tale*, who pulls her suitor Florizel's hat over her brow, making her boyish enough to escape undetected as she flees from his father toward her own, Jessica adopts disguise as a brief charade; and both figures defy patriarchal rules only to reinstate them.

Portia, however, does not assume disguise in order to pursue a wooer or, like Rosalind, to play gender games. As a married woman, she has no need to protect her virginity, as Julia does, from "the loose encounters of lascivious men" (*Two Gentlemen*, 2.7.41) or, like Viola, by serving a lord. Nor does she change her social position. Of all Shakespeare's cross-dressed heroines, she is the likeliest "feminist" candidate, one who leaves a household where she is "master" to take up a similarly powerful role in the public sphere where, as Balthazar, a "young doctor of Rome" and stand-in for the fictional Bellario, she saves the life of Antonio, her husband Bassanio's friend. During Shylock's trial, her disguise works primarily in sociolegal terms, adhering to rather than subverting patriarchal rules. The liberty she achieves coincides with the presence of a scapegoat character who cannot be assimilated into the play's comic society, suggesting that when an outsider threatens the social order, women attain more freedom within the group.[14]

But it is not Shylock's presence alone that gives Portia's disguise a different charge from those of other romantic heroines. Responding to Bassanio's claim that he would sacrifice his life and his wife to deliver Antonio by remarking, "Your wife would give you little thanks for that / If she were by to hear you make the offer" (4.1.284–85), she later demands from Bassanio the ring she has given him as payment for saving his friend's life, as does her "clerk" Nerissa, who claims *her* ring from Gratiano. Here, Portia resembles Henry V on Agincourt Eve, cloaking himself as "Harry Leroy" to test his subjects' fidelity (*Henry V*, 4.1). Like Henry's glove exchange with Williams – and also like her father's device of the three caskets – Portia's demand for the ring sets up a loyalty test with objects, playing a double ring trick that confirms both husbands' commitment to marriage bonds. Although her experience in a law court enables her readjudication of marital relationships, that occurs *after* she has removed her disguise but continues to sustain her gender performance. Perhaps most significantly, the issue of fidelity, so often mapped on to women's bodies in the early modern drama, gets worked out on *men*'s bodies – a gender reversal effected by a woman putting on male disguise.

"I am not that I play"

Uniquely among Shakespearean heroines, Viola assumes sexual disguise at the outset of her role, from which all the play's misunderstandings and plot complications arise. Whereas Portia's disguise gives her social power, Viola disguises herself as a eunuch – neither woman *nor* man, an identity expressly suited to the boy player's body, to the character's role as a go-between, and to a play about *young* people. Incorporating her brother's identity into her performance as Cesario, she plays Sebastian *and* herself, moving from shipwrecked sister to Illyria's world-turned-upside-down, which licenses a "What-You-Will" indifference to fixing gender that punctures any idea of a "true" masculinity or femininity. Unlike Portia, who *acts* or intervenes in situations, Viola/Cesario remains a figure to whom events happen and who permits "Time" to untangle *Twelfth Night*'s knotty plot. Like Feste, she travels between manorial households; also like Feste, she finds everyone *at* her to perform this or that – service that the play defines both as a mutual bond between master and servant and as the passionate attachment of love.

Acting Orsino's part in a proxy wooing explicitly focused on what performing bodies say and might *do* ("much," according to Olivia), she appears as a girlish youth, prompting Olivia's desire, not for Orsino but for a husband *un*masculine enough for her to master (1.5).[15] To Orsino, obsessed with Olivia, she seems a boyish girl: citing her "smooth and rubious" lip and "maiden's organ," all "semblative a woman's part," he even voices the culture's notion that boys begin as girls, only later becoming males (1.4.31–33). Later, defending women's truth in loving, she speaks of her own history as "a blank," voicing herself and her brother as one (2.4.109–20). Whether with Olivia or Orsino, she mediates literary and performative fantasies of masculinity and femininity through the *tabula rasa* of an indeterminate gender identity. Most "*her*self" when mourning her brother Sebastian (1.2), in soliloquy (2.2), when fooling with Feste (3.1), and when she finally faces

Sebastian (5.1), Viola/Cesario is less a coherent Stanislavskian, psychologically based persona than a mercurial performer whose gender remains tenuously constituted, adaptable to circumstance – and to "the whirligig of time."

Although she plays "complete twin" only until she learns that Sebastian may be alive, her disguise further enhances gender ambiguities throughout the play's finale. When, mistaking her for Sebastian, Olivia calls her husband, she confesses her love for Orsino, but only when Sebastian appears does "One face, one voice [and] one habit" become "two persons," and it is he who names her as Viola, "outing" her as a woman. All the ensuing reconciliations of self and other are staged around this central image of twinning, in which homoerotic desires – Olivia's for Viola/Cesario; Orsino's for Cesario/Viola – dissolve toward, though not fully "into," heterosexual unions. For, although the close defuses one homoerotic bond by turning Olivia and Viola into sisters-in-law, it also continues to sustain the "both/and" meanings of *Twelfth Night*'s orgy-like circulations of homosocial desire. Acknowledging Cesario's new identity ("Give my thy hand / And let me see thee in thy woman's weeds"), Orsino transforms Viola from servant to mistress to ring a further change on the dutiful servitude and submission associated with both roles (5.1.265–66).[16] Yet Shakespeare upsets the convention that would mark her as female by retaining her servant's attire: like sonnet 20's "master-mistress of my passion," she still participates in the *theatrical* ambivalence that "pricked [her] out for [doubly-gendered] pleasure" (line 13). Moreover, Orsino's (and the play's) final lines affirm her masculine persona:

> Cesario, come –
> For so you shall be while you are a man;
> But when in other habits you are seen,
> Orsino's mistress, and his fancy's queen.
> (5.1.172–75)

While acknowledging that, at least in the imaginary, there is no difference between men and women as desiring subjects, Orsino's lines also point to a theatrical trick: at least in early modern stagings, keeping Cesario/Viola's "singular" character in boy's dress may be designed as much to exhibit the performer's ability at twinning genders as to sustain homoerotic play. As Lisa Jardine suggests, readers and spectators tend to import present-day gender politics and confusions into *Twelfth Night*'s narrative, overreading its erotic investments as their own,[17] and, like Viola in *Shakespeare in Love*, imagine a "transvestite theatre" that blurs distinctions between play and world.

Laurie Osborne's fascinating study of *Twelfth Night*'s nineteenth-century performance editions reveals a not entirely dissimilar confusion that underscores the problematic status of cross-gender disguise in that period's stagings, which adopted a double-edged anxiety about role, performer, and performance. On the one hand, the most extensive editing aims at defending Viola's character from the implications of disguise; on the other, productions appeared eager both to conceal and exploit the lure of "breeches" parts. Despite his distaste for what he saw as an unseemly fascination for cross-dressed roles, Leigh Hunt's mid-century review of Maria Tree's Viola praises her legs, not her acting: she appeared as a sexualized spectacle rather than as a performer. In keeping with the century's finely tuned sensibilities, editors downplay the potential transgressiveness of Viola's disguise by eliminating her lines about its devilish "wickedness" (2.2.25–26), which conflicted with her perceived delicacy of mind. They also mute her exchanges with Olivia, revise her participation in Orsino's household, and trim Orsino's damning of women's love to focus on Viola's idealized love, especially her "patience on a monument" speech (2.5.109–17). In attempting to secure her ideal femininity, editors also eliminate lines which either call attention to her as an actress playing a part or stress her feminine sexual vulnerability, for both came too close to the nineteenth-century perception that actresses who displayed their bodies publicly in male disguise were sexually tainted. As Osborne writes, "The transvestite actress, with her strong economic draw and her erotic appeal to both sexes, challenged emerging gender hierarchies of public versus private and exceeded the heterosexual oppositions of male desire and female submission."[18]

More contemporary performances not only demonstrate an increasing lack of anxiety about fixing gender (at least in Viola's case) but also invest more fully in framing her male disguise to suit cultural fashions and trends. Once the second World War's social disruptions brought the image of the "masculine" woman who wore pants inside and outside the home into view, theatrical trousers no longer marked women actors as "transvestite" performers. For thirty years after Beatrix Lehmann's 1947 Cesario "appeared every inch a man," Violas were praised less as feminine ideals than for their skills at acting "the boy eternal." Dorothy Tutin's 1958 Viola/Cesario, in Cavalier costume, seemed "touchingly young and boyish"; and in 1966, Diana Rigg, the black-leather-clad Emma Peel of TV's *Avengers* behind her, resembled pantomime's "big, strapping principal boy." But by 1974, reviewers seemed fully to accept Viola/Cesario's double gender: Irving Wardle saw Jane Lapotaire as a "neutral androgynous presence, a blank screen on which others project their fantasies," while Peter Ansorge, observing that she yielded to Orsino's embraces as a page-boy and even wanted to satisfy Olivia as a woman, imagined her as a perplexed modern woman.[19]

Yet even as the twentieth century waned, in an age where popular culture idols flaunt gender ambiguities, performance, cross-dressing, and homoerotics *à la* Shakespeare still proved potentially disruptive to the dominant view that bodies *ought* to conform to heterosexual norms. Trevor Nunn's 1996 film of *Twelfth Night*, for instance, invents a prologue that establishes cross-dressing as a fanciful charade: costumed as veiled "oriental" houris, Viola and Sebastian perform for a delighted shipboard audience, revealing themselves as sister and brother (Sebastian plucks off Viola's moustache; she fails to remove his real one) just as the storm threatens. If this performance cues spectators to read sexual disguise as improvisatory dissembling, the ensuing shipwreck and its aftermath – in which an anguished Viola tries to drown herself, then hides from Orsino's soliders in a cemetery where she watches Olivia visit *her* brother's grave and hears of Orsino – overnarrates her physical and psychic vulnerability in order to justify her transformation into Cesario. Viola's gaze at a photograph of herself and her brother then cues a title sequence that constructs her disguise through close-ups of body parts and dress: a hand picks up scissors and snippets of hair fall to the floor; hands unlace her corset, button trousers, stuffing out what she "lacks" with a sock, bind her breasts and button up her shirt – all under the approving eye of the Captain, who teaches her a manly swagger. Looking once more at her brother's image, she picks up the false moustache she had worn in the earlier charade, and the final shot shows her, back to the camera, striding toward a distant castle as twilight falls.

Both prologues clearly establish sexual disguise as a convention which plays beside, even cheats on, the film's prevailing realism. When, acting Orsino's embassy, Cesario/Viola (Imogen Stubbs) enters Olivia's carefully prepared candlelit sitting-room shrine, she is an uneasy observer, not a participant. Whereas other actors – Helena Bonham Carter's Olivia, Imelda Staunton's Maria, and Nigel Hawthorne's Malvolio – appear fully to inhabit their parts and to be fixed within the film's detailed Victorian *mise-en-scène*, Stubbs remains outside hers – perpetually young, malleable and unfixed, the "comedian" (or boy-player) Olivia suspects her to be (1.5.121) as well as a potential stand-in for a (youthful) spectator. Rather than looking at the "character", Cesario/Viola, a spectator is constantly intercepted by Stubbs' presence as a late twentieth-century performer, a strategy that defuses any hint of sexual transgression and also mutes the playfulness of gender. Elsewhere, with Orsino, the film stages body jokes and moments of "put-on" male performance that threaten to expose her identity, her desire for Orsino or both: at fencing practice, Stubbs shies away from the instructor's hand touching her breast; when Orsino puts his arm around her shoulders, she punches him in "manly" camaraderie; asked to scrub his back as he lolls in a bath, she sneaks an admiring look at his nude body. Only when Orsino's comments on women's inability to love as men prompt her to confess her love does she drop her alienated position and control their exchange: in the "patience on a monument" speech, Stubbs and "Viola" suddenly fuse, moving Orsino deeply. Curiously – and appropriately, given the film's Victorian setting – precisely the speech that nineteenth-century performances foregrounded as expressing Viola's ideal femininity ensures her body's "truth." That moment also reassures (mainstream) spectators that the "right" bodies will couple in comedy's happy ending, where the film asserts its final negotiation between Stubbs' dissembling performer and "Viola" by turning her into an icon of femininity. Adorned in a beautiful ball gown, she participates in a celebratory dance that frames her history with two "dress-up" occasions, the one a sham, the other "for real."

A gender of her own

Although written before *Twelfth Night*, which raids its strategies of sexual disguise, especially in foregrounding the boy player's figure, *As You Like It* displays an even more radical investment in sexual disguise and gender performance. Tied to plot, Viola/Cesario's figure is embedded within the fictional action called *Twelfth Night*, but in *As You Like It* "Rosalind for Ganymed" *is* the play: her role displaces plot with a series of turns or music-hall-like routines. This distinction between the pleasures and processes of theatre, governed by the author's text, and performance, governed by the actor, surfaces in *As You Like It*'s early modern publishing history. An August 1600 entry in the Stationers' Register lists it among several plays "to be staied," and it was not printed until the 1623 folio, leading some editors to assume that the Lord Chamberlain's Men considered it a theatrical property too valuable to be shared.[20] Taking that conjecture a step further suggests that the *literary* text was no substitute for the extratextual pleasures of its enactment: indeed, *As You Like It* juxtaposes literary culture to theatrical entertainment, playing the one against the other.

Early on, the fictional heroine Rosalind is banished from the Duke's court (and the stage) because she will elicit an audience's pity (1.3.75–77), with the result that fiction and "character" are pushed to the margins, foregrounding the interaction between the performer and the fictional Rosalind as the central theatrical action. In Arden, a realm already marked by the pastoral convention of courtiers disguising themselves as shepherds, "Rosalind for Ganymed" reshapes that milieu into one where romantic fictions dissolve into popular performance: while Orlando's verses write Rosalind as an idealized fictional beloved, "Ganymed" performs verbal acrobatics which deflate his texts (3.2; 4.1). Even the name of her disguise turns on literary as well as colloquial connotations ("Jove's own page" [1.3.118]; a male prostitute), wrapping both into a figure for the boy player – the embodiment of homoerotic attraction, at least as imagined by early modern antitheatrical writers. Noting how the text repeatedly stresses the player's *boy*-ness, Lesley Anne Soule names him "Cocky Roscius" or "Cocky Ros," catching up the adolescent male performer's skill at assuming a radically double persona, simultaneously heterosexual and homoerotic, capable of mediating and mocking gender identities and of being superior to and wielding power over the fiction.[21] Allied to timelessness ("There's no clock in the forest" [3.2.275–76]) and time-wasting, Cocky Ros performs a series of digressions not unlike those of Hamlet, her tragic opposite, whose *inability* to act (though not to perform) also results in displaying language as secular magic and delays closure. The Rosalind–Celia relationship stages the interplay of two youths sending up the serious business of love and marriage; the Rosalind–Touchstone relationship, that between a young comedian and an older clown, evokes the camaraderie of fellow performers. Counseling Phebe and Silvius, Cocky Ros "proves a busy actor" (3.4.50), playing her male rival and herself in a pageant that nearly risks double exposure (3.4). In the most famous scenes (3.2; 4.1), Orlando plays straight man to Ganymed, but when Orlando "can live no longer by thinking," Cocky Ros becomes yet another performer (his last appearance in male attire), a magician-conjuror who "can do strange things," even make the "real" Rosalind appear (5.2.45, 53). She is, of course, only an illusion, an iconic Rosalind-as-bride who speaks in formulaic riddles – "To you I give myself, for I am yours"; "I'll have no father . . . [or] husband, if you be not he . . . nor [to Phebe] wed woman, if you be not she" (5.4.105–13) – suggesting that she exists only in others' possession of her.

The traits marking "Rosalind" as an ideologically desirable actor – charisma, apparent naturalness, spontaneity, skill at making impersonation seem "real" – translate easily into those of an ideally desirable woman – a fantasy figure of feminine allure and mystery garbed in masculine attire on to whom spectators map their own gender performances, their own desires for erotic mobility.[22] Although how early modern spectators responded to the boy player's "Cocky Ros" can only be conjectured, performances from the nineteenth century forward clearly have prompted playgoers' desires both for "Rosalind" and for actors' "real" bodies. Ada Rehan's 1889 Rosalind, for instance, performed an array of "feminine" behaviors that blurred distinctions between role and self to stress normative heterosexual desire, turning "Ganymed" into a shared joke. Discovering that Orlando is nearby, she is "ashamed at being caught out of her petticoats"; later, offering to cure Orlando, she "creeps beside him, nudg[ing] his elbow with her own" and, at "Nay, you must call me Rosalind," she "foolishly swings her hands to and fro – he does the same – then both glance slyly at each other, burst[ing] into a laugh." When Orlando arrives late, she greets him "with a pout and almost sulky cry"; at his departure, "she sinks her head on his shoulder as if about to faint," then "waves her handkerchief and kisses her fingers after him."[23] Admiring her "gleeful animal spirits," her skill as a "radically natural performer" and her "gypsy charm," William Winter considered her to personify "the actual woman of Shakespeare's dream."[24]

Winter's desire to transport Shakespeare's idealized character into a fantasy of theatrical performance as (masculine) wish-fulfillment peaks with Vanessa Redgrave's 1960 Rosalind. Almost without exception, critics praise her radiance and "feminine magic": "immensely natural, [she] might be any of our daughters." When, J. W. Lambert writes, she "escapes from her boy's disguise, snatch[ing] off her cap so that her hair tumbles like a flock of goldfinches into sunshine, [she] strikes a silver note"; delighted at seeing a "real woman" in the swinging sixties, Bernard Levin thought that "nothing at once more beautiful and more accomplished than her performance has ever met my sight." A decade later, however, nostalgia for Rosalind as the embodiment of a shared fantasy of femininity began to wane. Reviewing Eileen Atkins' 1974 performance, Michael Billington mentions how, in her "headband, fringed blouse, and crutch-hugging jeans, she seemed even more seductive as Ganymede than before"; and, given the production's boldly frontal, declamatory style, Susan Fleetwood's 1980 Rosalind appeared more as a performance than as a "character." Indeed, critics singled out Sinead Cusack's Celia, whose bravura display of domestic chores – mending a garment, straightening the edges of a picnic cloth – just before the mock-wedding (4.1) naturalized her body as that of a model wife, offsetting Fleetwood's overtly athletic Rosalind.[25]

Trapped in their own stereotypes of essential sexuality and performative conventions, especially that of pantomime's "principal boy," critics have increasingly appeared divided over whether a particular Rosalind appears as "good girl" or "good boy." Part Ariel, part Peter Pan, Rosalinds who slap their thighs, put their hands in their pockets, and adopt one-leg-up, one-leg-down or arms akimbo poses exemplify a tradition of gender limbo: reduced to behavioral clichés, Rosalind becomes, as Lindsay Duguid writes, "a gender all her own."[26] Juliet Stevenson's 1985 Rosalind for Ganymed – bowler-hatted, dressed in baggy white trousers with scarlet braces, punctuating her lines with a Charlie Chaplin cane – broke that mould with a vigorous, iconoclastic performance which anticipates Soule's image of "Cocky Ros." Yet, although program excerpts citing Jung's idea of the animus/anima cued spectators to view Rosalind and Orlando as "each having something of the other's sexual nature," most reviewers faulted Stevenson for expending energy on externals and for lacking "the true voice of passion." Only the *Listener's* critic, more fully engaged with a "what if" world where imagination has free rein, saw "an actor seriously dallying with a woman-girl-boy-girl."[27]

Consider, now, another performance, Adrian Lester's Rosalind in Cheek by Jowl's all-male *As You Like It* (1991–5). When, dressed in a loose shirt belted over trousers, vest, brown trousers, and straw hat, she first met Orlando in Arden, her "Do you hear, forester?" (3.2.271–72) was akin to the lady leaping out of the cake to a musical flourish – wantonly inviting, yet all of a flutter. Disconcerted, Orlando turned to the voice he thought he had heard before and saw – Ganymed. Furious that he did not recognize her ("Not know me? You're clutching my portrait that I hung around your neck at the wrestling!"), Rosalind's jaw set: the disguise which she'd been ready to throw off ("What shall I do with my doublet and hose?" [3.2.200–01]) became a gauntlet thrown down before him. As Orlando's tutorials in knowing her began, her (superficial) *female* disguise gradually penetrated the (deep, culturally normative) *male* disguise – that of the myths which lovers perpetrate when they say they will die for love. Just as "Rosalind" was stripped away, so was "Orlando." Discarding her straw hat for Celia's ruffled apron, she dressed for allure – "Come, woo me, woo me, for now I am in a holiday humour, and like enough to consent" (4.1.59–60). As Orlando knelt before her, touching Rosalind's portrait and vowing to kiss before he spoke, she tied the apron on him, snatched it back as she again "put [him] to entreaty" and then tossed it away, her voice breaking, on "Well, in her person I say I will not have you" (4.1.79). Clutching his verses, Orlando's "Then in mine own person I die!" (4.1.80) prompted her to comfort him with the tales of famous lovers and, again donning the apron, to play Rosalind "in a more coming-on disposition." As they knelt before Celia, she whipped off the apron, mischievously turning it into a wedding veil. Convinced that he was "cured," she entwined him between her legs, felt his arms and grabbed his waist in frank desire – "Now tell me how long you would have her" – but when he shouted "For ever and a day!" (4.1.120–22), she turned impatiently away ("Hasn't he learned *anything*?") and stood, apron in hand, to lecture on male and female attitudes to wooing, wedding, and cuckolding. She was about to discard Orlando's crumpled verses ("At last we're rid of these"), but when Orlando suddenly recalled his appointment with the Duke and tried to leave, she feigned death and rattled off warnings on fidelity which Orlando took for a joke – yet he nonetheless kissed her forehead as he said "Adieu," making her giddy with delight.[28]

In this apotheosis of costume-as-gender property, Celia's "stolen" apron became an interchangeable sign of "feminine" submissiveness that marked the breaks between "Rosalind" and "Ganymed" (and between "Orlando sick" and "Orlando cured") – in a brilliant bit of comic mismatch that reversed the joke of how you put the pants on someone. As Peter Holland writes, "Gender became a construct of performance, and sexuality was placed in the hands of character, not actor... Performing gender became a game."[29] That Irving Wardle could align Lester's Rosalind with Vanessa Redgrave's suggests how his winning performance played her as *he* liked it, even if, as some noted, it remained a performance of a woman seen through a man's eyes.[30] Yet how could it be otherwise? If it is only by watching a "real" transvestite performance that spectators can recuperate the frisson of gender violations and the swerving erotics that travel readily from one body to another, then this production certainly highlights what, since the early seventeenth century, audiences may have been missing. This is not to suggest that either the production or Lester's performance attempted to convey an aura of "Shakespearean authenticity" often evoked as one standard for measuring contemporary performances. Rather, at least to John Peter, the performance revealed the present through the lens of the past: *As You Like It*, he writes, "is not about sexuality – hetero-, homo-, bi- or trans – but about love, which both transcends sexuality and includes it."[31]

Peter's remarks offer one gloss on Rosalind's Epilogue, perhaps the play's most radical performative moment and the speech regularly cited in literary-critical discussions of *As You Like It*'s gender games.[32] Although Epilogues usually are social conventions which apologize for the play (in this case, also for the speaker) and invite applause, Rosalind's turns social convention into erotic invitation. Just beyond the point where comic form fixes both gender and erotic play in heterosexual coupling, as the fiction travels on its edge, the speaker addresses male and female spectators – "I charge you, O women, for the love you bear to men ... I charge you, O men, for the love you bear to women" – setting up a triangular structure that joins performer, character, and spectator to the play-as-fiction and to the "play" that extends *As You Like It*'s gender games into a shared space beyond it. Simultaneously, "If I were a woman" acknowledges the erotic ambiguity of gender performances – whether occurring on or off stage or between same-sexed or differently sexed bodies (Ep. 10–12; 14–15). In reasserting *As You Like It*'s gender premise, that "if" also plays off an earlier exchange. Just after "Rosalind for Ganymed" exits, Touchstone enters to instruct Jaques in the seven degrees of the lie, all of which turn on "If you said so, then I said so": as he puts it, "Your 'if' is your only peacemaker; much virtue in 'if' " (5.4.90–92). His digression covers (and prepares for) a costume change: when he finishes, "Rosalind" reappears. Speaking the Epilogue, she incorporates Touchstone's "if" into Rosalind for Ganymed's role as magician ("My way is to conjure you" [Ep. 9]). The play's ending, then, is shaped not just by conventions of comic closure but also by two performances: one by the older clown, one by the young comedian Cocky Ros – a strategy that the later *Twelfth Night* reverses, highlighting the Cesario/Viola performer within the play proper and letting Feste sing the Epilogue.

When the adolescent boy player, neither woman nor man, performed the Epilogue, "If I were a woman" asserted two "truths": the indeterminacy of his body as well as that circulating in his performance of "Rosalind for Ganymed." But when a woman speaks it, *As You Like It* suddenly becomes something else, opening up a gap between present performance and a ghosted past. Helena Faucit, a nineteenth-century Rosalind, writes that, while it was "fit enough for ... a boy-actor of women's parts in Shakespeare's time, it is altogether out of tone with the Lady Rosalind." Citing her desire to lose herself in the ideal character and a distaste for addressing spectators as herself, she speaks of doing her best "to illustrate how the high-toned winning woman reasserted herself in Rosalind, when she laid aside her doublet and hose."[33] Although more recent performers acknowledge the flexible separation of role and body, prompt books across the centuries rarely mark the passage; rather, it remains unmanaged – the actor's private preserve. And that is precisely the point. For *As You Like It* gives an especially poignant "local habitation and a name" (*Dream*, 5.1.17) to how Shakespeare's theatre of gender, always exceeding its texts, turns on performing bodies, and on a kind of "if".

NOTES

1 See Marc Norman and Tom Stoppard, *Shakespeare in Love* (New York: Miramax Film Corp and Universal Studios, 1998).
2 Citations follow *The Norton Shakespeare* (New York: W. W. Norton, 1997).
3 Bruce R. Smith, "Making a Difference: Male/Male 'Desire' in Tragedy, Comedy, and Tragi-Comedy," in Susan Zimmerman (ed.), *Erotic Politics: Desire on the Renaissance Stage* (London: Routledge, 1991), p. 129.
4 Thomas Heywood, *An Apology for Actors*, 1612, ed. Arthur Freeman (New York: Garland, 1973), C3v.
5 See, for example, Jean E. Howard, *The Stage and Social Struggle in Early Modern England* (London: Routledge, 1994), pp. 94–104; Stephen Orgel, "Nobody's Perfect: or Why did the English Stage take Boys for Women?," *South Atlantic Quarterly* 88 (1989): 7–29; Stephen Greenblatt, *Shakespearean Negotiations: the Circulation of Social Energy in Renaissance England* (Berkeley: University of California Press, 1988); and Lisa Jardine, "Boy Actors, Female Roles, and Elizabethan Eroticism," in David Scott Kastan and Peter Stallybrass (eds.), *Staging the Renaissance: Reinterpretations of Elizabethan and Jacobean Drama* (London: Routledge, 1991), pp. 57–67. See also David Cressy, *Travesties and Transgressions in Tudor and Stuart England* (Oxford: Oxford University Press, 2000), pp. 92–115.
6 Bruce R. Smith, *The Acoustic World of Early Modern England: Attending to the O-Factor* (Chicago: University of Chicago Press, 1999), p. 232.

7 Peter Stallybrass, "Worn Worlds: Clothes and Identity on the Renaissance Stage," in Margreta de Grazia, Maureen Quilligan and Peter Stallybrass (eds.), *Subject and Object in Renaissance Culture* (Cambridge: Cambridge University Press, 1996), p. 312.

8 See Kathleen McCluskie, "The Act, the Role, and the Actor: Boy Actresses on the Elizabethan Stage," *New Theatre Quarterly* 3 (1978): 120–30.

9 Judith Butler, *Gender Trouble: Feminism and the Subversion of Identity* (London: Routledge, 1990), pp. 140–41.

10 See Valerie Traub, *Desire and Anxiety: Circulations of Sexuality in Shakespearean Drama* (London: Routledge, 1992), pp. 117–44. Traub's term neatly substitutes for "boy actor," which applied more to Hamlet's "little eyases" (the choirboy players) and so infantilizes both the adolescent male actor and the woman performer.

11 Lorraine Helms, "Playing the Woman's Part: Feminist Criticism and Shakespearean Performances," in Sue-Ellen Case (ed.), *Performing Feminisms: Feminist Critical Theory and Theatre* (Baltimore: Johns Hopkins University Press, 1990), p. 198.

12 Marjorie Garber, *Vested Interests: Cross-Dressing and Cultural Anxiety* (London: Routledge, 1992), pp. 32–40; and Catherine Belsey, "Disrupting Sexual Difference: Meaning and Gender in the Comedies," in John Drakakis (ed.), *Alternative Shakespeares* (London: Methuen, 1985), pp. 183–84.

13 Traub, *Desire and Anxiety*, pp. 121–22.

14 Katherine Maus, introduction to *The Merchant of Venice*, Norton Shakespeare, p. 1087.

15 See Alan Sinfield, *Faultlines: Cultural Materialism and the Politics of Dissident Reading* (Berkeley: University of California Press, 1992), pp. 66–69; see also Eric Mallin, *Inscribing the Time: Shakespeare and the End of Elizabethan England* (Berkeley: University of California Press, 1997), pp. 167–220.

16 See Lisa Jardine, "Twins and Travesties: Gender, Dependency and Sexual Availability in *Twelfth Night*," in Zimmerman (ed.), *Erotic Politics*, pp. 27–38.

17 Lisa Jardine, *Reading Shakespeare Historically* (London: Routledge, 1996), p. 77.

18 Laurie E. Osborne, *The Trick of Singularity: "Twelfth Night" and the Performance Editions* (Iowa City: University of Iowa Press, 1996), pp. 72–73, 102, 104, 163.

19 Reviewers' comments cited in Penny Gay, *As She Likes It: Shakespeare's Unruly Women* (London: Routledge, 1994), pp. 18–20, 25, 31, 37.

20 Mary Hamer, "Shakespeare's Rosalind and Her Public Image" *Theatre Research International* 12 (1986): 108.

21 Lesley Anne Soule, "Subverting Rosalind: Cocky Ros in the Forest of Arden," *New Theatre Quarterly* 26 (1991): 126–36; the following paragraph also draws on Soule's theatrically alert reading.

22 Ibid., p. 127; and Hamer, "Shakespeare's Rosalind," p. 109.

23 Prompt copy for *As You Like It* as arranged by Augustin Daly (privately printed, 1890), n.p.

24 William Winter, *Shadows of the Stage* (New York: Macmillan, 1893), pp. 161–63, 168–69.

25 All citations from volumes of press cuttings in the Shakespeare Centre Library.
26 Lindsay Duguid, *TLS* (8 May 1992); Peter Holland, *English Shakespeares: Shakespeare on the English Stage in the 1990s* (Cambridge: Cambridge University Press, 1997), p. 133.
27 For more revealing accounts, see Carol Rutter, *Clamorous Voices: Shakespeare's Women Today* (London: Women's Press, 1988), pp. 97–121; and Russell Jackson and Robert Smallwood (eds.), *Players of Shakespeare 2* (Cambridge: Cambridge University Press, 1988), pp. 55–72.
28 My thanks to Carol Rutter for details not reproduced on the Open University videotape featuring Declan Donellan's production (London: Routledge, 1996).
29 Holland, *English Shakespeares*, p. 91.
30 Reviews cited from *Theatre Record* 15 (1995): 66.
31 John Peter, *Sunday Times* (8 December 1991).
32 See, for instance, Traub, *Desire and Anxiety*, p. 128; Garber, *Vested Interests*, p. 76; Belsey, "Disrupting Sexual Difference," pp. 180–81.
33 Helena Faucit Martin, *On Rosalind* (privately printed, c. 1885), p. 74.

12

ANTHONY MILLER

Matters of state

Shakespeare's comedies touch on "matters of state" in two ways: the workings of law or the exercise of authority may give them a threatening or problematic edge; and, despite their exotic settings and fantastic actions, some of the comedies also bear the impress of the political conditions and anxieties of early modern England. Four plays – *The Comedy of Errors*, *The Merchant of Venice*, *Measure for Measure*, and *The Tempest* – turn dramatically on legal or political questions. In three of them, persons appear under guard or in chains, and death sentences impend; *The Tempest* employs the invisible or virtual chains of Prospero's magic, and death is a possible though unspoken penalty for his traitorous brother. All four plays climax in scenes of trial or judgment. In all, the principle of mercy or the bounty of fortune eventually overrides or skirts or deflects the rigors of law – at least on the face of it, and at least for some persons. Yet both justice and mercy prove questionable, through their arbitrariness, their incompleteness, or their very theatricality. The same four plays, like most Shakespearean comedies, are set in remote or fabulous realms – Ephesus, Venice, Vienna, and "an uninhabited island" somewhere between Tunis and Naples – where things are sometimes delightfully and sometimes disturbingly different. But these places would also have had a familiar aspect for Elizabethan and Jacobean playgoers. They are versions of London or England, or of their possible futures, and their dukes shadow England's rulers, or their menacing foes and rivals. No less than modern audiences and critics, Shakespeare's original audiences were alert to the political resonances of plays – their "application," as it was called.[1] These four comedies offer ample materials for the practice of "application."

The action of *The Comedy of Errors* is framed by the sentence of death passed on Egeon in the first scene and commuted in the last. Less extreme disasters overtake Antipholus of Ephesus, who is imprisoned for debt and diagnosed as insane, while the twin slaves are continually menaced and frequently visited with violence. In one sense, these are all fantastical threats in a fanciful fiction, but an Elizabethan audience may have recognized in them discomfiting historical realities.

The "enmity and discord" between Syracuse and Ephesus correspond in their detail to the state of war that existed between England and Spain at the date of *The Comedy of Errors*. In 1586, Philip II had placed an embargo on trade with England, ordered Spanish ports to seize English shipping, and instructed authorities to arrest Englishmen and confiscate their goods.[2] Shakespeare's cities have similarly decreed "To admit no traffic to our adverse towns"; if a citizen of the one is found in the "marts and fairs" or the territorial waters of the other,

> he dies,
> His goods confiscate to the Duke's dispose,
> Unless a thousand marks be levied
> To quit the penalty and ransom him.
> (*Errors*, I.i.19–22)[3]

The Spanish embargo was widely flouted. Local authorities permitted favored English merchants to remain in the country; like Antipholus of Syracuse in Ephesus, other Englishmen risked entry to Spain by assuming a neutral nationality (Loomie, "Religion," p. 29). Nevertheless, English sailors and merchants captured in Spanish waters or even on the high seas might find themselves detained by the authorities and at risk of death. Though the number of such deaths was quite small, contemporary books and pamphlets give a more lurid and fearful impression. In *The travailes of an Englishman* (1591), Job Hortop witnesses the execution of two fellow Englishmen and suffers twenty years in Spanish galleys and prisons; among the *Strange and Wonderful Things happened to Richard Hasleton* (1595) were the experiences of being tortured and left for dead in a Spanish prison and later whipped through the streets on the back of an ass.

Though the national enmity was based on religion, Englishmen believed that Spanish persecution was in practice motivated by profit. Queen Elizabeth complained that Spanish "malice and gain" sought to "entrap and confiscate the goods of her subjects."[4] John Foxe tells how an English merchant had been executed when he refused to reveal the location of his goods, evidence that the Spanish "do nothing but seek their own private gain and commodity."[5] Ephesian law likewise ensures that Egeon's capture will profit the authorities: to escape execution, he must pay a thousand marks' ransom; if he is executed, his goods will be "confiscate to the Duke's dispose." In Shakespeare's text, Syracusan law exactly reciprocates Ephesian, a political twinning that mirrors the play's familial twinnings. Elizabethan England did not enact identical laws to Spain, but it did reciprocate some Spanish practices. After the Armada campaign of 1588, the authorities held for ransom captive Spaniards of means, and executed the rest. Even some Englishmen considered these summary executions, like the executions of the Duke of Syracuse, to be "Sprung from . . . rancorous outrage."[6] In 1588 also, two priests of the Roman Church convicted of treasonous traffic with Spain were executed at Hollywell Priory, adjacent to the Theatre at Shoreditch. When staging the near execution of Egeon and the intervention of the Abbess in *The Comedy of Errors*, Shakespeare may allude to the topography of this neighborhood, and hence to the past and present menaces and revenges of Anglo-Spanish enmity.[7]

Shakespeare's Syracusans are wary of Ephesus:

> They say this town is full of cozenage:
> As nimble jugglers that deceive the eye,
> Dark-working sorcerers that change the mind,
> Soul-killing witches that deform the body,
> Disguised cheaters, prating mountebanks.
>
> (1.2.97–101)

Protestant Englishmen held the same views of Spain's Catholicism, which they regarded partly as superstitious hocus-pocus, partly as a potential conduit for devilish influence. Foxe related many examples of sorcerer popes who "by conjuration, compacted with the devil to be made pope," or engaged in "diabolical practices of conjurings, charms, and filthy sorceries" (*Acts*, II, 94, 125; cf. II, 95–96, 121; III, 185). Samuel Harsnett would in 1603 write *A Declaration of Egregious Popish Impostures*, denouncing the Papist pretence of exorcising devils. The absurdity of Papistry is embodied in Shakespeare's Doctor Pinch, who attempts ineffectually to exorcise Antipholus of Ephesus "by all the saints in heaven," and is dismissed as a "doting wizard." The threat of Papist authority figures and their murky sources of power materializes when Shakespeare entrusts the management of the dénouement to an abbess. In the notionally non-Christian setting of the ancient Mediterranean, the Abbess cannot be associated specifically with Papistry, but she surely carries some of its marks. If so, her wisdom and benevolence reverse the anti-Papist expectations of an English audience. With the nimbleness of Ephesus' own jugglers, Shakespeare first gives Catholicism a human face, then finds for the Abbess a different and more reassuring role, as the long-lost wife of Egeon, and therefore neither a nun by vocation nor even a challengingly autonomous female.

The oppressive law that threatens Egeon is forgotten for most of *The Comedy of Errors*, but its main action introduces other forms of law, which help tie the delightfully exasperating knots of the plot, and complement the poetry of enchantment with a harsh materiality. When Antipholus of Ephesus finds himself arrested for debt, he is entrusted to a jailer who is terrifyingly described by Dromio of Syracuse: "A devil in an everlasting garment . . . One whose hard heart is button'd up with steel; . . . One that before the judgment carries poor souls to hell" (4.2.33–40). The English folklore of the Spanish Inquisition, with its monstrous persecutions and infernal prisons, helps endow this figure with part of his terror.

Legalized forms of binding and beating fill the text. Antipholus of Ephesus commissions a gold chain necklace, destined first for his wife and later for his courtesan, but which instead descends like a charm on Antipholus of Syracuse. This emblem of love's sweet bonds and of bountiful fortune transforms into an item of legal evidence against Antipholus of Ephesus in an action for debt. Not only does the chain bring about his arrest: when he rails against the legal error he faces the threat of being literally "bound and laid in some dark room" as a madman. As well as the chain, Antipholus of Ephesus orders a rope, with which to beat his apparently unfaithful wife and her confederates. In the event, he succeeds in beating only his slave Dromio, who is then also bound, probably with the same rope. The rope that beats and binds is the emblem of the violence by which authority is exercised. "When I am cold, he heats me with beating; when I am warm, he cools me with beating. I am wak'd with it when I sleep, rais'd with it when I sit, driven out of doors with it when I go from home, welcom'd home with it when I return" (4.4.32–37): Dromio's beatings are partly the matter of physical farce, partly an evocation of the legal condition of Greco-Roman slavery.

Here too the Spanish menace casts its shadow. Had the Spanish invasion succeeded, Englishmen believed that they would have suffered the degradations of slavery. Thomas Deloney produced a blood-curdling *Ballet of the straunge and most cruell Whippes which the Spanyards had prepared to whippe and torment English men and women* (1588); another Armada pamphlet tells of "certain Irons grauen with markes, to be heated for the marking of all the children in their faces, being vnder seuen yeeres of age."[8] The Spanish branding of American slaves was denounced as a demonic form of inscription: "the faces of these men . . . have been, by our sins, transformed into paper."[9] The same image is applied to the whippings in *The Comedy of Errors*: "If the skin were parchment, and the blows you gave were ink" (3.1.13). On the other hand, owning or trading slaves was not altogether unknown or unthinkable to Englishmen. Sir William Hawkins, a hero of the Armada campaign, trafficked prosperously in slaves; there were proposals in England to enslave captured American Indians; throughout the sixteenth century, proposals had been floated to institute a form of slavery as a solution to the social problems caused by England's own "sturdy beggars" (Hunt, "Slavery," p. 39).

There was therefore an element of ideological displacement in the English practice of treating slavery as an instance of Spanish barbarism. In *The Comedy of Errors* there is a contrary tendency to naturalize or to accept slavery. In the Roman comedies that provide the model for *The Comedy of Errors*, slaves win or buy their way out of slavery. In Shakespeare's version the Dromios remain slaves at the end: the play's providential dénouement does not extend to this degree of enfranchisement. To render slavery a matter of comedy is, when practiced by Englishmen, to make it acceptable, and, when practiced by England's enemies, to exorcise its threat.

The Merchant of Venice is governed by legalisms: contracts, wills, marriage oaths; fidelity to bonds and release from bonds. These features of civil law turn into matters of state when Shylock's attempt to claim Antonio's bond collides with the laws of Venice. The collision reveals starkly that the Venetian state uses law to privilege its Christian citizens and enrich itself. At the play's momentous peripeteia, when Shylock's persecution of Antonio is turned back on himself, the scales of justice tip abruptly and precipitously, and Venice reveals an unexpected political ruthlessness. The transformation corresponds to the historical double nature of the city, which was proverbial for frivolity and license but also admired for its formidable naval strength and its unrelenting judicial severity.

The argumentation and pleading that pervade the play position the audience as judge or jury, weighing up conflicting words and actions. But the profusion and contradictions of these features also perplex judgment. Portia's aphorism "Nothing is good, I see, without respect" (that is, judgments vary according to circumstances) summarizes the operation of law in *The Merchant of Venice*. There is one law for Christians and another law for aliens. In Act 4, legalism is used punitively, to condemn and humiliate Shylock; in Act 5, it is used playfully, to tease and forgive Bassanio. Shylock's insistent appeals to his bond and to law manifest in one "respect" an inhuman legalism; in another they show that a Jew in Christendom depends on a system of laws for his rights and his status. Shylock's conduct toward Antonio in particular is given a variety of explanations. His decision to pursue the prosecution follows Jessica's flight, suggesting that it is a function of rage and powerlessness. Antonio gives a different explanation: he has redeemed debtors from Shylock's malignant power. Shylock's own summary is that his hatred for Antonio is arbitrary and irrational. This "overdetermined" multiplicity of motives suggests that Shakespeare experienced some unease with the role of Shylock, and it problematizes the task of judgment that the play simultaneously invites.

As the trial scene approaches and unfolds, Shylock's pursuit of Antonio makes law more and more the weapon of a furious revenge – exactly the reverse of the conventional Renaissance view of law's purpose, to restrain and civilize revenge. With Shylock on the point of taking Antonio's life, the action reveals the legal system as a flimsy thing, dangerously susceptible to misuse. In *The Merchant of Venice*, however, law is not only the customary comic source of threat; law, not fortune, is also the source of redress. Law and state power are not canceled or outwitted; they themselves produce the resolution. But in this process the redirected law partakes disturbingly of Shylock's own misuse, and law itself becomes endowed with a degree of chicanery, the aspect of comedy that delights in "getting away with it." Portia's rescue of Antonio and prosecution of Shylock hinge on a clever reading of the bond, a brilliant *coup de théâtre* but improbable law. If the original contract were legally enforceable (which it would not be in any sane legal system), then the difficulty of taking the exact weight of flesh and the necessity of shedding blood would be recognized as inherent in its terms. Even Portia's request that Shylock furnish a doctor proves to be less a gesture of charity than an engine of incrimination.

The confrontation between Shylock and Portia in the trial scene has been thematized as New Testament mercy superseding Old Testament law, but the play conforms only with difficulty to this dichotomy. Portia insists on enforcing the law against Shylock, until the Duke intervenes. Even then, her mercy has a bullying quality, very different from the ethereal entity, dropping as the gentle rain from heaven, of her eloquent encomium. Shylock discerns this kind of fissure when he argues that Christians talk humility but practice revenge, or asks why the Venetians do not demonstrate their mercy by releasing the slaves who row their galleys – and on whom the city's security, wealth, and system of justice therefore depend (3.1.68–73; 4.1.90–98). The final legal judgment on Shylock translates into the harshest terms the forgiveness and unexpected bounty that customarily ends a comedy: Shylock is forgiven at the expense of his religious identity and economic freedom. In an inversion of comic convention, the miserly father is put into the position of the young lover, a powerless "ward" of the state and of Antonio. This bitter version of comic forgiveness is superseded formally, but cannot be erased emotionally, by the light-hearted trial, judgment, and forgiveness of Bassanio and Gratiano at Belmont.

How might Elizabethan Englishmen have envisaged the Venetian state? The city of Venice, with its important community of Jewish moneylenders, exemplified an economy built on trade instead of land, and a society that incorporated a cosmopolitan population. In 1589 the volatile relations between Venice and its Jewish population had entered a new phase in which

Jews were granted increased religious freedom and personal protection. In such a state, as in the multicultural states of the twenty-first century, shared customs or traditions become less important and the protections of law more important:

> If you deny it, let the danger light
> Upon your charter and your city's freedom!
> . . . If you deny me, fie upon your law!
> There is no force in the decrees of Venice.
> (4.1.38–39, 101–02)

Not that Venice was a liberal polity. The city was proverbially severe in punishing sedition and treason; in emergencies, it imposed special taxes or forced loans on Jews; and citizens were discouraged from contact with the Jewish population – hence the institution of the Jewish ghetto, whose name probably originated in Venice.[10] Though England, or at any rate London, increasingly shared the characteristics of Venice, the Elizabethan regime attempted to contain them within traditional political and social forms. *The Merchant of Venice* is shot through with the anxieties aroused by economic and social change. Wealth is unstable, and may at any moment vanish in shipwreck or by state decree; the fear of miscegenation appears in Portia's unwelcome Moorish suitors and in the uncomfortable marriage of Lorenzo and Jessica; the punishment of Shylock also registers the fear that a cosmopolitan state must harbor secret enemies.

Nevertheless, Shakespeare allows Shylock a measure of dignity and a number of cogent speeches in his own defense. The play's conflicted treatment of its villain-victim has historical precedents. In Italy popes occasionally denounced anti-Semitism, shrewdly recognizing it as the product of economic resentment and rivalry.[11] In Shakespeare's London a Portugese Jew, Roderigo Lopez, became a leading doctor and eventually chief physician to Queen Elizabeth. Lopez was implicated in a Spanish plot to assassinate the queen, and he was condemned and executed in 1594. The role of Shylock in *The Merchant of Venice* may well cater to popular interest in this *cause célèbre*. Here too the record shows a division of attitudes. At his execution, Lopez is said to have declared that "he loved the Queen as well as he loved *Jesus Christ*; which coming from a man of the Jewish profession moved no small laughter in the Standers-by." Even a Christianized Jew remained by definition treacherous, and his punishment an occasion for the vengeful rejoicing voiced by Shakespeare's Gratiano. Queen Elizabeth, however, at first defended "the poor man . . . whose innocence she knew well enough," and later delayed signing his death warrant; after his death, she allowed his family to retain much of the property that was, like Shylock's, legally forfeit to the state.[12] Shakespeare's stage permits a similar double response: the spectacle of the condemned Jew might be viewed with mirthful triumph or with compassion.[13]

Shylock's forced conversion might also have drawn a double response. London in the 1590s saw outbreaks of hostility toward aliens, who were believed to be present in much greater numbers than was actually the case, and who, like Shylock, were accused of enriching themselves at natives' expense and of devising treasons against the state.[14] At the end of Shakespeare's play, the challengingly diverse and tolerant Venice of historical fact responds to these anxieties by metamorphosing into a more comprehensible and reassuring model of enforced uniformity. On the other hand, Shylock's offense and its punishment might represent distinctly un-English, continental, and Papist practices. By condemning Shylock because he intended to take the life of a citizen, even though he did not actually do so, Venetian law functions in an opposite way to law in *Measure for Measure*, which acquits Angelo because he did not actually commit fornication, even though he not only intended to do so but acted in the belief that he was doing so. English law likewise generally confined itself to actions, not intentions, and the English Reformation was generally satisfied with outward conformity. Queen Elizabeth was said to have declared that she "would not open windows into men's souls."[15] To an English audience, the Venetian law might suggest the conditions of continental Catholicism, which sought to examine private beliefs through its Inquisitions and in particular had a history of forcing the conversion of Jews (Calimani, *Ghetto*, pp. 41–42).

In *Measure for Measure*, the traditional comic opposition between law and license is reconfigured to produce the play's distinctive acerbity. The attempt to police sex is greeted with the critique of the untameable flesh: "Does your worship mean to geld and splay all the youth of the city?"; "it is impossible to extirp it quite, friar, till eating and drinking be put down" (2.1.230–31; 3.2.102–03). In this play, however, sex manifests itself practically as prostitution and its diseases, or as Angelo's exploitative and tortured advances to Isabella, or as the Duke's entrapping of Angelo into sexual relations with Mariana. Even the harmless young lovers Claudio and Juliet dutifully repent of their sexual misdemeanor. The history of Angelo enacts another classic comic demonstration, the human frailty of the judicial authority who claims the right to punish frailty in others. The self-controlled and dispassionate man of justice proves to have passions after all, and privately flouts the law that he publicly enforces. The irruption of Angelo's passion is not, however, pleasantly ludicrous or genially forgivable; it is too much like the lust delineated in Shakespeare's sonnet 129, "perjur'd, murd'rous, bloody, full of blame, / Savage, extreme, rude, cruel, not to trust." When Isabella declares that she will denounce Angelo, his answer is chilling: "Who will believe thee, Isabel?" (2.4.154). After Isabella has apparently given Angelo her body in exchange for Claudio's life, he treacherously orders Claudio's death all the same. When he is publicly shamed, Angelo begs for death rather than forgiveness: to the last, his role threatens to disrupt comic convention. All these things imbue the Angelo plot with an ominous darkness.

The play subjects to distinctive treatment another legal entanglement, the threatened execution of Claudio "for getting Madame Julietta with child." This is the improbable penalty for a forgivable offense that an audience of a comedy expects to see lightly overturned, but the threat of death receives heavy emphasis and prevails long into the play. The disguised Duke repeatedly assures Claudio that he must die, and Isabella that he has died, until his survival is revealed and his pardon announced in the play's closing moments. These are comedic deceptions pursued to an unusual extremity, constituting a severe test for their victims. If Isabella rises to the heroic charity of praying for Angelo's pardon, Claudio performs less nobly. He vacillates between accepting death and dreading it, and he finally begs Isabella to save him by surrendering her honor to Angelo. The play's *jeune premier* is not as worthless as Bertram in *All's Well That Ends Well*, but he is decidedly unheroic, a suggestible and very ordinary young man.

Though *Measure for Measure* eventually allows the flesh to evade the strictures of a harsh law, this is a comedy unusually suspicious of license and release. Sexual promiscuity and other forms of liberty (such as Lucio's slanderous verbal liberty) are so out of control in Shakespeare's Vienna that most characters welcome restraint, or at least acknowledge its necessity. For the penitent Claudio,

> As surfeit is the father of much fast,
> So every scope by the immoderate use
> Turns to restraint.
>
> (1.2.125–27)

Isabella enters a convent, and seeks a yet "more strict restraint" than her sisterhood enjoins. Mariana immures herself, and apologizes for enjoying even the consolation of music. Shades of the prison-house close upon this play as upon no other Shakespearean comedy. Four scenes take place in prison; a provost, or jailer, has a significant role, and an executioner and a condemned criminal have cameo roles; the plot turns on the death of a prisoner, whose severed head appears as a stage property, a startling incursion of death into the domain of comedy.

In guiding, or attempting to guide, the action toward the welcome and equitable outcome of comedy, Shakespeare's disguised Duke also aims to

restore law and respect for authority. Much in the Duke's character and activities appears to be suggested by the historical figure of King James I, or
James' manual of kingly conduct, *Basilicon Doron*, as well as other Renaissance writings on princely rule, such as Machiavelli's *The Prince*. Yet it is
difficult to regard the Duke as an ideal or even a notably competent ruler,
still less as the "power divine" that the guilty Angelo discerns. Though the
Duke's efforts are well intentioned, they are also problematic in their almost
desperate improvisations, double standards, and risible misjudgments. The
Duke appoints Angelo as his deputy and vanishes into the disguise of a friar
largely because his lax government has produced Vienna's excessive liberty,
a result against which King James warns.[16] The Duke's appointment of a
deputy to incur the opprobrium that will accompany the restoration of law
enacts a stratagem notoriously admired by Machiavelli. Cesare Borgia ap-
pointed as governor "a man of cruelty, but at the same time of great energy."
Borgia then set out to show "that if any cruelties had been practised, they
had not originated with him, but had resulted altogether from the harsh nature of his minister," and had his governor put to death – a fate that hangs
tantalisingly over Angelo in the last act.[17] The Duke has another reason for
appointing Angelo. He wishes to observe "if power change purpose: / What
our seemers be" (1.3.54). His observation of Angelo follows James' injunc-
tions that a king must acquaint himself at first hand with the "nature and
humours" of his subjects, and "Bee a daily watch-man ouer your seruants,
that they obey your lawes precisely" (*Political Writings*, pp. 31, 37).

The Duke engineers Angelo's unknowing assignation with Mariana so that
he will believe he has succeeded in coercing Isabella. The Duke confidently
awaits the arrival of Angelo's order for Claudio's release; instead there arrives the order for his execution. The Duke next plans to have Barnardine
executed in place of Claudio; this expedient too fails when Barnardine proves
deaf to the Duke's confidently proffered religious counsels. Only then does
a corpse materialize that bears a fortuitous resemblance to Claudio. The repeated frustration of the Duke's stratagems and their eventual cumbersome
execution are surely designed to emphasize the limits of his mastery over
people and events. Lucio's ability to disconcert the Duke with his slanders
also suggests a ruler lacking in self-assurance. Finally, the ethics of the Duke's
solutions are discomfiting. The sexual intimacy between Angelo and Mariana
seems to replicate the intimacy for which Claudio and Juliet are condemned.
The end of the play produces not only a series of mostly mismatched marriages, but also the pardon and release of a defiantly unreconstructed criminal. The Barnardine who is freed to wander loose in Vienna may represent the
obduracy of flesh against legal and spiritual ministrations, but he is hardly
the harmless representative expected in a comedy.

The Duke's management of the dénouement does have, at least for his stage audience, the *éclat* that Machiavelli recommends: "It is also important for a prince to give striking examples of his interior administration . . . when an occasion presents itself to reward or punish any one who has in civil affairs either rendered great service to the state, or committed some crime, so that it may be much talked about" (*Chief Works*, I, 82). The Duke also exemplifies James' repeated injunction that a king should hear directly his people's complaints and should support the poor and distressed against oppressors (*Political Writings*, pp. 24, 28, 31–32, 45). For the theatre audience his preparations, over several scenes, are excessively busy, and the performance, with its multiple entrances and exits, is contrived and creaky. Lucio's irreverent commentaries continually threaten to steal the Duke's show, and Lucio's characterization of the "fantastical Duke of dark corners" is a dangerously apt description of the Duke's whole procedure, from disguise to plotting to dénouement. King James' teaching that "a King is as one set on a stage whose smallest actions and gestures, all the people gazingly doe behold" (*Political Writings*, p. 49) has been much quoted. It is not always recognized that James regards this prominence as problematic, because people see only the king's exterior and do not understand his interior motives. *Measure for Measure* makes the audience privileged viewers of the king's secret conduct, but the result is not reassuring. The Duke may seem like a masterful ruler to his subjects, but the audience sees how flimsy is this self-presentation.

Shakespeare's Vienna embodies many of the features that induced anxiety in the overpopulated and potentially ungovernable metropolis that Jacobean London was turning into. London's authorities also contended with uncontrollable prostitution in the suburbs outside the city's jurisdiction, and royal authorities with a military caste were discontented by King James' policy of peace with England's traditional Hapsburg foe. The choice of Vienna, however, sets *Measure for Measure* in a strikingly alien milieu, a center of Hapsburg power. In this setting, the Duke's disguise as a friar reminds the audience of the alliance between the Hapsburg Empire and counter-Reformation Catholicism. Shakespeare's Duke may suggest specifically the monastically inclined Archduke Albert, contemporary governor of the Austrian Netherlands,[18] or the Emperor Charles V, who had retired to a monastery after his abdication in 1556. The Vienna associated with these figures stands for the menaces that James' peace risked loosing on England. The idle soldiers of the second scene might turn their attention to the unfinished mission of suppressing Protestantism; any concession to Catholic powers might see the entry to England of meddlesome friars, who were known to be the initiators and instruments of inquisition. Though in other plays Shakespeare displays benevolent friars, a ruler garbed as a friar would be a threatening figure to an English public.

He would be all the more so for a London theatre audience, who might recognize in the rule of the Duke-friar and his "precise" deputy the lineaments of those theocratic regimes that were invariably hostile to theatrical entertainments. One example was the former regime of the friar Savonarola at Florence. Another was the present regime at Geneva, established by Calvin, now under the leadership of Théodore de Bèze, and the subject of revived admiration around the date of *Measure for Measure* for its providential self-defense on the night of the Escalade (1602) and the subsequent treaty of St-Jullien (1603). A third was the regime of moral policing that English Puritans sought to install in London itself.[19] The play debates a *quaestio* that the disputatious James would have delighted in, and that had local and contemporary reverberations: whether a ruler may reform the morals of his people? The examples of both Angelo and the Duke suggest that totalizing schemes of ethical management will issue at worst in tyranny, at best in very limited success.

More than any other comedy of Shakespeare, *The Tempest* foregrounds matters of state and government; yet on examination its political fable proves elusive. For a "liberal humanist" criticism, interested in individual autonomy and emphasizing ethics rather than politics, this elusiveness endows Shakespeare with a suprapolitical stature, exemplifying what Coleridge called the "wonderful philosophic impartiality in Shakespeare's politics."[20] For a "materialist" or politically oriented criticism, emphasizing class structures, and analyzing in the play the operation of a colonialist ideology, its elusiveness may rather exemplify the way in which an ideology is capable of disguising itself, entertaining exceptions and conceding weaknesses or injustices in order to underpin the more effectively its necessity. Hence *The Tempest* contains allusions to England's American colonies, but blurs them by its Italian characters and Mediterranean setting. Prospero has the marks of a colonial ruler, but he has not settled on his island voluntarily, and he leaves it at the first opportunity. Caliban has the marks of a colonial subject, but at points in the text he is classed as a nonhuman monster, to whom the concept of colonialization would not apply. Such manipulations of the dramatic material might suggest that the play's political content is merely matter for a fanciful entertainment. Stuart masques show however that fanciful entertainments could readily serve the purpose of political myth-making. A colonialist ideology is well served by representing a reluctant settler and a bestial native, a cast that makes colonialism a self-sacrificing taming of brutishness – the belief with which many colonizers have consciously entered on their project.

The Tempest also directly debates the issues of colonialism. Prospero claims that divine providence has brought him to the island; that Caliban is ungrateful, unteachable, good only for menial tasks; and that Caliban is the illegitimate child of Sycorax and the devil, and thus has no claim to inherit the island. In these circumstances, Prospero has the right to rule, and the magic by which he enforces his rule witnesses to a superiority that is ethical as well as technological. This is a very convenient story for Prospero, but Caliban tells a counterstory. He claims the island by prior occupancy and by descent from his mother Sycorax; that Prospero bribed Caliban into teaching him how to survive on the island, but then betrayed Caliban's trust and turned him into a slave. In this version, Prospero is as much a usurper on the island as Antonio in Milan, or the English colonists in Virginia: "I am subject to a tyrant, / A sorcerer, that by his cunning hath / Cheated me of the island" (3.2.42–44). Caliban's history of betrayal echoes the related history of slave-trading. African princes sent to Europe for their education were instead sold into slavery. The first Africans whose presence in England is definitely attested were slaves brought there in 1555, "so that on their return to Africa, they would 'be a helpe to Englishmen' as interpreters."[21] Sir John Hawkins obtained 300 slaves "partly by the sworde, and partly by other meanes" – means that are ominously unstated. Their sale in the Indies brought Hawkins a freight worthy of Prospero's banquet or Ariel's songs: "ginger, sugar, and some quantitie of pearles."[22] The opposition between Prospero and Caliban finds expression in their exchange of curses or threats on Caliban's first entrance. Emotionally, the two operate on the same level of childish retributiveness, but materially Prospero has the advantage. As in the Renaissance Americas, where the new settlers had superior weaponry, and as in all sites of imperial conquest, Prospero's "magic," the play's code for technology, means that his threats will succeed, whereas Caliban's curses are empty.

Whatever his rights, Caliban adopts the subordinate position of the colonized subject, even toward the degraded Stephano and Trinculo. On one reading, this assumes that colonized populations are not only quasibestial but naturally slavish. On another reading, Caliban's conduct is the result of a cultural encounter in which he is disadvantaged. Caliban's status as slave, rapist, and drunkard may simply show the position in which he is put when confronted by a more powerful culture with different customs. The ability of colonial rule to persuade its subjects to interiorize their subordination is demonstrated in Caliban's lyrical appreciation of the island:

> The clouds methought would open, and show riches
> Ready to drop upon me, that when I wak'd
> I cried to dream again.
>
> (3.2.141–43)

Caliban's noises are presumably the musical products of Prospero's magic, or the melodies of his indentured servant Ariel. Caliban has fallen in love with the conditions of his own imprisonment and persecution. The ultimate success of the colonizer is to make the colonized subject find beauty and solace in his subjection. Yet this submission is countered by Caliban's ability to fashion the colonizer's tools of domination into means of resistance: "You taught me language, and my profit on't / Is, I know how to curse" (1.2.363–64). If Caliban's curses are ineffectual, his later rebellion against Prospero shows a shrewd sense of the need to act against the material source of his power: "Burn but his books."

The political interest of *The Tempest* is not directed only at colonialism. It also treats broader principles and problems of government, ostensibly in the dukedoms and kingdoms of Italy, the earliest models of Renaissance statecraft, though also with bearings on the England of James I. The overarching action of the play concerns Prospero's enterprise of regaining his dukedom of Milan and arranging the marriage between Miranda and Ferdinand that will ensure a succession. This action generates a range of educative or coercive attempts to fashion worthy magistrates, and idealistic discourses on perfect commonwealths. The figure of Prospero embodies James' aspiration to the status of philosopher-king, while his past and present career demonstrates the risks of political negligence in such a role and the limitations imposed on it by human recalcitrance. Prospero's choleric relations with his two island servants, and their grievances against him, have features in common with the disputes between James and his parliaments, while his education of Ferdinand may refer to the high hopes held out for James' heir apparent, Prince Henry.[23]

In the process of redressing his exile, Prospero is obliged to thwart two further rebellions. In their attempt on Prospero's life, Caliban, Stephano, and Trinculo stage an example of the popular uprising dreaded by the authorities of early modern England. In an example of the dynastic *coup d'état* that was in reality a greater threat to Renaissance rulers, Antonio and Sebastian, who had dethroned Prospero, now attempt to kill Alonso, who was implicated in the dethronement. As he masters and overcomes these schemes, Prospero deals peremptorily and harshly with the base characters, but quite mildly with his peers, whom he attempts to educate and bring to repentance through the experience of loss and suffering, through terrifying spectacles, and through admonition. Like the Duke's plans in *Measure for Measure*, Prospero's plans do not operate with perfect smoothness, and the play ends with his project less complete than he would wish. Prospero is successful with Alonso, who believes for most of the play that his political crimes have been punished by the loss of his son in the opening shipwreck. But

Prospero fails with Antonio and perhaps with Sebastian, who by all appearances return to Italy ethically unreconstructed. In an eloquent stage image, Prospero addresses and instructs one by one the subjects of his educative project, but these subjects are all in a state of trance. The words of the magus may penetrate their minds, or he may be speaking to the deaf.

As the Duke in *Measure for Measure* is particularly troubled by Lucio, whose slanders he cannot control, so Prospero seems excessively troubled by Caliban. The thought of Caliban's rebellion makes him cut short his betrothal masque for Ferdinand and Miranda, even though his magical powers are easily capable of routing Caliban. When Prospero fulminates about "a born devil, on whose nature / Nurture can never stick" (4.1.188–89), he could be speaking of Antonio as much as Caliban. Prospero's failure with the "savage and deformed slave" stands for his failure with his own civilized but deeply corrupt brother, which he cannot so readily admit. Both failures arise from the intractable material of a fallen human nature. When in the last scene Prospero acknowledges Caliban as his servant, his words, "this thing of darkness I / Acknowledge mine" (5.1.275–76) insist primarily on the separateness and bizarre unlikeness of master and servant, but also have a resonance that acknowledges their affinity. Prospero seems to acknowledge the Caliban in himself, as he has been forced reluctantly to acknowledge the unregenerate Antonio as his brother.

It was always recognized that statecraft was a means of controlling, and perhaps even correcting, the waywardness of that fallen nature. In his impositions on the youthful Ferdinand, Prospero seems more successful. Prospero forces Ferdinand to perform menial labor and to practice sexual temperance, disciplines that will prove him an ethically worthy husband of Miranda and eventually a politically worthy ruler of Naples and Milan. Ferdinand's role is the main focus for the play's many echoes of Virgil's *Aeneid*, a poem that likewise combines the promise of empire and exemplifies the careful self-cultivation necessary in an ideal prince. Yet when the young lovers are "discovered" to the other noble characters, Miranda claims to catch Ferdinand cheating in their chess game, a trivial but ominous offense – unless one takes the Machiavellian view that a prince needs to know when and how to cheat skilfully. *The Tempest* also holds out Utopian ideals, in which humanity, and nature at large, recover (in Christian terms) their unfallen condition or (in classical terms) the Golden Age. Gonzalo' account of how he would ideally govern the island (which paraphrases Montaigne's optimistic imaginings of pre-colonial America), and the winterless perfection of Prospero's broken betrothal masque for Ferdinand and Miranda, are evidently not compatible with the human material presented in the play.

Nevertheless their imaginative power witnesses to the necessary dream of a better society.

NOTES

1 See, for example, Ben Jonson's dedication to *Volpone*, *Ben Jonson*, ed. C. H. Herford and Percy and Evelyn Simpson, 11 vols. (Oxford: Clarendon Press, 1925–51), V, 18–19.

2 Albert J. Loomie, "Religion and Elizabethan Commerce with Spain," *Catholic Historical Review* 50 (1964): 28–30.

3 References to Shakespeare to G. Blakemore Evans *et al.* (eds.), *The Riverside Shakespeare*, 2nd edn (Boston and New York: Houghton Mifflin Company, 1997).

4 Pauline Croft, "Englishmen and the Spanish Inquisition 1558–1625," *English Historical Review* 87 (1972): 254.

5 *The Acts and Monuments of John Foxe*, ed. George Townsend, 8 vols. (London: Seeley, Burnside and Seeley, 1843–49), VIII, 513.

6 Colin Martin and Geoffrey Parker, *The Spanish Armada* (London: Hamish Hamilton, 1988), pp. 231–50.

7 T. W. Baldwin, *William Shakespeare Adapts a Hanging* (Princeton: Princeton University Press, 1931).

8 *The Copie of a Letter . . . declaring the state of England* (1588), sig. E4.

9 Quoted in Maurice Hunt, "Slavery, English Servitude, and *The Comedy of Errors*," *English Literary Renaissance* 27 (1997): 35.

10 David C. McPherson, *Shakespeare, Jonson, and the Myth of Venice* (Newark: University of Delaware Press, and London and Cranbury, N.J.: Associated University Presses, 1990), pp. 36, 45.

11 Riccardo Calimani, *The Ghetto of Venice*, trans. Katherine Silberblatt Wolfthal (Milan: Rusconi, 1988), pp. 24–25.

12 David S. Katz, *The Jews in the History of England 1485–1850* (Oxford: Clarendon Press, 1994), pp. 86–100.

13 In a case of 1596, the English legal system treated two Jewish defendants with conspicuous fairness: C. J. Sisson, "A Colony of Jews in Shakespeare's London," *Essays and Studies* 23 (1938): 41–51.

14 James S. Shapiro, *Shakespeare and the Jews* (New York: Columbia University Press, 1996), pp. 180–89.

15 *The Works of Francis Bacon*, ed. J. Spedding, R. L. Ellis, and D. D. Heath, 14 vols. (London: Longman, 1857–74), VIII, 98; cf. VI, 298.

16 *King James VI and I: Political Writings*, ed. Johann P. Sommerville (Cambridge: Cambridge University Press, 1994), p. 22.

17 Niccolò Machiavelli, *The Chief Works and Others*, trans. Allan Gilbert, 3 vols. (Durham and London: Duke University Press, 1958), I, 31.

18 Leah S. Marcus, *Puzzling Shakespeare* (Berkeley and Los Angeles: University of California Press, 1988), pp. 190–200.

19 See John Spurr, *English Puritanism 1603–89* (Basingstoke: Macmillan, 1998), pp. 72–78. For English laws and social practices in the area of sex, see Martin Ingram, *Church Courts, Sex and Marriage in England, 1570–1640* (Cambridge: Cambridge University Press, 1987), especially pp. 219–37.

20 Samuel Taylor Coleridge, *Shakespearean Criticism*, ed. T. M. Raysor, 2 vols. (London: J. M. Dent, and New York: Dutton, 1960), I, 79.
21 Folarin Shyllon, *Black People in Britain 1555–1833* (Oxford, New York and Ibadan: Oxford University Press, 1977), pp. 6, 45.
22 Richard Hakluyt, *The Principal Navigations . . . of the English Nation*, 12 vols. (Glasgow: James MacLehose, 1903–05), X, 8.
23 Donna B. Hamilton, *Virgil and "The Tempest" : The Politics of Imitation* (Columbus: Ohio State University Press, 1990), pp. 37–40, 44–55.

13

MICHAEL O'CONNELL

The experiment of romance

Shakespeare's "romances," the four plays written toward the close of his theatrical career, can be seen as his most experimental and, in some respects, his most daring theatrical ventures. They elude easy definition as comedy, tragedy, or history. *Pericles, Cymbeline, The Winter's Tale,* and *The Tempest* constitute in modern critical discourse a grouping of plays set off from the rest of his dramatic works. But what they share generically, and indeed what they are, may not be entirely self-evident. The first folio of 1623, which printed all of them but *Pericles* (added in the third folio of 1664), is no help. It placed *The Tempest* and *The Winter's Tale* among the comedies and *Cymbeline* among the tragedies. Clearly all are comedies in the formal sense in that they end not in death but in the happiness of reunions and/or promised marriages. Another generic term for them is "tragicomedy," but this does not so much define them as simply describe the mixture of threatened tragedy and comic conclusion each contains. While historically the individual plays have been appreciated and performed – *The Tempest* in particular because of its apparent self-referentiality in seeming to relate Shakespeare's own art to Prospero's magic – earlier readers and audiences often found them, in terms of Shakespeare's career, an apparent falling off from the intensity and gravity of the great tragedies. It is, in fact, an accomplishment of twentieth-century criticism to have rediscovered the sophistication and seriousness of the four plays and to find fascination in their interrelatedness.[1]

The plays were first termed romances just over a century ago by the Irish critic Edward Dowden, when he celebrated what he took to be their achieved serenity in relation to the preceding tragedies: "The dissonances are resolved into harmony; the spirit of the plays is one of large benignity; they tell of the blessedness of the forgiveness of injuries; they show how the broken bonds between heart and heart may be repaired and reunited; each play closes with a victory of love."[2] While such idealizing, which constructed a comforting biographical narrative for Shakespeare, is little to our taste now, the term itself has stuck because all four plays do indeed employ such romance motifs as shipwreck, lost children, disguises, pastoral interludes, apparent death, and final reunions. And except for *The Tempest*, they all spread their plots over vast tracts of time and space; even *The Tempest*, while ostentatiously observing the Aristotelian unities of time and place, extends its actual story over a dozen years as it condenses this "backstory" to exposition.

Romance, while difficult to define as a narrative genre, has in fact proved a rich and useful term for describing these plays, and I want in part to offer an argument about how Shakespeare deployed the tradition of romance in building these plays. But it is my primary contention that these works constitute an experimental form of theatre, that each of them is distinctive, even idiosyncratic, in its manipulation of the conventions of romance. One characteristic they share is self-consciousness about their relationship to the romance tradition. "Like an old tale still," remarks Third Gentleman in *The Winter's Tale* (5.2.61) as the improbabilities of the recognition scene of Leontes and the long-lost Perdita are narrated.[3] In its own way, each of the plays both acknowledges the "old-tale" character of its narrative and foregrounds its own equally self-aware theatricality. In doing so the plays appear to adumbrate a built-in critique of romance that is an element of their experimental character. Mere parody is never the point of this recognition of artificiality. Rather, what fascinates about the four plays is that at the same time as they acknowledge artificiality, they give the impression of great seriousness in their undoing of tragic separation and injury; the recognition scenes have a seriousness about them that seems to challenge even the acknowledged artificiality. The four plays, in quite different and separate ways, engage the issues explored in the tragedies. In particular, the themes and psychological patterns explored in *Othello*, *King Lear*, and *Macbeth* return again and again in the romances, as if obsessively querying whether tragic conclusions are a dramatic inevitability of those thematics.

We can take Ben Jonson's contentious and negative reaction to the romances as contemporary evidence of their experimental character. In the induction to *Bartholomew Fair*, itself experimental in a number of ways, Jonson has his spokesman, the Bookholder, indicate what the audience will *not* find in his play: there is no "servant-monster" or "a nest of antics." Jonson "is loth to make nature afraid in his plays, like those that beget Tales, Tempests, and such like drolleries, to mix his head with other men's heels, let the concupiscence of jigs and dances reign as strong as it will amongst you."[4] The "servant-monster" is clearly Caliban, and the "nest of antics" refers almost as obviously to the dancers of *The Tempest*, either Ariel's sprites or the reapers who dance after the wedding masque. In both *The Winter's Tale* and *The Tempest* Shakespeare mixes his head with other men's heels and includes country dances. Jonson was writing this in 1614, hard upon the success of these plays. But some fifteen years later the character of Shakespeare's late plays would still irritate him. While counseling himself to "leave the loathed stage" in his "Ode to Himself," he insists that "some moldy tale, / Like *Pericles*" will please mere playgoers, as his own plays have not done. By this date *Pericles* was indeed long in the theatrical tooth, but the moldiness inheres as well in the character of the play itself, "a song that old was sung" in the words of the narrating Gower that begin the play. Jonson seems to be objecting to those very characteristics of the plays that link them with romance, that they are mere "tales" and lack mimetic connection to an identifiable reality. In this regard a figure like Caliban, indeterminate between human and subhuman, is particularly objectionable. The dancing that punctuates the pastoral discussion of Act 4 of *The Winter's Tale* may look like mere entertainment, unconnected to the serious business of advancing the plot. We can further infer Jonson's objections to the way the first three romances egregiously violate the unities of time and place in the self-conscious way *The Tempest* fulfills them. Early in the play (1.2.239) Prospero asks Ariel the time and how long they have for the actions that must be performed; at the beginning of Act 5 he again asks the time of Ariel and learns that all is to be completed on schedule. Surely this is designed to call amused attention to the play's observance of the formal structures – at the same time the play projects a magically constructed storm, spirits under the control of a magus with fantastic power, the "servant monster" with a witch for a mother, not to mention the mere coincidence of all Prospero's enemies gathered on his island in a moment. Does the breaking off of Prospero's betrothal masque in the midst of a dance of "certain reapers" suggest a response, perhaps ironic, to Jonson's objection to dancing and visual spectacle – expressed later in the sneer at the "concupiscence of jigs and dances"? Do these elements of *The Tempest* suggest something of the artistic conversation out of which the play emerged? Whether or not he was entertained by the fulfilling of the unities in *The Tempest*, Jonson's comments indicate that he was not persuaded by the experimentation. But at the very least, the playful references to time indicate that the experimentation is not gratuitous but connected to questions of the role of romance and mimesis on the Jacobean stage. Shakespeare sets before his audience (including Ben!) the extremes of romance improbability *and* the punctilious observance of the unities.

By the time Shakespeare came to write *Pericles*, romance was a vast and varied tradition. On the one hand it could be understood as "high," if by that term we can refer to works connected with antiquity or aimed at a readership that might be considered cultivated. The Greek romances had been translated into English, first the *Aethiopica* of Heliodorus by Thomas Underdowne in 1569, then *Daphnis and Cloe* by Angel Day in 1587 and

Clitophon and Leucippe of Achilles Tatius by William Burton in 1597. Sir Philip Sidney had already mined this vein, as well as sixteenth-century Italian imitations, in his *Arcadia*, which he completed in its initial form in 1580, then revised over the next several years. Spenser's *Faerie Queene* (1590 and 1596) blended chivalric romance with the Italian romance epics of Ariosto and Tasso. Robert Greene's *Pandosto* (1588) would supply Shakespeare with the narrative of *The Winter's Tale*. John Gower's tale of Apollonius of Tyre, from the *Confessio Amantis*, together with Lawrence Twine's version of it, *The Pattern of Painful Adventures*, is the narrative source of *Pericles*. But all these represent only a small bay of what Peter Womack has recently called "a sea of stories," the vast tradition of saints' lives and chivalric tales.⁵ Scouring this sea, one does not so much find the "narrative sources" of Shakespeare's romances as numerous analogues, a particular kind of story and a particular kind of spirit. During the 1570s and 1580s romance was a popular tradition in the theatres. While only three such plays survive, some thirty-one have titles that suggest that they are romantic narratives.⁶ These are the plays that Sir Philip Sidney complains of in the *Apology for Poetry*. While the surviving plays are naïve in their dramaturgy and characterization, they were clearly effective theater in their day. *Clyomon and Clamydes* has a well-managed and fast-paced plot, concluding with reconciliations and recognitions that anticipate Shakespeare's comedies and romances.⁷ *The Rare Triumphs of Love and Fortune*, performed at court in 1582, unfolds a plot with the turns and twists characteristic of romance that illustrate the alternating influence of the goddesses of love and fortune. It too has plot motifs that remind one of Shakespeare's romances, particularly *The Tempest* and *Cymbeline*. We cannot know for sure whether Shakespeare knew these plays; perhaps he had seen them performed when he first came to London. But his turn toward romance represents a return to a dramatic type that must have looked decidedly outmoded in 1607.

But romance had even more archaic, and possibly ideological roots. At an early point, saints' lives had taken on the character of romance. The third-century *Acts of Paul and Thecla* is perhaps the first of these, telling of a young aristocratic woman who becomes rapt by St. Paul's teaching on virginity, renounces her prospective husband, and follows Paul, enduring heroic suffering and twice miraculously avoiding execution. The story freely mixes romance motives with details from the stories of Paul in Acts of the Apostles. If not a precedent, the legend is simply the first of many narratives of saints that follow patterns of separation, endurance, divine preservation, and eventual recognition and reconciliation with families. *The Golden Legend* of Jacobus de Voragine collects a vast number of these hagiographies. One such is the story of St. Agnes, whose virtue transforms the brothel into which she is thrown into a place of prayer, a striking analog to Marina's trials in *Pericles* and the conversions she prompts. Another hagiographical romance is that of St. Eustace, a Roman general who has a vision of the crucified Christ between the antlers of a stag, is converted, and undergoes Job-like suffering, including separation from his wife and young sons. Fifteen years later, after an anonymous life as a shepherd, Eustace is rediscovered by the emperor and is successively reunited with his wife and sons. The legend of Mary Magdalene told of her voyage to Marseilles, her conversion of the king and queen there and her intercession through which the queen conceives a child. In an episode analogous to the loss of Thaisa and Marina in *Pericles*, the queen dies in childbirth during a storm at sea, and she and her son are put ashore on a deserted isle. Both are miraculously preserved by the Magdalene's prayer, and the king is reunited with them on his return voyage. This latter legend is the subject of *Mary Magdalene* in the Digby manuscript, an elaborate and spectacular late fifteenth-century play. In fact saints' plays are likely to have been one of the most common and popular of late-medieval theatrical genres – the titles of some sixty-six plays about thirty-eight different saints are known, though only a small handful of texts survive – and were typically played in towns and parishes.[8] Some of these plays survived in performance into the 1560s. So a cultural memory, if not actual memories, of these dramatic mixtures of romance, allegory, and miracle endured into the time of Shakespeare's experimentation with new dramatic possibilities. It is to this cultural memory that Gower gestures at the beginning of *Pericles*, when he speaks of a world of archaic story. Himself embodying this tradition, "Ancient Gower" sings a song that "hath been sung at festivals, / On ember eves and holi[-ales]." This evocation of a world of pre-Reformation Catholic festival conveys a nostalgic sense of remembrance of hagiographic narratives that "lords and ladies" have read as "restoratives." The strangeness of this experimentation is acknowledged in Gower's hope that his audience, born in "latter times, / When wit's more ripe" (1.chorus.5–12), may still find pleasure in a return to such archaic performance.

While each of the plays engages romance in a separate and even idiosyncratic way, it is possible to make some generalizations about what they make of its varied character. Romance stands for transformation in all four plays, transformations enacted within the characters that enable an emergence from tragic rigidity. In this regard, Sidney's *Arcadia* might seem to offer the antithesis of what Shakespeare found in romance. For there the disguisings of the heroes are emphatically disconnected from any inward changes. Pyrocles transforms himself into the Amazon Philoclea, and Musidorus into the shepherd Dorus, but neither of these transformations is allowed to suggest an enlarged sympathy in the character so changed. Pyrocles exhibits no feminization of his consciousness, and the change of gender is understood throughout to be a degradation of his male identity. Even more striking is the class rigidity apparent in the attitude toward the actual shepherds of the book. For Musidorus, the role of shepherd is simply a disguise, and far from showing any interest in a nonaristocratic way of constructing the self, he mocks and humiliates the shepherd Dametas. The mockery is also Sidney's and extends to the entire family of Dametas, who are shown as foolish, rustic boors, devoid of human dignity. If Shakespeare took anything from Sidney's experimentation with romance, it must have been the negative example of such psychological rigidity among the disguised aristocrats. This is not the case in Spenser's *The Faerie Queene*, where in the sixth book the knight Calidore gratefully takes on the life and manners of a shepherd and is enlarged in the process. Still, it is the hagiographic tradition that most abundantly supplied the sense that abasement to a lower status had positive implications for growth and emergence from psychic fixation and paralysis. Here the abasement of diminished social position expressed the gospel values of the necessary humiliation of the proud and at the same time necessitated a period of trial and purgation. In the saints' lives, abasement could demonstrate patience and fortitude or purge the guilt of earlier sin.

Of the four plays, *Pericles*, the first written (perhaps as early as 1606, but by 1608), experiments most extensively with romance structures. The play is the first in which romance patterns pervade, that fully sets out to be a romance. It may be too much to say that Shakespeare "discovers" romance in *Pericles*; in fact, it might be more accurate to say that here romance discovers Shakespeare. The complex state of the text suggests that he came to the play after it had been at least partially written, that the first two acts of the play may have initially been composed by another playwright and that Shakespeare was either rewriting a play that already existed or was given a partially written text to complete.[9] So it is possible that the romance design of the play may have been handed to Shakespeare rather than formed by his own immediate choice. If so, it cannot have been an uncongenial matching of playwright to material. Romance elements and motifs occur with some frequency in the earlier plays. For all its farcical enjoyment of mistaken identities, romance grounds the plot of *The Comedy of Errors*, emerging most seriously in the wonder of a reconciliation of long-separated spouses at its conclusion. The pastoralism of *As You Like It,* and the sea-separated twins of *Twelfth Night* make evident that romance frequently lurks visibly in the comedies. Even *King Lear* seems about to enter the country of romance before turning toward its relentlessly tragic end. But *Pericles* clearly *is* a romance. The characters, while vivid, are idealized, conceived of in terms of their overall function in a plot that approaches the mythic. Storms at sea – no fewer than three – seem like allegorical images of the perils of mortal life. In what seems an almost parodic romance motif, the heroine is saved from death by the arrival of pirates, who, conveying her from frying pan to fire, sell her to a brothel. Moreover, a conscious archaism pervades the play: "ancient Gower" is brought forth not only as prologue but as a narrative framer of each act. Never before and never again does Shakespeare use this device to suggest that his enacted play emerges from an old story – and at its conclusion recedes back into it.[10] "Ancient Gower," appearing at the beginning of each act and at the end of the play, is both a figure from the fourteenth-century past and a device to circumscribe enactment by narration. Three times he gestures toward a dumb-show to illustrate what he speaks, a dramatic device that was at least twenty years out of fashion in 1608. What this does is to foreground enactment, *theatre*, in relation to an ancient narrative. In his first appearance Gower evokes the very phenomenon of theatre: he himself has come from "ancient ashes" to his present embodiment, "assuming man's infirmities," that he may "glad your ear, and please your eyes." The double epistemology of theatre, language *and* sight, is a deep preoccupation of Shakespeare's self-reflexive representations of his own art, apparent comically, for example, in Bottom's frequent transpositions in *Midsummer Night's Dream* ("I see a voice: now will I to the chink, / To spy an I can hear my Thisbe's face" [5.1.192–93]).[11] *Pericles* is a play in which the relationship of ear and eye, of language and visual embodiment, is paramount: "Your ears unto your eyes I'll reconcile" (4.4.22), Gower says introducing the final dumb-show of Pericles' visit to the feigned tomb of Marina.

The play contains a number of strikingly visual constructions and images, beginning with the opening scene in which the grim, severed heads of former suitors look down on the dazzling beauty of Antiochus' daughter. The parade of the richly attired knights before the tournament at Pentapolis and the storm at sea during which Marina is born are other such moments of high theatrical spectacle. If dumb-shows are juxtaposed to verbal narration to suggest the uncompleted elements of theatre, then Pericles himself becomes such a dumb-show after his losses strip him of happiness and perhaps even reason: with overgrown hair and beard, he becomes simply an image, aphasic and dependent on Helicanus to define his mute sorrow. Marina's speech, her narration of a life tragic in a way exactly complementary to Pericles', begins to heal him, returning his use of language. But Marina's visual appearance as well, her physical replication of her mother, triggers the recognition. Both ear and eye, phenomenologically coequal in our response to theatre, are necessary in the healing of Pericles. But the analysis of narration and the visual that is implicit in the play's experimental theatricality is not confined to speech and bodily presence; it is a striking characteristic of the play that it uses music in an equally imagistic way. The moments of greatest wonder in the play, those in which romance intends to adumbrate a connection between human agency and mystic powers, are accompanied by music. The music of a viol, "the rough and woeful music that we have" (3.2.88), accompanies Cerimon's ministrations that bring Thaisa back from her apparent death. Marina's singing to Pericles begins her cure of his mute lethargy, though at first he seems not to respond. Music, unheard by Lysimachus, but presumably marked by the audience, accompanies Diana's appearance to Pericles when she bids him to go to her temple at Ephesus and tell his story.

Though the play was in all likelihood taken up by Shakespeare in an earlier form, it does achieve a certain thematic neatness in its experimentation with romance patterns. The strange image of incest that clouds Pericles' sense of the world at the beginning of the play finds its thematic response in Pericles' exclamation to Marina at the anagnorisis: "Thou that beget'st him that did thee beget" (5.1.195). The saintly virtue of Marina, overcoming the corruption of the brothel (in scenes of comic realism that lighten the somber tone of the play), redeems Pericles from the despair that the world had led him to. While not allegorical, the hagiographic element extends a quasireligious sense to romance's claim that a child may psychologically cure the spiritual malaise of her parent. If Pericles follows St. Eustace in playing a Job-like role in the world, all is given back to him in the reconciliations that romance allows.

Cymbeline and *The Winter's Tale* represent a different type of experimentation, similar in beginning with a tragic plot that is not based on romance but then using romance structures to complicate events and ultimately turn tragedy to comedy. The plays are also alike in centering their tragic plots on male jealousy, in both cases a husband's unfounded jealousy of his virtuous wife. But the two plays differ greatly in their ways of using romance. *Cymbeline* weaves together three separate stories, drawn from separate sources, and creates a plot of such dizzying complexity that a concluding scene of 485 lines is devoted to resolving no fewer than ten different plot complications. The tragic narrative, of Jachimo's trickery of Posthumus and the jealousy that drives him to the verge of insanity, is drawn from Boccaccio's *Decameron* and fills the opening two acts. It is not until Act 3 scene 3 that the romance plot enters the play, a story of stolen royal children brought up in the wilderness unaware of their identity. A third plot, quasihistorical, frames the other two, the revolt of King Cymbeline from Rome at the time of Caesar Augustus. An extraordinary number of potential sources can be found for the various plot and character motifs of the play, among them two of the romances from the 1580s. *The Rare Triumphs of Love and*

Fortune, acted at court in 1582, supplies an apparent source for the situation of Imogen and Posthumus at the beginning of the play; a princess, suggestively named Fidelia, in love with a worthy but lesser-born man (named, oddly for Shakespeare's next play, Hermione) who was brought to court but banished for his relationship with the princess. And *Clyomon and Clamydes* may supply the hint for the lurid moment when Imogen/Fidele finds the headless Cloten and because of his clothes mistakes him for Posthumus: in the old play the heroine Neronis, dressed as a shepherd boy, sees the golden shield of her lover, Clyomon, beside the grave of the false Thrasellus and thinks it marks Clyomon's grave; only the descent of Providence saves her from suicide at this point. Both of these old plays were written in fourteeners, a clumsy seven-beat line, and this, curiously, is the verse used for the scene where Posthumus' dead family appear to him and appeal to Jupiter for an end to his sorrows. It may be that this spectacular scene is also to be understood as a throwback to the dramaturgy of the 1580s.

The pastoral world of rugged self-sufficiency is represented somewhat conventionally through Belarius' understanding of its honest humility in relation to court and city. When Imogen disguised as the boy Fidele arrives, she expects hostility for her daring to steal food, but instead encounters hospitality in a world of more humane values. The dominant pastoral note is nature over nurture. The princes, her brothers, immediately feel a bond with her and express their sudden affection for the new-arrived "boy." At the same time their princely natures chafe against their rustication and long for chivalric experience and exercise. But the most transformative element in the pastoral world of the play is death. Imogen has been brought to Wales by Pisanio to be shown the letter from Posthumus that orders her death, an experience that makes her long to die. And she undergoes a temporary death after ingesting the Queen's poison. Cloten finds death at the hands of Guiderius. Posthumus, in his guilt desiring death, is thought dead by Imogen who mistakes Cloten's headless body for his. The most poignant moment in the play is the brothers' discovery of the apparently dead Imogen/Fidele, announced by "solemn music" played by Arviragus, who then enters (Lear-like) with her in his arms. The song that the brothers sing over her portrays death as the better pastoral:

Fear no more the frown o' th' great,
　　Thou art past the tyrant's stroke;
Care no more to clothe and eat,
　　To thee the reed is as the oak.
The sceptre, learning, physic, must
All follow this and come to dust.

(4.2.264–69)

This sense of death as the leveler that chastises human pride, as a refuge from suffering, and, in symbolic enactment, as a restorer of value extends beyond the Welsh pastoral world. Amid the complexities of the play's ending the threat of death appears designed to shock characters toward penitence and healing. There is, it must be admitted, a good deal of artificiality in this, an artificiality that the play acknowledges when Posthumus, having just confessed his supposed murder of Imogen and yearning for torture and death, exclaims "Shall 's have a play of this? Thou scornful page, / There lie thy part" (5.5.228–29) when the still-disguised Imogen tries to interrupt him. He strikes her and she falls, apparently dead as far as the audience can know. Pisanio, who knows her identity, cries out that only now has Posthumus killed Imogen. She is not dead, of course, and to our relief "rises" – again! – from death. The trick on the audience, while it restages what is the psychic reality of Posthumus' crime, seems implicitly to admit the role of theatrical art in what romance is being asked to accomplish in the play. Here only the egregiously evil characters, Cloten and the Queen, die, and others are allowed symbolic deaths that regenerate their lives and renew love. The art of romance clears up the tragic errors, one by one, and creates happiness from despair.

The Winter's Tale, certainly the most powerful and challenging of the romances, follows the pattern of *Cymbeline* in beginning with a tragic plot, then developing romance structures to explore how tragedy may be reversed. The first three acts seem a full-scale tragedy of a jealousy that not only destroys a marriage and a friendship, but kills one child, casts out another, and leaves a kingdom barren of succession. Moreover, the apparent death of Hermione affords no room for a comic conclusion. There is no hint that the tragic circumstances will engage romance until the end of the third act, when the innocent baby is ejected and becomes a foundling. But the play avoids the complications of multiple plots and sources of *Cymbeline* and instead allows romance motifs – a storm, a marauding bear, discovery of the foundling by shepherds – to emerge with a mild irony that is not parody, but not high seriousness either. From the moment in Act 3 scene 3 that Antigonus exits, famously pursued by a bear, and the shepherd enters grumbling about youth, the play turns on its heel and suddenly opens to comic possibility. "Heavy matters, heavy matters," the shepherd says to his son, who has seen the shipwreck and the half-eaten Antigonus, but he could also be speaking to the audience of the previous three acts and the havoc wrought by Leontes' jealousy. "But look thee here, boy. Now bless thyself; thou met'st with things dying, I with things new-born" (3.3.111–13), he says of his discovery of the infant Perdita.

From this point on the play experiments with romance elements as an antidote to the rigidity of tragic error. Leontes' sin seems infinite in its offense, and Paulina tells him that repentance can never undo what has been done: "A thousand knees, / Ten thousand years together, naked, fasting, / Upon a barren mountain, and still winter / In storm perpetual, could not move the gods to look that way thou wert" (3.2.210–14). Time is the first of these elements, but it is also space, slipping over sixteen years and depositing the play in Bohemia, an emphatic violation of two of the unities. Once the play is delivered to pastoral Bohemia, time becomes something entirely different from what it had been in the first three acts, springtime rather than winter of course, but altogether different dramatically. It has no urgency and seemingly nothing to accomplish in advancing the plot. Autolycus' tricking of the shepherd looks like a parody of a parish play on the Good Samaritan, but has no consequence. The evocation of a village sheepshearing festival is allowed to encompass the lyric love dialogues of Perdita and Florizel, a debate on nature and art over the hybridized gillyvors, a dance of shepherds and shepherdesses, Autolycus' impersonation of a pedlar of ballads and a rustic performance of one of them, another dance of twelve satyrs, and finally the betrothal of Perdita and the disguised Florizel. Only the last, and its enraged interruption by Polixenes, calls the play back to its business and reminds us what the green world, and the lovers, need to accomplish. Of the 842 lines of the pastoral Act 4 scene 4, fewer than 100 are devoted to the plot, and the disparity is even greater when we think of stage time. By the end of the long scene, with Perdita and Florizel packed off to Sicily, we think we know how the play will end, how romance patterns of recovered children, the passing of time, and the love of the younger generation will restore the succession of Sicily and the friendship of Leontes and Polixenes. But the experimentation with romance, and particularly pastoral, has also been an experimentation with dramatic modes and dramatic representation. Again and again the play self-reflexively reminds us that we are part of a theatrical experience, that tragic events and the possibility of their undoing are also part of a process that art seeks to encompass. The turn to romance modes has a self-consciousness about it that admits its artfulness – and at the same time asserts the "truth" of its claims.

The Winter's Tale concludes with Shakespeare's greatest *coup de théâtre*, the scene in which the audience learns, at the same moment the characters learn, that Hermione is not dead, that she has been alive and sustained by Paulina in the hope that the oracle will be fulfilled. That this is announced through her posing as what we are led to believe is a statue of the "dead" queen, a statue that comes to life, places an intense focus on the issue of theatre, what theatre is and what it can demand of an audience. We are, of course, cheated of the scene we were expecting, the discovery of Perdita and her recognition by Leontes, and instead learn of their meeting in a scene of exposition that makes a great deal of the fact that we are *not* witnessing it;

the language of the narrating characters emphasizes what the *eyes* of the audience have missed.[12] The reason why we are so cheated, of course, is that all the emphasis is to fall on the statue scene, in which our eyes are successively deceived, then opened to the theatrical life that is bestowed on the seemingly inanimate statue. The "statue" was said to have been sculpted by "that rare Italian master, Julio Romano" (5.2.97), who is reputed to be so perfect in his art that he could steal Nature's practice of creating life, "had he himself eternity and could put breath into his work" (5.2.98–99). By implication, the divine sculptor of the actor playing Hermione does have eternity and indeed breathes life into his "art." But so in a sense can the playwright, whose stock-in-trade are the human bodies that he presumes to fashion into mimetic representations of human life. The actual art of Hermione's "return" to life is that of theatre itself – of playwright, actors, and stage – and an art that is verbal, visual, and embodied. As in the scenes expressing a moment of wonder in the other two plays, music also accompanies Hermione's "descent" into full theatrical life. Paulina's command to Leontes, "It is requir'd / You do awake your faith" (5.3.94–95), seems as much directed to the audience, which must give its assent to this most extraordinary of theatrical tricks that has been played on it. Theatrical performance gives testimony that the scene is among the most moving of Shakespeare's mature art. But the play goes to some trouble to suggest that its manipulations of the structures of romance are not only the constructions of art, but are tied to human agency, are not unconnected to what human life may be. Not only Hermione's endurance, but the fidelity of Camillo, Paulina's witness to Hermione's innocence and her insistent discipline of Leontes, and finally his own penitence – all these respond to the growth bestowed by Time and "great creating Nature" in the lives of Perdita and Florizel. Together they represent a world countering tragic error, accomplishing this by an art that is at once confident and highly self-aware.

The Tempest is perhaps the most evidently experimental of the plays in the way it deploys romance and fantasy and explores the boundaries of theatre. But instead of a developed romance story, it centers on the single figure of Prospero, placing elements of romance in his past (betrayal, near murder and survival after being cast away at sea), then having him construct, through magic, the romance world of the play. The first thing he fashions is the event that seems central to any romance narrative, the tempest that names the play. The spectacular opening scene is theatrical in the extreme – shouted language that creates with extraordinary precision the impression of a ship about to be dashed on to a lee shore, the movement of actors' bodies and noisy sound effects that both construct the stage as a windswept and moving deck. It is only after the scene ends in chaotic screams and shipwreck that we learn it was not "real." Storm and shipwreck are the trigger of romance, but here they are simply illusion, a vanity of Prospero's art. As audience we have been taken in by it. At this point the dramaturgy of the play changes altogether, and a long scene of exposition solves the "problem" of the unities through Prospero's narration of their past life to Miranda and through his quarrels with Ariel and Caliban. It may be hard to escape the feeling that there is something mildly parodic in this solution – Jonson is a master of this sort of exposition – especially in that Prospero asks Miranda twice whether her attention has wandered. Their story, of course, is near tragedy averted by preservation, the very grounds of romance. But henceforth all of the romance elements in the play will be constructions of Prospero. He will engineer and oversee the meeting of the lovers, who will be the means of the reconciliation of their fathers. He will ensure Ferdinand's fidelity by the pastoral trial of requiring him to cast off aristocratic niceness and perform Caliban's labor. Through Ariel he will avert the *Macbeth*-like assassination of Alonso by Antonio and Sebastian. He will drive the court party to the verge of madness by the masque of judgment into which they are drawn, opening the possibility for their repentance.

Through it all there is, again, a high degree of theatrical self-reflexivity. Gonzalo, who seems the embodiment of naïve goodness and optimism, praises the natural beauty of the isle. "How lush and lusty the grass looks! How green!" (2.1.53), he insists, as the actor gestures to the stage. "The ground indeed is tawny," sneers Antonio. "With an eye of green in't," adds Sebastian (2.2.55–56). Which is it? Audiences in the Globe depended not on scenery but on verbal scene-painting. Here the answer lies in a choice to be made between the characters, a choice that becomes not so much literal as moral. Ariel is Prospero's stage manager, creating various scenes and masques, leading characters about with his music. All sorts of strange visual things occur, the servant monster himself, and the wonderful composition when Trinculo creeps under Caliban's gaberdine and becomes "some monster of the isle with four legs" (2.2.65) – and two thirsty mouths. And twice more Prospero and Ariel create elaborate visual spectacle. The first is the banquet presented to the court party: to the accompaniment of "solemn and strange music" there enter "several strange shapes" who compose an elaborate still life and perform a dance about it "with gentle actions of salutations" (3.3.18–20) that invite the king and his company to partake; Alonso calls the vision "a kind of excellent dumb discourse" (3.3.39). The point of the vision is how the various members of the court react to it; at its disappearance Ariel denounces the guilt of the three "men of sin." The other spectacle is the betrothal masque that Prospero creates as an elaborate visual and musical blessing on Ferdinand and Miranda. "No tongue! All eyes! Be silent!"

(4.4.59) the lovers – and the audience – are commanded. The masque concludes with a dance of "certain reapers, properly habited," who join with the nymphs in their graceful performance. Or rather it does not conclude, because Prospero suddenly comes to himself, remembers Caliban and his confederates, and awkwardly stops it. The dancers look at one another and at Prospero in surprise and confusion, then walk off stage in disarray. As performance testifies, for a moment the play itself seems threatened. Prospero's own troubled and "beating mind" is linked to the interruption of what we were watching. The thought of mortality suddenly ties the whole endeavor of creating the masque – and of playwrighting itself – to the impermanence of the phenomenal world of "cloud-capp'd towers, the gorgeous palaces, / The solemn temples, the great globe itself" (4.1.152–53). Both the great and the lesser Globe will pass. Life is not far from a play.

The romance elements, the *creation* of romance, are very much a part of the self-reflexivity of theatre in *The Tempest*. Prospero has used romance motifs to structure what he wants from his enemies. But an audience may not be sure whether it is justice – and vengeance – or reconciliation that he intends. So there is something deeply moving in the moment (5.1.17–20) when Ariel asks Prospero to confront his humanity and make the choice of what is, essentially, the ethos of romance – in spite of the fact that not all the characters are certain to respond to his proffered forgiveness. Gonzalo would define the events as a perfect romance: Prospero was thrust from Milan so that his offspring would be kings of Naples, Ferdinand found Miranda when he himself was lost, Prospero his dukedom in a poor isle, "and all of us, ourselves, / When no man was his own" (5.1.205–13). But the silence of Antonio and Sebastian is ominous. So the renunciation of magic for a return to ordinary human powers represents *faith* in the endeavor of romance, rather than an absolute conviction that its solutions will always and inevitably prevail.

The epilogue, "Spoken by Prospero," makes the audience in some sense complicit in the reconciliations of romance, just as in *The Winter's Tale* the evocation of the spectators' faith in the possibility of a statue's coming to life made them participants in that play's end. The self-reflexivity of both plays implies the need for the audience to understand its necessary role in the conclusions of romance. And the self-critiquing character of romance elements in all four plays shows art willing to judge itself, to assert the truth of its claims and at the same time to preserve a skeptical awareness of itself as an imaginative construction. The four plays project alternatives to tragic resolution, and at the same time their experimental character renders always tentative their assertions of representation.

NOTES

1 Perhaps the most influential early study fo the four romances is that of G. Wilson Knight, *The Crown of Life: Essays in Interpretation of Shakespeare's Final Plays* (Oxford and New York: Oxford University Press, 1947).

2 Edward Dowden, *Introduction to Shakespeare* (London: Blackie and Son, 1893), p. 82.

3 All quotations from Shakespeare are from *The Riverside Shakespeare*, ed. G. Blakemore Evans *et al.* (Boston and New York: Houghton Mifflin Company, 1974).

4 Ben Jonson, *Bartholomew Fair*, ed. Eugene M. Waith (New Haven and London: Yale University Press, 1963), p. 32 (induction, lines 113–18).

5 Peter Womack, "Shakespeare and the Sea of Stories," *Journal of Medieval and Early Modern Studies* 29 (1999): 169–87.

6 See John Owen Isaac's appendix to his edition, *The Rare Triumphs of Love and Fortune* (New York and London: Garland, 1979), p. 201; this introduction also contains an account of the brief vogue of romance in the 1570s and 1580s.

7 *Clyomon and Clamydes: a Critical Edition*, ed. Betty J. Littleton (The Hague: Mouton, 1968).

8 See John Wasson, "The Secular Saint Plays of the Elizabethan Era," in *The Saint Play in Medieval Europe,* ed. Clifford Davidson (Kalamazoo: Medieval Institute Publications, 1986), p. 242. F. D. Hoeniger calls attention to the importance of the tradition of the saints' play in his introduction to the Arden edition of *Pericles* (London: Methuen, 1963), pp. lxxxviii–xci; see also Howard Felperin, *Shakespearean Romance* (Princeton: Princeton University Press, 1972), pp. 12–16.

9 See Hoeniger's introduction to the Arden edition of *Pericles*, pp. lii–lxiii, and Robert M. Adams, *Shakespeare: the Four Romances* (New York and London: W. W. Norton, 1989), pp. 28–35.

10 Only the chorus from *Henry V* would seem at all comparable to the use of Gower in *Pericles*, but there the chorus is used more to connect the narrative and encourage the audience to "eke out our performance with your mind," rather than to tie the play to ancient narrative and stylize its dramaturgy.

11 See Michael O'Connell, *The Idolatrous Eye: Iconoclasm and Theatre in Early Modern England* (Oxford and New York: Oxford University Press, 2000), pp. 130–32.

12 Ibid., pp. 139–42.

SELECT BIBLIOGRAPHY

Comedy: theory and tradition

Andrews, Richard, *Scripts and Scenarios: the Performance of Comedy in Renaissance Italy*. Cambridge: Cambridge University Press, 1993.

Bakhtin, Mihail, *Rabelais and his World*, trans. Hélène Iswolsky. Cambridge, Mass.: MIT Press, 1968.

Barton, Anne, *The Names of Comedy*. Toronto: University of Toronto Press, 1990.

Castelvetro, Lodovico, *Castelvetro on the Art of Poetry*, trans. Andrew Bongionro. Binghamton: Medieval and Renaissance Texts and Studies, 1984.

Cicero, *De Oratore*, trans. E. W. Sutton and H. Rackham. Cambridge, Mass.: Harvard University Press, 1942.

Colie, Rosalie L., *The Resources of Kind: Genre Theory in the Renaissance*. Berkeley: University of California Press, 1973.

Cordner, Michael, Peter Holland, and John Kerrigan (eds.), *English Comedy*. Cambridge: Cambridge University Press, 1994.

Frye, Northrop, "The Argument of Comedy," *English Institute Essays 1948*. New York: Columbia University Press, 1949.

Hardison, O. B. Jr., *et al.* (eds.), *Medieval Literary Criticism*. New York: Frederick Ungar Publishing, 1974.

Herrick, Marvin T., *Comic Theory in the Sixteenth Century*. Urbana: University of Illinois Press, 1964.

   Italian Comedy in the Renaissance. Urbana: University of Illinois Press, 1960.

Hunter, R. L., *The New Comedy of Greece and Rome*. Cambridge: Cambridge University Press, 1985.

Joubert, Laurent, *Treatise on Laughter*, trans. David de Rocher. Alabama: University of Alabama Press, 1980.

Konstan, David, *Roman Comedy*. Ithaca, N.Y.: Cornell University Press, 1983.

Lauter, Paul (ed.), *Theories of Comedy*. Garden City, N.Y.: Doubleday, 1964.

Lea, Kathleen M., *Italian Popular Comedy: a Study in the Commedia dell'Arte 1560–1620, with Special Reference to the English Stage*. 2 vols., Oxford: Clarendon Press, 1934.

Leggatt, Alexander, *English Stage Comedy 1490–1990: Five Centuries of a Genre*. London: Routledge, 1998.

Lewalski, Barbara (ed.), *Renaissance Genres: Essays on Theory, History, and Interpretation*. Harvard English Studies 14. Cambridge, Mass.: Harvard University Press, 1986.

Miola, Robert S., *Shakespeare and Classical Comedy*. Oxford: Clarendon Press, 1994.

Nelson, T. G. A., *Comedy: the Theory of Comedy in Literature, Drama, and Cinema*. Oxford: Oxford University Press, 1990.

Newman, Karen, *Shakespeare's Rhetoric of Comic Character: Dramatic Convention in Classical and Renaissance Comedy*. New York and London: Methuen, 1985.

Nicoll, Allardyce, *The World of Harlequin: a Critical Study of the Commedia dell'Arte*. Cambridge: Cambridge University Press, 1963.

Richards, Kenneth, and Laura Richards, *The Commedia dell'Arte: a Documentary History*. Oxford: Oxford University Press, 1990.

Salingar, Leo, *Shakespeare and the Traditions of Comedy*. Cambridge: Cambridge University Press, 1974.

Sypher, Wylie (ed.), *Comedy*. New York: Doubleday Anchor Books, 1956.

Soc and cultural contexts

Adair, Richard, *Courtship, Illegitimacy and Marriage in Early Modern England*. Manchester: Manchester University Press, 1996.

Bates, Catherine, *The Rhetoric of Courtship in Elizabethan Language and Literature*. Cambridge: Cambridge University Press, 1998.

Bell, Illona, *Elizabethan Women and the Poetry of Courtship*. Cambridge: Cambridge University Press, 1998.

Bristol, Michael, *Carnival and Theatre: Plebeian Culture and the Structure of Authority in Renaissance England*. London: Methuen, 1985.

Clements, Robert J., and Joseph Gibaldi, *Anatomy of the Novella: the European Tale Collection from Boccaccio to Cervantes*. New York: New York University Press, 1989.

Cook, Ann Jennalie, *Making a Match: Courtship in Shakespeare and his Society*. Princeton: Princeton University Press, 1991.

Cressey, David, *Travesties and Transgressions in Tudor and Stuart England*. Oxford: Oxford University Press, 2000.

Garber, Marjorie, *Vested Interests: Cross-Dressing and Cultural Anxiety*. London: Routledge, 1992.

Hedricks, Margo, and Patricia Parker (eds.), *Women, "Race," and Writing in the Early Modern Period*. London: Routledge, 1994.

Houlbrooke, Ralph, *The English Family, 1450–1700*. London: Longman, 1984.

Ingram, Martin, *Church Courts, Sex and Marriage in England, 1570–1640*. Cambridge: Cambridge University Press, 1987.

Laroque, François, *Shakespeare's Festive World: Elizabethan Seasonal Entertainment and the Professional Stage*. Cambridge: Cambridge University Press, 1991.

MacDonald, Joyce Green (ed.), *Race, Ethnicity, and Power in the Renaissance*. Rutherford, N. J.: Fairleigh Dickinson University Press, 1997.

Magnusson, Lynne, *Shakespeare and Social Dialogue: Dramatic Language and Elizabethan Letters*. Cambridge: Cambridge University Press, 1999.

Meader, William G., *Courtship in Shakespeare: its Relation to the Tradition of Courtly Love*. New York: King's Crown Press, 1971.

Riehle, Wolfgang, *Shakespeare, Plautus, and the Humanist Tradition*. Cambridge: D. S. Brewer, 1990.

Shapiro, James S., *Shakespeare and the Jews*. New York: Columbia University Press, 1996.

Smith, Bruce R., *The Acoustic World of Early Modern England: Attending to the O-Factor*. Chicago: University of Chicago Press, 1999.

Stone, Lawrence, *The Family, Sex and Marriage in England 1500–1800*. New York: Harper and Row, 1977.

Theatrical contexts

Beacham, Richard C., *The Roman Theatre and its Audience*. Cambridge, Mass.: Harvard University Press, 1992.

Brown, John Russell, and Bernard Harris (eds.), *Elizabethan Theatre*. New York: St. Martin's Press, 1967.

Clubb, Louise George, *Italian Drama in Shakespeare's Time*. New Haven and London: Yale University Press, 1989.

Dillon, Janette, *Language and Stage in Medieval and Renaissance England*. Cambridge: Cambridge University Press, 1998.

Henke, Robert, *Pastoral Transformations: Italian Tragicomedy and Shakespeare's Late Plays*. Newark: University of Delaware Press; London: Associated University Presses, 1997.

O'Connell, Michael. *The Idolatrous Eye: Iconoclasm and Theater in Early Modern England*. Oxford and New York: Oxford University Press, 2000.

Orgel, Stephen, *Impersonations: the Performance of Gender in Shakespeare's England*. Cambridge: Cambridge University Press, 1996.

Rose, Mary Beth, *The Expense of Spirit: Love and Sexuality in English Renaissance Drama*. Ithaca and London: Cornell University Press, 1988.

Smith, Bruce R., *Ancient Scripts and Modern Experience on the English Stage, 1500–1700*. Princeton: Princeton University Press, 1988.

Weimann, Robert, *Shakespeare and the Popular Tradition in the Theater*. Baltimore: Johns Hopkins University Press, 1978.

Wiles, David, *Shakespeare's Clown: Actor and Text in the Elizabethan Playhouse*. Cambridge: Cambridge University Press, 1987.

Shakespearean comedy

Adams, Robert M., *Shakespeare: Four Romances*. New York: W. W. Norton, 1989.

Barber, C. L., *Shakespeare's Festive Comedy: a Study of Dramatic Form and its Relation to Social Custom*. Princeton: Princeton University Press, 1959.

Berry, Edward, *Shakespeare's Comic Rites*. Cambridge: Cambridge University Press, 1984.

Bishop, T. G., *Shakespeare and the Theatre of Wonder*. Cambridge: Cambridge University Press, 1996.

Bloom, Harold (ed.), *William Shakespeare: Comedies and Romances*. New York: Chelsea House, 1986.

Bradbury, Malcolm, and David Palmer (eds.), *Shakespearean Comedy*. London: Edward Arnold, 1972.

Carroll, William C., *The Great Feast of Language in "Love's Labour's Lost."* Princeton: Princeton University Press, 1976.

   The Metamorphoses of Shakespearean Comedy. Princeton: Princeton University Press, 1985.

Charney, Maurice (ed.), *Shakespearean Comedy*. New York: New Literary Forum, 1980.

Elam, Keir, *Shakespeare's Universe of Discourse: Language–Games in the Comedies*. Cambridge: Cambridge University Press, 1984.

Evans, Bertrand, *Shakespeare's Comedies*. Oxford: Oxford University Press, 1960.

Frye, Northrop, *A Natural Perspective: the Development of Shakespearean Comedy and Romance*. New York: Harcourt, Brace and World, 1965.

   The Myth of Deliverance: Reflections on Shakespeare's Problem Comedies. Brighton: Harvester Press, 1983.

Gay, Penny, *As She Likes It: Shakespeare's Unruly Women*. London: Routledge, 1994.

Leggatt, Alexander, *Shakespeare's Comedy of Love*. London: Methuen, 1974.

Mowat, Barbara, *The Dramaturgy of Shakespeare's Romances*. Athens: University of Georgia Press, 1976.

Nevo, Ruth, *Comic Transformations in Shakespeare*. London: Methuen, 1980.

Ornstein, Robert, *Shakespeare's Comedies: from Roman Farce to Romantic Mystery*. Newark: University of Delaware Press, 1986.

Platt, Peter G., *Reason Diminished: Shakespeare and the Marvelous*. Lincoln, Neb., and London: University of Nebraska Press, 1997.

Rutter, Carol, *Clamorous Voices: Shakespeare's Women Today*. London: Women's Press, 1988.

Slights, Camille Wells, *Shakespeare's Comic Commonwealths*. Toronto, Buffalo, and London: University of Toronto Press, 1993.

Traub, Valerie, *Desire and Anxiety: Circulations of Sexuality in Shakespearean Drama*. London: Routledge, 1992.

INDEX

Printed in Great Britain
by Amazon.co.uk, Ltd.,
Marston Gate.